CU00731591

Such Deliberate Disguises:
The Art of Philip Larkin

Also available from Continuum:

Philip Larkin: Jazz Writings, ed. Richard Palmer and John White

Such Deliberate Disguises:
The Art of Philip Larkin

Richard Palmer

continuum

Continuum
The Tower Building
11 York Road
London SE1 7NX

80 Maiden Lane, Suite 704
New York
NY 10038

www.continuumbooks.com

© Richard Palmer 2008

Richard Palmer has asserted his right under the Copyright, Designs and
Patents Act, 1988, to be identified as Author of this work.

All rights reserved. No part of this publication may be reproduced or
transmitted in any form or by any means, electronic or mechanical,
including photocopying, recording, or any information storage or
retrieval system, without prior permission in writing from the publishers.

British Library Cataloguing-in-Publication Data
A catalogue record for this book is available from the British Library.

ISBN: 978-0-8264-9118-3 (hardback)
      978-1-8471-4025-8 (paperback)

Library of Congress Cataloging-in-Publication Data
A catalog record for this book is available from the Library of Congress.

Typeset by YHT Ltd, London
Printed and bound in Great Britain by Athenaeum Press Ltd,
Gateshead, Tyne and Wear

Contents

For Louise and Michael Tucker

Acknowledgements

This book has been long in gestation; it was conceived in 1998, and the first person I must acknowledge is Ann Palmer, for a debt that will never be forgotten. I thank her for her years-long loving support and tolerance of my innumerable hours at the computer and in libraries, and no less in this instance for her invigorating perceptions, especially those concerning Larkin's painterly qualities, in which area she is far better versed than I shall ever be.

James Booth and Anthony Thwaite have been consistently helpful in their correspondence and manuscript suggestions. I am no less grateful to John White: to a considerable extent, it was our 1998 *Reference Back: The Uncollected Jazz Writings of Philip Larkin 1940–84* that led me to write this book, and his comments have been invariably illuminating. Thanks are due to Istvan Racz, for commissioning me to write an essay for the 2004 Larkin Symposium in the Hungarian Journal of English and American Studies and then allowing me to use its (recast) material here. Belinda Hakes and Janet Brennan, in their capacity as editors of the Philip Larkin Society's journal, About Larkin, have been as pertinent as encouraging, and I also thank them for their permission to use my (again, recast) articles in this book.

One of the greatest pleasures of my professional life has been teaching Larkin to boys at Bedford School: Year 9 as well as sixth-formers. If I were to mention all those boys who have furnished new insights and responses to his poetry, this section would be very lengthy; they all know who they are, and I hope this 'blanket thank you' will suffice. I must also pay tribute to colleagues past and present in Bedford School's English Department: David Cundall, Tim Firth, Andrew Grimshaw, Catherine Wilson and, especially, Andrew Speedy.

I would also like to acknowledge the friendship, advice and lecturing opportunities afforded me by Colin Brezicki, Peter Carpenter, Stewart Cook, Tim Kirkup, Colin Poulden; the expert help of Brian Dyson and all the staff at the Larkin Suite in the Brynmor Jones Library at Hull University; the periodicals department of the Cambridge University Library; David Wheatley and Andrew Eastwood of the Philip Larkin Society; my Continuum editors Anna Sandeman and Colleen Coalter.

However, two people must be thanked above all others. First, my colleague, Linda Caldicott. Without her initial insights into Larkin's use of religious language, Chapter 6 would not have been conceived; without her further ideas and the energizing power they created it would have not been written. Elsewhere she has been as stringent as supportive, and full of illumination, and this book would have been the poorer and thinner without her invaluable contribution.

The same applies to Dr Michael Tucker. A scholar of distinction and prodigious range of expertise, he spent countless hours on the manuscript, providing a host of ideas and sources while also ensuring that mistakes and stylistic lapses were far fewer than they might have been; needless to say, those that remain are to my detriment, not his. His suggestions were invariably cogent, often revelatory: he has, quite simply, been invaluable. So have the friendship, hospitality and incisive contributions of his wife, Louise. No two people more deserve a Dedication.

Richard Palmer
Bedford–Brighton–Tenerife

Such Deliberate Disguises
T. S. Eliot, 'The Hollow Men'

There's not much to say about my work. When you've read a poem, that's it, it's quite clear what it all means.

Philip Larkin, *Observer* interview, 1979

Abbreviations

AWJ	*All What Jazz*
AWL	*A Writer's Life* (Andrew Motion)
CP	*Collected Poems*
FR	*Further Requirements*
ITAWJ	*'Introduction' to All What Jazz*
LJ	*Larkin's Jazz* (the earlier imprint of *Philip Larkin's Jazz Writings*)
PLJW	*Philip Larkin's Jazz Writings*
RfJ	*'Requiem For Jazz'*
RW	*Required Writing*
SL	*Selected Letters*

Preface

I came to Larkin back to front. My induction was via the distinguished poet and editor James Reeves and focused on 'Aubade', the last major poem that Larkin wrote.[1] As I started to steep myself in Larkin's work, I was of necessity moving backwards, and in no particularly organized way either. My first port of call was *Whitsun Weddings*; then *The Less Deceived*; then *All What Jazz*. After that came a full absorption in *High Windows* and the pieces collected in *Required Writing*; finally, in confirmatory back-to-front fashion, I read Larkin's two novels, *Jill* and *Girl in Winter*, and his first volume of poetry of 1945, *The North Ship*.

It was 1988 before my I completed my jigsaw-like achronological study of Larkin's work, and – a coincidence at once serendipitous and baleful – that was also the beginning of the end for the 'old' Larkin. His Memorial Service at Westminster Abbey in 1985 had attracted a huge congregation, in keeping with his status as England's most loved poet after John Betjeman.

Just three years later, Larkin's reputation was transformed by the appearance in quick succession of two major publications: the *Collected Poems* and the *Selected Letters* (both edited by Anthony Thwaite); five years after that, Andrew Motion's biography *A Writer's Life* was published, which did not just complete the transformation but kerosene-fuelled it.

Those three books will feature regularly in my text; what I want to say here is that for all the seismic and still-raging controversy that trilogy engendered, they did not illuminate three puzzles I had begun to see as central to an understanding of Larkin's work.

1. The mediocrity of virtually everything he wrote until the late 1940s.
2. The related but separately extraordinary change in his writing from that time. Not just his poetry but everything he wrote dramatizes a radical alteration in diction, purpose, tone, method and, above all, quality.
3. The obvious and central importance of jazz in his life and work: why had nobody attended to this?

The attempt to unravel those three mysteries informs the heart of this book. The need to do so is even more pressing given what has happened in 'Larkin Studies' over the last two decades. Following the publication of Motion's extensive but partial biography and a subsequent range of criticism which has focused on both narrowly personal and unduly politicized readings of the work, Larkin's critical stock has fallen, although his popularity with the general public remains high.

It is my view that this popularity is often based on a fundamental misreading of the work. In a world of high-flying theory and heavily self-conscious poetry, Larkin has often been appraised as an essentially simple poet, endlessly refreshing and rewarding by virtue of that very simplicity. Furthermore, his poetry is regarded by many as that of the disillusioned, the fearful and the sad; therein, so it is argued, lies his appeal – his work offers analgesic solace, especially to those who have freed themselves from the fetters or false consolations of religion. This 'popular Larkin', poet of both supermarket and suburb, but also beloved by certain cultural elites and featured in many a teaching syllabus, has attained almost mythical status in the public and critical mind.

A signal (albeit hostile) instance of such mythologization is to be found in Al Alvarez's essay 'The New Poetry, or Beyond The Gentility Principle' of 1962.[2] He quotes these words from Larkin's 'Church Going': 'Hatless, I take off / My cycle-clips in awkward reverence'; and continues:

> This, in concentrated form, is the image of the post-war Welfare state Englishman: shabby and not concerned with his appearance; poor – he has a bike, not a car; gauche but full of agnostic piety; underfed, underpaid, overtaxed, hopeless, bored, wry ... he is just like the man next door – in fact, he probably *is* the man next door.
>   Now, I am wholly in favour of restoring poetry to the realm of common sense. But there is always the delicate question of how common common sense should be ...

This not only misrepresents 'Church Going':[3] it centrally associates Larkin with the accusatory 'Gentility Principle' of Alvarez's title in a way I find bewildering. There may be deleteriously genteel passages in Larkin's early verse, but by the time of 'Church Going' (1954) he had developed a forensically exact diction and a toughness of treatment that strike me as the very opposite of what Alvarez detects. Moreover, the Identikit portrait of the poem's speaker is wildly at odds with both the sardonic, irreverent comedy of the poem's first two stanzas and the remarkably philosophical, individual and profound reflections that comprise the remaining five.

That local objection duly logged, the fact remains that myth *is* a fundamental property in Larkin's work; however, it operates at a level and in a fashion utterly distinct from those just outlined. So often seen as the poet of the quotidian, Larkin's work is at root driven by a mythic determination to shape his identity as an artist, and one cannot properly understand that work if this underlying force is not acknowledged in full.

As both man and poet, Larkin wore many masks. Not in the self-conscious way of either the existentialist thinker Søren Kierkegaard (1813–55), with his use of various pseudonyms, or the Portuguese poet Fernando Pessoa (1887–

1935), who created a variety of what he called 'heteronyms' to offset and complement the 'orthonym' that was the poet when he wrote in his own name. A central figure in European Modernism, Pessoa spoke of a 'drama in persons, not in acts'. Although Philip Larkin always wrote in his own name, it is essential to identify and understand the many masks he used, consciously or otherwise, in order to come closer to what he felt was his authentic voice.

Arguably the most serious flaw in all those who approach his work in a biographical frame of mind is the assumption that the 'I' in his poems – and many of them do feature the first person – is necessarily Philip Larkin. There are times when that is true – 'Self's the Man', 'Dockery and Son' and the regrettably infamous 'This be the Verse' come immediately to mind.[4] In the main, however, to assume that, as the (rather tiresome) modish phrase has it, 'What you see is what you get' applies in Larkin's case is as mistaken as assuming that, say, Iago or Lady Macbeth 'are' Shakespeare. In a fine lecture delivered some years ago, James Booth drew attention to Larkin's matchless ability to mock his own poeticisms without undermining what they actually say, pronouncing it 'organic, life-affirming comedy of Shakespearian proportions'.[5] I would use the same three adjectives in relation to his use of persona and mask – and the noun 'comedy' is also pertinent, in that there is a profoundly ludic streak in much of Larkin's writing (prose as well as poetry), not least in his playful delight in 'pretending to be me'.

One such deliberate disguise has led to considerable critical confusion, even wrong-headedness. Like many writers before and after him, Larkin was a formidable theoretician of his own work, and he has proved adept at predicating the terms in which his work should be discussed; or to put it another way, his *obiter dicta* have too often been blithely accepted at face value with nowhere near enough circumspection or analytical rigour. One such instance forms one of the two epigraphs to this book – a statement of almost stupefying disingenuousness which has been taken seriously by far too many.

Another is Larkin's 1965 revelation that he switched 'overnight' from Yeats to Hardy as his source of inspiration. That did not satisfy me 20 years ago, and it does so even less now; nevertheless, it is a point of view which demands an answer. My attempt at that can be found in Chapter 5; I introduce it here *via* Ernst Cassirer's words written over 50 years ago at a time when, coincidentally, Larkin had truly found his voice as a mature writer.

What poetry expresses is neither the mythic world-picture of gods and daemons, nor the logical truth of abstract determinations and relations. The world of poetry stands apart from both, as a world of illusion and fantasy – but it is just in this mode that the realm of pure feeling can find utterance, and can therewith attain its full and concrete actualisation. *Word and mythic image, which once confronted the human mind as hard realistic powers, have now cast off all reality and effectuality; they have become a light, bright ether in which the spirit can move without let or hindrance.* This liberation is achieved not because the mind throws aside the sensuous forms of word and image, but in that it uses them both as organs of its own, and thereby recognises them for what they really are: forms of its own self-revelation.[6] [My emphasis]

The italicized sentence, in particular, points to the change in Larkin's diction and preoccupations after he had completed his novels and *The North Ship*. Not immediately, but still with remarkable speed, he found a way to allow his own 'spirit' to 'move without let or hindrance'; paradoxically, at the same time he found a much more disciplined and mimetically enabling poetic lexis, thus combining freedom of spirit with rigorous craft in a fashion that had only fleetingly characterized his previous work.

The 'liberation' and 'spirit' of which Cassirer speaks were in Larkin's case remarkably symbiotic. It wasn't just that his Muse enabled him to explore 'the realm of pure feeling' in a fashion quite different from (indeed, largely absent in) his earlier writing. It also led him to a cognate of 'spirit' – a deep and abiding interest in *spirituality*. The 1946 'Going' and 'Wedding Wind' reverberate with religious and biblical connotations, and while those poems are not fully representative of the mature Larkin, they nevertheless point the way. He had freed himself of the inner-directed self that predominates in *The North Ship* and, rather like Robert Browning, found he could investigate through mask and persona states of existence that were not his own but which he understood, could penetrate and capture.

Larkin was also brave enough, as man and artist, to confront his own uncertainty. The three words which end 'Mr. Bleaney' – 'I don't know' – have an enormous resonance in terms of his *oeuvre*. One of his poems is entitled 'Ignorance'; many others project an engaged perplexity, be the focus marriage, religion, social mores and social change, or our species's defining mortality. Notwithstanding John Betjeman's affectionate tribute – 'I love Larkin: he's so gloriously *glum!*' – Larkin is hardly ever a gloomy poet and often a profoundly affirmative one: his stance and spirit of enquiry are not 'negative', 'morose' or any of the many other condescendingly limiting adjectives that have been applied to him. On the contrary, his work evinces a tough-minded honesty that distinguishes the truly adult man and artist. As Goethe put it:

To be uncertain is uncomfortable; but to be certain is ridiculous.

The mention of Betjeman was not just a passing reference: he has often been 'paired' with Larkin, and I explore that relation shortly. Before that, I want to look at Larkin's affinity with another British poet, R. S. Thomas.

At first glance, the connection seems eccentric – unless one takes the view that Larkin is as lugubrious in his way as Thomas is in his, and it should already be clear that I do not. Furthermore, Thomas does not strike me as lugubrious either; on the other hand, much of his poetry certainly dramatizes anguished faith, a persona pulled between belief and doubt – an inner conflict enacted in an unambiguously Christian context. So wherefore my suggested link with one of English poetry's more celebrated atheists?

While 'anguished' and of course 'Christian' do not characterize Larkin, he does in his inimitable fashion wrestle with spiritual matters as often as does Thomas. 'Going', 'Wants', 'Dockery and Son', 'Days', 'Water', 'The Explosion', 'Solar', 'Aubade' itself and perhaps above all 'Church Going' – all these and a significant number of other poems find Larkin investigating the attraction and mystery of the numinous in a compelling variety of ways. Perhaps because of his final disinterest, he does this more subtly and with a lighter touch than did Thomas or the similarly anguished Gerard Manley Hopkins (with whose work Larkin was certainly familiar). Despite such differences, however, a congruence can certainly be traced; in some ways, Larkin is closer to Thomas in both technique and concerns than to any of 'The Movement' figures with whom Larkin has been associated.[7] Apposite here are these 1939 reflections by the painter Joan Miró:

> If [as artists] we do not attempt to discover the religious essence, the magic sense of things, we will do no more than add new sources of degradation to those already offered to the people of today, which are beyond number.[8]

Thomas and Larkin went about such a mission in very separate ways, granted, but they are akin to an extent that cannot be said of Larkin's relation to Betjeman.[9]

Once again, that may seem an eccentric proposition: on the surface, those two poets had plenty in common. Both were popular, and both were fondly regarded as very 'English' poets; both used persona and mask; both were in their different ways social chroniclers; and both had a governing extra-literary passion – architecture for Betjeman, jazz for Larkin. And an additionally intriguing, localized link is Betjeman's 'Inevitable': not only does its title echo Larkin's last reported words, 'I am going to the inevitable,' but these lines in stanza two –

> Is he too ill to know that he's dying?
> And, if he does know, does he really care?

– are highly reminiscent in matter (if not in diction) of Larkin's 'The Old Fools', while stanza three's

> Speech becomes sacred near silence everlasting
> Oh if I *must* speak, have I words to say?

is analogous in its spiritual preoccupation to 'Church Going'.

Yet the differences between them are larger than the congruencies (discounting the fact that Betjeman accepted the Poet Laureateship whereas Larkin turned it down). Betjeman's masks were notably extrovert: he was used to the public persona and honorific self-presentation – as witness his many television appearances. More than once Larkin pronounced himself 'timid': he eschewed television almost entirely, was not comfortable recording his own work, and in sum created his mythology and its attendant masks in an introverted, even self-abnegating fashion.

They were also quite different as social chroniclers. Betjeman's strengths in this respect are well known and rightly fêted; Larkin's have hardly been considered, let alone fully recognized, and I wish to redress that at once.

Much has been written over the years about Larkin's 'Englishness'; since the appearance of the *Selected Letters* and *A Writer's Life*, much of that commentary has been distinctly unflattering. The concept itself has always irritated me: too often it leads to imprecise cultural attitudinizing at the direct expense of how the writing in question actually works, what it's about and why it appeals. (Evelyn Waugh and P. G. Wodehouse have been notable casualties in that regard.) However, in Larkin's case there *is* an undoubted 'Englishness' about his work – a muscular, revelatory, even priceless one – and to explore it I want to draw on Nikolaus Pevsner's classic survey, *The Englishness of English Art*.

The governing thesis of that book (whose first incarnation was as the Reith Lectures in 1955, the year Larkin's first mature collection, *The Less Deceived*, was published) hinges on the idea that English art is best approached through Complementary Opposites, exemplified by the formal house and the picturesque garden, and by the contrasting approaches of Turner and Constable. And at one point Pevsner produces a series of judgements and reflections that are almost uncannily apposite to Larkin's own style and preoccupations.

> [T]he English portrait also keeps long silences, and when it speaks, speaks in a low voice, just as the Englishman does to this day, and as indeed the muffled sound of the English language seems to demand. Or, to put it differently, the English portrait conceals more than it reveals, and what it reveals, it reveals with studied understatement. These men and women [in the portraits] illustrate what Jane Austen ... calls 'The true English style' by 'burying under a calmness that seems all but indifference, the real attachment'.[10] 'Dr. Livingstone, I presume' is the *locus classicus* of this aspect of Englishness ...[11]

It is not just that passage which makes Pevsner's book a valuable source in appraising Larkin's poetic method and voice. It so happens that the only then-contemporary artist whom he mentions is Henry Moore; were Pevsner writing the book today, it is probable that his focus would be directed at Tracey Emin or Damien Hirst. Just as the artistic landscape has changed over those 50 years, so has the social landscape – and an unwitting bonus of Larkin's mature verse is that it offers a notably dense and precisely detailed account of the social history of the time.

I have taught adults all my working life, but for 35 years my main job has been as a secondary school teacher; I don't believe I would have become fully aware of this rich dimension in Larkin's work were it not for that fact. Until I taught his poems regularly to younger students, it never occurred to me that the world Larkin described and the language he used to do so were historically confined or 'parochial'. If it wasn't exactly *my* world, I could recognize it at once, having been a child in the 1950s (*The Less Deceived*) and a burgeoning adult in the 1960s (*The Whitsun Weddings*). In the same way, his idioms and his slang were instantly familiar, all the more pleasing for being so in the midst of work that demanded such close attention and exact decoding.

However, when I began using his poems on a systematic basis with sixth-formers and more junior pupils too, I soon realized that our difference in age was, for once, crucial. It became apparent that far more vocabulary-explanation-&-clarification was going to be needed than I had anticipated: there were a host of things that even the brightest and most well-informed student did not know. Amongst all else, that prompted the poignant reflection that many poems distinguished for their idiomatic flair and a near-infallible sense of linguistic pertinence now require substantial glossing to make them fully comprehensible. And it is further clear to me that such glossing will need to be increasingly multi-layered.

It's not merely things like 'stewed', 'plugging at the four aways' and the kind of 1950s fashions described in 'The Whitsun Weddings' that puzzle, nor (to many) the arcane references to jazz records and jazz musicians. Just as redolent of a past age are what ambulances actually looked like 40 years ago – sleek, sinister, instantly alarming; the sheet music central to 'Love Songs In Age' (almost all my students think that 'played' indicates records, even iPods); the culture of the Western that drives the final stanza of 'A Study of Reading Habits', or that of Enid Blyton's Famous Five, which has an important incidental role in 'I Remember, I Remember'; virtually every reference in 'The Large Cool Store' and, self-evidently, 'MCMXIV'; all three sections of 'Livings'; the governing mentions of 'the Beatles' and 'Chatterley' in 'Annus Mirabilis'; even 'pithead' and 'slagheap' in 'The Explosion'.[12]

Nor does the complexity end there. Locale and topographical description; social customs, habits, expectations and values; attitudes to sex, money, empire, subsidized art, work, religion – all these are subject to frequent and superficially dramatic change. It would be absurd to suggest that the England Larkin described from 1950 to 1975 is nowhere to be found any more; however, many assumptions that underlie or inform his poems now need fairly lengthy explanation to a young audience. Because those assumptions remain vibrant, and because he realizes them so well in poetic form, that need to explain is not a problem: it becomes indeed an added pleasure, for teacher and class alike. But nowadays poems like 'Toads' and 'Toads Revisited', 'Self's the Man', 'Dockery and Son', 'Show Saturday' and the unfinished 'The Dance' require as much sociological as literary commentary, even if the latter is soon able to prevail as it should.

Before I further develop this survey of half-buried treasures, there is one poem which, ironically, needs no sociological glossing for today's young: 'Going, Going'. They know exactly what he's talking about and at once: I have used the poem to good effect in Citizenship classes as well as English ones, since it has such an evident sociopolitical thrust.

I say 'ironically' because to my mind the poem suffers from being, simply, *wrong*. 'Going, Going' was written at the behest of the Department of the Environment, who wished to increase public awareness of 'green' issues.[13] The poem is expertly crafted (the ellipsis early in stanza six signalling an abrupt switch of focus is particularly felicitous) and often powerfully expressed. The trouble is, 'the whole / Boiling' has not become 'bricked in'; not only did his baleful prophecy not 'happen, soon': it hasn't happened at all. But then being a prophet was not Larkin's métier,[14] which was rather the meticulous, unique observation of how things are.

Or how they *were*: his poems 'show us what we have as it once was' and communicate, too, a sense of 'Such absences!'. The unusual triptych of portraits captured in 'Livings' is a compelling example. 'I' memorializes the agricultural travelling salesman who thinks it 'time for change, in nineteen twenty-nine', a last line of stunning power, evoking the imminent Depression just as precisely as it does the fustily unique ambience of the 1920s 'Hotel'.[15] 'II' features a lighthouse-keeper, but there's nothing 'glum' about this portrayal of what has been termed 'the loneliest job in the world': the poem is robustly joyous, cherishing in its own way the 'secret, bestial peace!' that is championed at the end of 'The Card Players'. And 'III', in addition to its insights into the rarefied world of High Table dinner at an Oxford college, epitomizes an important Larkin trait on which I shall be focusing regularly – his *sprezzatura* nature. That term, coined by Castligione in *The Courtier*, indicates the conscious determination to wear one's learning and gifts lightly – another use of 'mask' at which Larkin was supremely adept.

Larkin the 'accidental social historian' is arguably at his finest in 'The Building'. A poem of great power and range in both its emotional and spiritual concerns, it also captures the *sui generis*, uncomfortable and fear-inducing ethos of the modern hospital. In that respect it is both timeless and precisely historical, as in such moments as 'rows of steel chairs', 'the ripped mags', 'kids' chalk games' and 'girls with hair-dos fetch / Their separates from the cleaners.' The poem's greatness transcends such considerations, certainly, but they are nonetheless part of that greatness – a judgement which can be applied to a host of other Larkin pieces too.

'Sunny Prestatyn', for all its many qualities, is not quite such a towering achievement as 'The Building'. But it quintessentially illustrates why Betjeman and Larkin are so different as social historians and commentators. Betjeman could be not just tart but acidic – think of 'Come friendly bombs . . .' – but his was a sensibility that could not have conceived of 'Sunny Prestatyn', let alone delivered it. Larkin's poem is driven by rage at hypocrisy, a deep if obliquely stated sympathy for the disadvantaged and the infirm, and a scathing awareness of commercial lying accompanied by a healthy empathy with those who take to vandalism in their response to it. It may seem an odd thing to say about the man who once said, 'Oh, I adore Mrs Thatcher', but Larkin the poet's soul was a radical, even Romantic one.

Just as decisive in separating rather than linking Betjeman and Larkin are those aforementioned 'extracurricular' interests. The former's passion for architecture was no less sincere and authoritative than Larkin's love for jazz, and it has been critically glossed in a detailed and edifying way. My strong suspicion is that such an approving response derives from a like-minded admiration in Betjeman's readers for the subject of his absorption. That cannot possibly be said about Larkin's jazz.

At the start of this Preface I outlined three puzzles which I have always seen as central to an understanding of Larkin's work. The first two are, ultimately, matters of opinion or interpretation. The third is a scandalous matter of *fact*. Twenty-plus years since his death, none of his now-many biographers[16] and only a tiny number of his multitudinous critics have addressed the enduring love of Larkin's life. He cared about and loved jazz more than poetry or any form of literature; more than his various women; more than his work. While all those things were, *pace* any number of post-Motion and post-*Letters* accusations and innuendos, honourably and seriously important to him, jazz transcended them all.

It is no accident that long after his poetic Muse had deserted him ('Aubade' the exception proving the rule) he continued to write with zeal, insight and surgical skill about jazz music; it is likewise no accident that the first truly auspicious piece he composed was his 1940 'The Art Of Jazz'. Occasionally impenetrable and pompous it may be, but its crusading seriousness of purpose puts the post-adolescent posturing of *The North Ship* and the prolix arch nonsense that is his 'Brunette Coleman' *oeuvre* into stark perspective.

You cannot fully understand Larkin's work unless and until you honour and absorb that defining passion. It is not just that he was and remains one of the most acute, scholarly and enduring jazz critics extant. Even more important is the 'ear' that made him such, for it informed everything that is best about his work. It was his greatest asset as a writer, but he took a long time to find it, or rather to take full and decisive advantage of it. In one of his *Daily Telegraph* columns devoted to the review of jazz records he wrote:

> He [the critic] must hold on to the principle that the only reason for praising a work is that it pleases, and the way to develop his critical sense is to be more acutely aware of whether he is being pleased or not.[17]

Significantly, the piece was entitled 'How Am I To Know?'. By this time – 1966 – Larkin not only knew what pleased him as a listener (though he was much more catholic than many have acknowledged): he had long known what most pleased him *as a writer*. He ended another jazz piece, a 1981 essay on Duke Ellington, by quoting its subject thus:

The band you run has got to please the audience. The band I run has got to please me.[18]

Larkin's eventual practice and success are distinctly analogous. The mature Larkin's ear for speech-rhythms, idiom and, simply, what best resounds is of the highest order. But he didn't get there until he had acknowledged the Pleasure Principle in terms of his own inner satisfaction; once he did so, his poetry was transformed and – not at all coincidentally – quickly latched onto by the reading public.

Jazz was therefore a primally enabling force in Larkin's personal and professional life as well as his greatest joy. But his writings on the subject make as much use of mask and persona as do his poems. The still widespread and total ignorance of his jazz work or the failure to appreciate the rhythms of his career is not entirely the fault of others. 'Oh, play that thing' he wrote in 'For Sidney Bechet', and to this reader/listener, those four words resonate almost endlessly. Larkin was, by all accounts, a halfway decent jazz drummer and an adequate blues pianist; but in an overall sense, there have been very few better, more artful 'players' than Philip Larkin, Writer. That defining deceptiveness is epitomized by his writings on jazz, which is where I begin this survey.

Author's Note: It will be abundantly evident by now how important and variously illuminating I consider Larkin's writings on jazz to be. However, those readers whose interest in or knowledge of the music is slight might wish to peruse the later chapters first. I have sought to make each chapter self-contained, and while of course there are governing motifs and strands of argument informing the book as a whole, each section can I hope be read piecemeal without significant loss of understanding or response.

Part 1

Larkin's Jazz: 'An Enormous Yes'

Chapter 1

Prologue: 'Useful to Get That Learnt'

Why begin with the jazz? It's a big risk: most of Larkin's readers regard his love of jazz as a charming but irrelevant quirk, roughly equivalent to trainspotting or stamp-collecting.

John White[1]

Just so. If 20 years after his death Larkin's poems are even better known than when he was alive, his jazz criticism remains largely a closed – in many cases never-opened – book.

One reason for beginning with jazz is that it was the longest-lived and most durable of the things that drove him, as both man and writer. It was the subject of arguably his first significant piece ('The Art of Jazz') and he continued to write vigorously about it years after his poetic muse had withered. If it would be presumptuous to call jazz the love of his life, it can certainly be seen as his lifeline, or as the soundtrack to that life. Moreover, his writer's voice is predicated in jazz: its rhythms, its ambiguities and paradoxes, its humour and its sheer common humanity.

Secondly, Larkin's jazz writings repudiate two slurs which have enjoyed widespread currency of late – that he was an anti-modernist Philistine and a closet racist. One can go further: if his jazz work had been properly attended to by Larkin's detractors, including Andrew Motion, such canards might never have been conceived. The 1999 publication of what is now *Philip Larkin: Jazz Writings*[2] and work by other commentators have somewhat redressed that particular balance; however, they have only adjusted the overall picture, not its detail. When it comes to the specifics, there seems to have been virtually no increase in conversance: two recent and otherwise valuable surveys of Larkin's work virtually ignore jazz altogether.[3] Shortly before he embarked on his first jazz reviews, Larkin wrote 'Ignorance' (1955): the noun is still all too sadly appropriate when it comes to appraisal of his jazz writing.

Moreover, that 'ignorance' is in many cases perverse rather than merely uninformed. To this day, most literary critics of Larkin freely – on occasion *proudly* – admit their lack of interest in jazz or their incapacity to judge Larkin's writings on the subject. Conversely and equally, a sizeable number of jazz critics consider Larkin a hopeless Mouldy Fig, someone who got off the train in about 1945 and could do little more thereafter than sneer foolishly down the track.[4] In both cases the verdict can only be one of abject laziness. Each stance does both Larkin and his readers major disservice, being equally wrong and pernicious in its differing way. Each has helped sustain the neglect of what Larkin had to say about something that mattered passionately to him for 50 years, and each has contrived to lend that neglect a spurious dignity.

The jazz that mattered to Larkin was typified by Duke Ellington,[5] Sidney Bechet (for whom he would later write a poem[6]) and above all Louis Armstrong. These masters of orchestral colour and solo virtuosity epitomize an art of tough joy, deceptive emotional range and complexity, and above all rhythmic élan. When in 1969 Peter Crawley (Faber & Faber's sales director) asked Larkin to provide some autobiographical reflections which might help promote the manuscript which became *All What Jazz*, he responded with:

> I became a jazz addict at the age of 12 or 13, listened avidly to all the dance bands of the day and tried to learn to play the drums, began collecting records, and ... have never ceased to be an enthusiast ... I think jazz was the emotional excitement peculiar to my generation ('in another age it might have been drink or drugs, religion or poetry'[7]) ... (*SL*, p. 416)

As a youth in Coventry in the 1930s, Larkin had first listened to British dance bands like Harry Roy's on the radio, eagerly awaiting a 'hot' break from a sideman. At the local Hippodrome, he was entranced by the antics (and paraphernalia) of the resident drummer, and persuaded his parents to buy him 'an elementary drum kit and a set of tuition records by Max Abrams', on which he 'battered away contentedly, spending less time on the rudiments than in improvising an accompaniment to records'. As he recalled:

> I was, in essence, hooked on jazz even before I heard any . . . *what got me was the rhythm*.[8] That simple trick of the suspended beat, that had made the slaves shuffle in Congo Square on Saturday nights, was something that never palled. (*AWJ*, p. 16; my italics)

As his 1984 appearance on *Desert Island Discs* reveals, Larkin was familiar with and loved a wide range of music.[9] His choices included a Newcastle street song and Elgar's First Symphony; Tallis's 40-part motet (*Spem in Alium*) and Handel's 'Praise the Lord' from *Solomon*. However, the programme left no doubt that it was Larkin's jazz choices – including Armstrong and Billie Holiday – that meant most to him. When asked which single choice he would plump for if so compelled, he replied:

> It would have to be one of the jazz records. I can't live without jazz.[10]

In essence, Larkin loved jazz because (as he said immediately afterwards) 'it is so full of life and so invigorating'.

However, by the time he made that 1984 remark, the nature of jazz had long changed radically from the music which had once so entranced him. Originally a popular and dance-centred art form, jazz had metamorphosed into an overtly art-conscious, esoteric affair. Over 20 years ago I characterized such latter-day jazz as 'the twilight art',[11] and time would seem to have increased rather than diminished the force of that metaphor.

As just noted, it was not always thus. *Pace* a number of jazz historians, even at the height of its popularity jazz was never the preferred music of the masses.[12] But it remains the case that the basic idioms of jazz had spread all over the world by 1940: as Larkin puts it, 'that incredible argot that in the first half of the 20th century spoke to all nations and all intelligences equally'.[13] There is no doubt that when the young Philip Larkin was first captivated by what he heard on the wireless and on records, jazz enjoyed a considerable currency, especially in its more diluted incarnations. And that was still the case when he began his 11-year stint as the *Daily Telegraph*'s jazz critic in 1961.

Within half a dozen years all that had changed utterly. By the time Larkin's stint came to an end in 1971, jazz was in a crucially depressed state, a state which arguably deepened during the remaining years of his life. A minority taste had inexorably become an esoteric one, and by 1985 the cultural significance of jazz (not to mention its 'feel good factor') had shrunk almost to invisibility. It is therefore unsurprising that jazz *is* a closed book to so many otherwise cultivated and highly educated people – and in that respect there is nothing special about Larkin's contemporary readers.

Moreover, although the 'Record Diary' which forms the bulk of *All What Jazz*, and most of the pieces collected in *Philip Larkin: Jazz Writings*, reveal a commitment to jazz that approximates proselytizing zeal, it would not be difficult to infer from Larkin's remarks elsewhere that he thought that jazz had died, that it had become a museum piece, and that the only recourse was to treasure the artefacts that remained.[14] Many enthusiasts disagreed with him and continue to do so; that said, one cannot readily imagine how jazz will prosper and develop in this new century. All its greatest figures are dead, and cannot be replaced: there will be no new Louis Armstrong, Duke Ellington or Dizzy Gillespie.

That may not exercise many readers overmuch. However, it exercised Larkin: he regarded jazz as 'high art'. That was most obviously so when he addressed his lifelong favourites: Bechet, Bix Beiderbecke, Bessie Smith, early Ellington and early Count Basie, and, supremely, Armstrong, whom he once described without irony or playfulness as 'an enormously important cultural figure in our century, more important than Picasso in my opinion'.[15] But even the jazz he did not particularly care for, or actively disliked, he still took seriously as art. He had no time for poor musicianship or frivolity – 'facetious' is arguably the most damning word in Larkin's critical vocabulary – but otherwise his appraisal of jazz musicians was invariably sympathetic and morally approbatory.

Illuminating though such aesthetic and ideological attitudes are, they were and are secondary to the most important consideration of all: pleasure. For some 50 years, jazz was a profound and enduring source of delight for Larkin. The 1940 'The Art of Jazz'[16] ascribes to the music a cultural importance somewhat Jungian in thrust, and his last piece, written a year before his death, celebrates both the joys and dignity of 'this unique art'.[17] In between, he confessed during the late 1950s that the only book reviews he felt like doing were the jazz ones sent him by *Truth*[18] (and shortly afterwards the *Guardian*), and at no time did he regard such work as 'Required Writing' in any pejorative sense.

Furthermore, he wanted to spread the word. He quotes with ringing approval New Orleans trombonist Jim Robinson's celebration of jazz, 'Everyone in the world should know this',[19] and that commitment stayed with him to the end. With the major exception of 'Aubade' (1976), Larkin wrote little poetry of real note in the last ten years of his life, but he was still reviewing jazz books in 1984. Just two years before that, he wrote 'Pleasing the People' (on Armstrong), which is among the most fervently eloquent pieces he wrote anywhere.[20]

Plainly, therefore, jazz mattered very much to Larkin. But why should it matter to his readers? I devote the rest of this opening section to an attempt to outline some answers to that question. There are several such, and in many respects they illuminate Larkin the Poet as much as they do the nature of jazz and Larkin's impassioned delight in it.

Five fundamental questions

1. How many poems did Larkin write about jazz?
2. Is there a 'jazz flavour' to any of his other poems?
3. Why is jazz significant? Why did Larkin think so? ...
4. ... And why did he place so much stress on it as a *recorded* art?
5. Why do we need to understand Larkin the jazz fan to appreciate him properly as a poet?

Larkin wrote just five poems which centre on or significantly address jazz: 'Two Guitar Pieces' (1946), 'Reasons for Attendance' (1953), 'For Sidney Bechet' (1954), 'Reference Back' (1955) and the unfinished 'The Dance' (abandoned in 1964). The second question is a more nebulous matter, but 'Days' (1953) and 'Church Going' (1954) have rhythmic and dynamic properties that can be associated with jazz, and something analogous could be said about 'Fiction and the Reading Public' (1954) and 'Love Songs in Age' (1957).

However, not only does a single-figure total hardly suggest a governing theme or even a governing preoccupation: apart from 'Two Guitar Pieces', all the poems in question were written after Larkin had turned 30. We now know that the young Larkin was a highly prolific writer, and realization that his prentice poems did not remotely touch on the subject might strike some as disconcerting, given his baptism into jazz in his early teens. In fact, there are several literary reasons for that: they are as complex as important, and will be addressed in due course. For now, and with the third question in mind, there is just one exception to that 'jazz dearth' in his early work, and it is crucial.

'The Art of Jazz' is not cited in Bloomfield's *Bibliography*, nor does Larkin's typescript indicate for whom it was written or where it appeared. However, it prompted these illuminating comments from Andrew Motion:

> The significance of the essay lies in the way it values the depths rather than the surfaces of jazz. It shows that Larkin was willing to see that art needs to be both immediate and profound, to have elements of obviousness as well as obscurity, and if necessary to record these things in different tones of voice. In doing so, the essay sets out many of the principles which were to govern his mature writing ... (*AWL*, p. 57)

John White and I unearthed the essay in the collection of Larkin's papers held at Hull University, and it became the final piece in *Reference Back* (now *PLJW*). In our 1999 introduction we commented that although the piece is not well written for the most part, there is a raw passion to his proselytizing that impresses despite the prose. But I would now say that we (or at any rate I) did not sufficiently draw attention to these sentences:

> The predicament in which the unconscious is finding itself today is reflected in the general upheaval in all the arts, and particularly in the emergence of a new art, American Jazz music ... The modern unconscious has chosen to symbolize its predicament of subjugation through the music of a subject people; its predicament of imprisonment through the unvarying monotony of 4/4 rhythm; its panic at its predicament through the arresting texture of the Jazz tone.
>
> ... The decay of ritual having sundered conscious from unconscious, Jazz is the new art of the unconscious, and is therefore improvised, for it cannot call upon consciousness to express its own divorce from consciousness.
>
> ... In Jazz the unconscious describes itself almost in its own terms. Though we find it in a certain number of the conventional artistic emotions – the 'moods' of Ellington, the conscious beauty of Beiderbecke, the romanticism of Armstrong – if we move nearer the centre of the music we discover stranger qualities: the pure confidence of Frank Teschmaker [*sic*], the cantabile of Sidney Bechet, and the elemental, dancing gaiety of Pee Wee Russell. Here is the unconscious describing its own beauty and balance, as in Mozart, forever caged in the prison of four beats to the bar ... [T]he unconscious is in a new state, and has a new need, and has produced a new art to satisfy that need, and it is as well that we should understand.

That final sentence alone is enough to dispel any notion of Larkin as anti-modernist, as are the earlier reflections on subjugation and artistic imprisonment.[21] The last clause of all virtually answers on its own my third question, 'Why did Larkin think jazz significant?'; to that can be added these remarks Larkin made to Jim Sutton in 1939:

> You simply can't think of Jazz after Beethoven. It's a physical impossibility ... Not that I pretend to 'understand' it. It conveys nothing definite. But it's just 'big', that's all. Jazz isn't big ... [22]

It would be a mistake to see that last remark as either critical or dismissive. Larkin was trying to persuade Sutton that jazz is essentially a miniaturist art. This would especially inform his writings on the music's most distinguished composer, Ellington, whose more extended later works Larkin invariably found inferior to his shorter pieces. Some of that is due to the fact that he – and Ellington – grew up in jazz with the 78 and its (absolute maximum) playing time of four minutes. It also explains, in part, Larkin's antipathy to trumpeter Miles Davis and, especially, tenor saxophonist John Coltrane: he thought many of their performances simply too long to sustain attention.

What attracted Larkin to jazz at its best, as he experienced it, was the ways in which the power of the unconscious (which he addressed in his 1940 piece) had been distilled into the sort of forms that could speak of both joy and pain, rage and beauty, yearning and affirmation, fulfilment out of and despite adversity. The jazz that he loved was a music which spoke through simple forms – e.g. the 12-bar blues and the 32-bar popular song. Whatever the form, such jazz handled sentiment while eschewing sentimentality[23] and spoke to all manner of people.[24] It had the common touch without being vulgar, and as such would have said a great deal to Larkin about the potentiality of poetry in his own time.[25]

Larkin's perception of jazz's particular scale is telling in many ways. It points to something definitive in his own mature poetry – the ability to distil with concentrated force multiple ideas (and multiple tonal effects) within a short lyric: he never had any interest in the epic.[26] He is also quite right to dissociate jazz from classical music in the way that he does. Jazz has never been able to compete in terms of either harmonic sophistication or scale of composition: its chief and unique virtues lie elsewhere, and are almost invariably best effected on small rather than large canvases. It is no accident that, as will become evident, those virtues also attend all that is best in Larkin's work.

Contrary to the conventional wisdom that sees Larkin as essentially an anti-modernist, the jazz vein in his work allows us to apprehend to what extent he was, in fact, strikingly modernist in ambition and achievement. Along with film, jazz is often called the modernist art form par excellence. What the architect Mies van de Rohe said of modernist architecture – 'Less is more' – applies equally to the jazz that Larkin loved and championed.[27]

All modernist art looks for a new power-to-weight ratio in its elements; jazz is exemplary in this respect. A great improviser like tenor saxophonist Lester Young could float through the chord changes of a popular song in a funda-mentally different way from the equally important Coleman Hawkins (often called 'the father of the tenor saxophone'), who swaggered through every song he played, his huge sound matched by his harmonic and rhythmic imperiousness. The trajectory of a Young solo is quite other: lithe, caressing the beat rather than driving it, dancing with supple but understated grace. Whatever their stylistic differences, Hawkins and Young contributed equally (albeit discretely) to what might be termed the mythology of the tenor sax-ophone as arguably the most expressive of all jazz instruments.

The search for an analogously mythic power has exercised many a twentieth-century poet, and that search could be undertaken down varying routes. There are three poets, more or less Larkin's contemporaries, whom I would place alongside him in the first rank of poetic achievement: Ted Hughes, Seamus Heaney and Sylvia Plath. When you read the other three you are left in no doubt that you are in the presence of 'A Poet': that is, someone who among all else is very obviously performing, declaiming, demanding your attention. There is, of course, nothing wrong with that: if they choose to dramatize their search by writing as if in front of a bank of microphones, or from a podium, or a wired-for-sound psychiatrist's couch, that is perfectly all right. Ostentation has been a key part of the poet's game from the Greeks onwards, and it is both fun and edifying.

Larkin is rarely if ever like that. If Hughes thunders, Heaney lectures and Plath raves – and those verbs are employed with admiration, not condescension – Larkin seems to *confide*. In a very significant majority of his mature poems, the scene is as it were a fireside conversation between you and him – or rather, him and you. Larkin's feel for the ordinary rhythms of speech has rarely been surpassed, and in that respect his approach resembles the idiomatic, seemingly casual touch of Lester Young. One might compare Larkin's multi-toned achievement in this regard with that of Seamus Heaney: as Heaney is to Hawkins, so is Larkin to Young. The power of myth can be conjured by both a measured march and a lissom feint.

The jazz that would eventually feed Larkin's poetry so nourishingly was itself fed by many sources. The peculiar genius of jazz hinges on a number of apparently paradoxical hybrids. It is in essence a marriage of the European and the African, as might be expected of a music whose origins lie in American slavery. Its formal, melodic and harmonic base is European while its rhythmic one is African. Trumpeter Dizzy Gillespie happened upon a more idiomatic way of putting it when his quintet recorded 'Something Old, Something New' in 1963. The programme was a beautifully judged mixture of revisited (and revivified) bebop classics and invigorating new compositions; it can additionally be said that the title has an even greater resonance than the excellent individual performances themselves.

That defining hybrid sets the pattern for further contrasting congruencies. Jazz is an improvised music, yet most of its arrangements are written down or pre-ordained. It is a music of direct, ostensibly simple emotional appeal whose ways of achieving that effect were from the outset highly complex and went on becoming more so. It is about both the quest for authenticity and the use of masks; it is simultaneously high art and good-time music; it embraces profundity while loathing pretension; it is deeply serious while (usually) eschewing solemnity. It is often thought of as raucously extrovert music, yet its use of space, silence and tension-and-release is often as subtle as it is enabling.

A further paradox is that the origins of jazz are in stark sociological and technological contrast to its full twentieth-century incarnation. Conceived in

slavery via the spiritual and field-holler, its post-Civil War development –
including the creation of that most definitive jazz form, the 12-bar blues –
burgeoned in a setting that was still rural, primitive, harshly disenfranchised:
as Larkin observes, it was absolutely 'the music of a subject people'. Yet by the
time the (white) Original Dixieland Jazz Band (ODJB) cut the first-ever jazz
recordings in 1917, the music was the preserve of the cities – their dance-halls,
brothels, clubs and private houses.

And that inaugural ODJB Chicago recording session had an even more
fundamental significance. From that time forth, jazz would have a symbiotic
relationship with technology: their histories are inseparable. Whatever cur-
rently fashionable weight is given to the oral tradition, and despite the never-
ending reflections by both musicians and critics on the virtues of 'live' jazz
over studio dates, recordings have been the music's very lifeblood. Larkin
himself took that truth a signal step further: he hardly ever attended a jazz
concert or any other live gig, and in September 1970, reviewing Derek Langridge's *Your Jazz Collection*, he quotes with approval this stern observation by
the author:

> 'live' listening to jazz has drastic limitations. In time it cuts off the past, in space it
> reduces to the accident of where one lives … The real jazz lover must be a record
> collector.[28]

From technology to musical technique. Jazz is as technically advanced as any
other musical genre: the best jazz musicians are dedicated craftsmen just as
their classical counterparts are, every bit as adept, and in a number of cases
they have extended the capability of the instruments in question (especially
the saxophone family). The great jazz bassist Ray Brown once commented
caustically, 'Some people think we just roll out of bed one morning able to
play the D-flat scale.' Recalling his 15-year partnership with pianist Oscar
Peterson he further observed,

> We worked at it every day, every night. And if you want to be that good playing jazz,
> you have to work at it all the time. We did a variety of things, and Oscar wrote some
> hard music; but he didn't write it down. We had to memorise all of it … And Oscar
> would play a tune in one key one night and walk in and play the whole arrangement
> in another key a week later.[29]

Mention of Peterson leads me to another matter that is central to the
achievement of Philip Larkin, Writer. The pianist happens to be my favourite
of all jazzmen, just as Larkin is my favourite twentieth-century poet, but it is
neither chauvinism nor whimsy which prompts the suggestion that they are
considerably alike. Both are virtuosos – Peterson dazzlingly so, Larkin altogether more quietly – and that virtuosity has caused many observers either to
dismiss or misunderstand them. Here is guitarist Herb Ellis, a member of
Peterson's Trio for five years,[30] on his boss:

We were very conscious of the reviews Oscar got. They all said the same thing, in essence. It's cold, it's mechanical. Granted he's a technician of the piano, they said, but he's got no definitive style. First of all, they're not really hearing him. They're not hearing the depth of it. They're only hearing the surface. They're only hearing a lot of notes ... [and] they arrive at the conclusion that if you have a tendency to play a lot of notes, it's got to be cold. They miss the point. They just miss the whole point. I've played with a lot of people, and a lot of piano players. I've never played with anybody who had more depth and more emotion and feeling in his playing. He can play so hot and so deep and earthy that it just *shakes* you when you're playing with him. Ray and I have come off the stand just shook up. I mean, he is *heavy*. If you're not up to hearing it, well that's your loss. I won't even discuss it with anybody, because there's nothing to discuss.[31]

Maybe it's not the first word one might associate with Larkin, but he is 'heavy' too – in the sense that his virtuosity can compel, captivate and 'shake' readers into new apprehensions, even newly discovered emotions. Those who hear only Peterson's profusion of notes and not the depths and textures which underscore them are comparable to those who can only apprehend Larkin the Little Englander or Larkin the Parnassian Ron Glum.[32]

Of course, for such views to be 'corrected' requires access to things recorded, whatever the medium. I know quite a few jazz enthusiasts who, left cold by Peterson in concert, came to hear something other than technical supremacy in his work through immersion in his records. The parallel with Larkin's poems is only a loose one; nevertheless, I have also encountered more than a few readers who have had their minds radically changed about the quality or meaning (sometimes both) of a Larkin poem by a similarly focused absorption. The point is important for two reasons. As noted, Larkin thought the true jazz fan must be a record collector, but he also challenged the truism that poetry is before all else a *public* medium. He disliked poetry readings (especially when compelled to perform himself) because he felt that so much in the poems, whether his or anyone's of any merit, was automatically lost. One needs to read as well as hear, and at one's own pace, not the speaker's. Larkin referred to himself as 'timid' more than once, but it was not shyness or introversion that made him champion the private experience over the instant public one: it was a hard-nosed aesthetic awareness of what high art is and how it works.[33]

Two main considerations, then, determined my decision to 'start with the jazz'. The first is that a decisive majority of Larkin's readers, whether lay or professional, are only marginally conversant with that area of his work. As a devout jazz enthusiast myself, I would want to rectify that anyway, but I also think such remedial enlightenment is long overdue for rather less parochial reasons. Larkin's Jazz matters even if you're tone-deaf, unaware of or disapprove of the whole genre. His love of the music was all-informing, his understanding of it immense; for those reasons alone, anyone interested in his life needs to take proper note of it. But jazz also casts considerable light on his poetry; his cultural and social attitudes; and on two remarkable properties which I have come to think crucial to his overall achievement as both poet and critic: a governing if steely Romanticism, and what I will call a 'subterranean modernism'. As already intimated, that last idea flies in the face of both the received wisdom about him and many of his *obiter dicta*, and it requires a thorough exploration.

It makes sense to begin that task by examining Larkin's 'Introduction' to *All What Jazz*, since it is by far the best-known of his jazz pieces. But it is an apt point of departure for a quite separate reason as well. Sophocles observes in *Oedipus Rex* that 'Troubles hurt the most when they are self-inflicted'; I fear that Larkin's most celebrated jazz piece illustrates that truth all too poignantly.

Chapter 2

All What Jazz: Larkin's Most Expensive Mistake

Actually, I like to think of myself as quite funny, and I hope this comes through in my writing.[1]

Why did he think adding meant increase? To me it was dilution.[2]

Jokes are splendid things. Why should they be cheap?[3]

Prelude

Speaking as a teacher, I know of no writer (outside Shakespeare) who engenders more fun – including outright laughter – than Philip Larkin. His work engenders a good deal else, naturally, but one of the reasons why he goes down equally well with students is the rich variety of his wit. Needless to say, his calculated scatology is a major asset: youthful learners respond with immediate pleasure to this, whether it take the form of mildish oaths (e.g. in 'Toads', 'Poetry of Departures'), stronger stuff ('A Study of Reading Habits', 'Sunny Prestatyn') or the full-bore obscenity that regularly informs *High Windows*. Occasionally, as one might expect, their amusement has a sniggering dimension; invariably, though, the self-satisfied giggle at being allowed to read 'naughty words' in class soon gives way to an awareness of why such diction is enablingly apposite and of how Larkin's humour serves his most serious purposes.

That is as right as it is satisfying to witness. John White called Larkin 'the funniest man I have ever known or expect to know';[4] in addition, I have always thought it no accident that the Larkin of middle age bore a striking facial resemblance to the great Eric Morecambe. Nowhere is that more noticeable than on the cover to *All What Jazz* (hereinafter *AWJ*) – which is as fitting as poignant and fundamental to the primary thesis of this book.

Larkin's multiple masks and governing deceptiveness have been all too successful – by which I mean that, while those properties are responsible for so much that is fertile and stimulating, they have also sponsored palpable mis-understandings of his work and of him as a human being. To get to the core of Philip Larkin the man, we need to dismantle the particular deception that is *AWJ*, simply because jazz was the most important thing in his life – not just the jazz he loved but the art form itself. And very few Larkin acolytes, be they professional critics or otherwise, seem to have grasped that fundamental fact.

When I wrote 'poignant' just above, I was prompted by the thought that while the 'Introduction' to *AWJ* is arguably the most resplendently witty of Larkin's works, many of its best jokes failed to register, and that as an overall jest it backfired badly, effecting long-term damage on him both as a sensibility and as an intellectual. Larkin the Jazz Enthusiast may be thoroughly familiar to anyone conversant with the poet's life and work, but Larkin the Jazz *Critic* is known only as the figure who wrote that 'Introduction': a handful of exceptions duly admitted, none of those acolytes knows (or is even significantly aware of) the bulk of *AWJ*'s text. And as this section's title reluctantly signals, the blame for that must be laid chiefly at Larkin's own door.

Larkin's 'Record Diary'

Larkin the poet made his name with *The Less Deceived* in 1955. Larkin the jazz critic made his debut two years later as a book reviewer for first *Truth* and then the *Guardian*, the *Observer*, the *New Statesman* and other journals. He had written over a dozen such pieces when Donald Mitchell of the *Daily Telegraph* commissioned him to write a monthly column reviewing jazz records – an audacious initiative on two counts. It was surprising that an always-conservative national newspaper would want jazz records reviewed at all, and additionally enterprising in entrusting the task not to a practising musician but a poet, albeit one of growing renown.

Mitchell was doubly shrewd. He knew that the young Larkin had been captivated by the pre-war jazz he had heard on the wireless and on records; he was also aware that jazz continued to enjoy considerable currency, especially in its more diluted incarnations. In 1961, UK traditionalist bands were hot property: The Temperance Seven reached number one in the charts,[5] and there were significant hits for Acker Bilk, Kenny Ball and Terry Lightfoot. No less significant were top-ten appearances by modernists John Dankworth ('African Waltz') and Dave Brubeck ('Take Five'). In addition, there was a profusion of jazz-*tinged* successes. The zanily propulsive Marcels[6] and pianist Floyd Cramer ('On The Rebound') reached number one; both Ray Charles ('Hit The Road Jack') and Bobby Darin ('Lazy River') came close;[7] there were also hits for Nat Cole, Harry Belafonte and Cleo Laine. 1962 saw more major sellers from Bilk, Ball and Brubeck, Quincy Jones ('Soul Bossa Nova'), John Barry's decidedly jazz-flavoured 'James Bond Theme', tenor saxophonist Stan Getz (in the Top Ten on both sides of the Atlantic with 'Desafinado') and number one hits from the vulgar but jazz-oriented Bee Bumble & The Stingers ('Nut Rocker') and Charles, whose 'I Can't Stop Loving You' may not qualify as a jazz performance but was nonetheless a record by a major jazzman.

In short, jazz was still observably part of the common culture it had inhabited from the outset, and in its own aesthetic terms was arguably in its prime.

That at any rate is the view of saxophonist and critic Dave Gelly, writing in 1996:

> Looking back on the 1956–60 period ... it seems an impossibly rich and burgeoning time for jazz. From George Lewis to Miles Davis, almost every style could be experienced live, played by its authentic masters. The very oldest jazz musicians had barely reached the age of seventy, and most were in the prime of life. The one element common to all [was] a kind of expansiveness, an ease and lightness of spirit that comes from knowing one's trade and exercising it in congenial company, without fuss or formality. Across the gulf of the years, and in a very different time, such unpretentious eloquence can be unbearably touching.[8]

Missing here is a roll-call of those who died during the latter 1950s – among them Charlie Parker, Art Tatum, Lester Young and Billie Holiday; the 1957 demise of Norman Granz's Jazz at the Philharmonic; the separate sojourns away from American jazz undertaken by Stan Getz (playing in Scandinavia) and Sonny Rollins (on extended sabbatical in New York). But Gelly's account is persuasive. Jazz may never have had a sustainable claim to be any nation's pop music, but its health as a minority art form was good. It had survived the advent of rock 'n' roll, the creation of a new market for the young and the evolution of the 'teenager' (a word not coined until the late 1940s). New and exciting things seemed to be just around the corner.

They were for Larkin too. He was gratified by Mitchell's invitation,[9] and from the outset the columns testify how inspired the initiative proved. The prose abounds in *joie de vivre*, and Larkin's judgements display a genial rigour that extends to the appraisal of artists he did not particularly like and whom he would vilify, directly or by implication, in *ITAWJ*. If his first and third columns (February and April 1961) centre on his 'proper ground' – traditional jazz and the blues – March finds him giving an unreserved welcome to the reissue of Benny Goodman's 1938 Carnegie Hall Concert and a cautious one to the Modern Jazz Quartet's involvement in 'Third Stream Music'; May carries an affectionate look at the British trad boom, also reviewing albums by Duke Ellington, Johnny Hodges, Count Basie and modernists Dizzy Gillespie and Clifford Brown. That final brace may not elicit unambiguous enthusiasm but they are hardly dismissed: Larkin toys fondly with the idea of Gillespie becoming Ellington's solo trumpet, and Brown's playing is characterized by 'mellow agility'. But any surprise at such perceptible warmth is as nothing when one turns to the next piece.

Entitled 'Bechet and Bird', it contains Larkin's first substantial discussion of alto saxophonist Charlie Parker's music, and it requires specific contextualization. In the 'Introduction' Larkin has *inter alia* these things to say about Parker:

> I used to think that anyone hearing a Parker record would guess he was a drug addict ... compulsively fast and showy, [he] couldn't play four bars without

resorting to a peculiarly irritating five-note cliché from a pre-war song called 'The Woody Woopecker Song'. His tone ... was thin and sometimes shrill ... The substitution of bloodless note-patterns for some cheerful or sentimental popular song as a basis for improvisation ... was a retrograde step, but worse still was the deliberately-contrived eccentricity of the phrasing and harmonies. (*AWJ*, pp. 20–1)

To absorb that and then turn to the June 1961 column printed 20 pages later is a disorienting experience, and not just for the novitiate:

Parker ... had when he died, aged 34, seen jazz refashion itself pretty well in his image and heard his own solos coming back at him from a thousand horns. His technique and invention were prodigious, whereas no one would pretend that Bechet had any more of either than he needed. Yet both alike ... display unquestioned individual authority, unclouded and absolute. This is jazz and this is Bechet (or Parker) playing it ...

... From the first staggering cadenza in the Parker–Gillespie 'Night in Tunisia' we [encounter] Parker in such fast flight that only Gillespie could follow him ... One has the impression of a man who not only could translate his ideas into notes at superhuman speed, but who was simultaneously aware of half a dozen ways of resolving any given musical situation, and could somehow refer to all of them in passing beyond it ... In his extended solos in 'Groovin' High' and 'Confirmation' idea succeeds idea so unhesitatingly that the hearer acquits him of any premeditated desire to astonish. Clearly, his problem was how to get it out fast enough.

... But on the evidence of these solos alone it would be absurd to call Parker's music a reaction. As well call leaping salmon a reaction.

Can this be the musician many would have us believe Larkin *hated*? As David Wheatley has pointed out, 'The other two P's in his infernal trilogy, Pound and Picasso, never moved Larkin to praise like that.'[10]

Those first five columns set the tone (in all senses) for their successors. These next extracts span 1961–8.

1. The Modern Jazz Quartet has sometimes been condemned for an inbred academicism emanating from its leader, John Lewis, in whose hushed and respected aura vibra-harpist Milt Jackson is to be seen struggling like a fly in amber. To me, their music has a natural swing under its shimmering restraint. (p. 46)

2. [Gillespie's] solo on the 1946 'Night In Tunisia' ... [is] still tremendous; free, rocketing phrases, each punched out powerful and precise. Beside him, the rest of the group seems hardly to have emerged from the John Kirby era. (p. 58)

3. 'Tough Tenors' ... offers the sinuous-sinewy styles of [Eddie 'Lockjaw'] Davis and [Johnny] Griffin romping like young otters at play. (p. 76)

4. Paul Desmond has been called the Godfrey Winn of the [alto], but in 'Take Ten' his limpidity is never limp. (p. 107)

5. Jacques Loussier on 'Play Bach: Numéro Quatre' [comprises] tasteless expanses of real Bach themes distracted with aimless bits of syncopation [which] seem the acme of pallid vulgarity. (p. 116)
6. Bill Evans ... [on] 'Sunday at the Village Vanguard' seemed to me precious rather than valuable ... (p. 138)
7. If [Albert] Ayler's tenor sounds at times like a cello being scraped with a wet rubber galosh ... [his work is] no crazier than some European art music. (p. 152)
8. For my taste Tatum is rather like a dressmaker who, having seen how pretty one frill looks, makes a dress bearing ninety-nine ... (p. 156)
9. [Archie] Shepp and [John] Tchicai dingeing away ... (p. 162)
10. [On] 'Angry Tenors' ... [Ben] Webster is silky and delightful, and about as angry as a chocolate soufflé. (p. 200)

If those examples are selective rather than random – bypassing not only the musicians Larkin most loved but also Miles Davis and his undoubted *bête noire* John Coltrane – they are safely representative of what became *AWJ*'s main text and subtitle, 'A Record Diary' (henceforth *ARD*), and strikingly at odds with *ITAWJ* in both tone and judgement. All the musicians cited (apart from Tatum and Webster) are modernist in persuasion, an aesthetic Larkin is supposed to have detested. No such virulent antipathy is deducible; even the references to avant-gardists Ayler, Shepp and Tchicai are jaunty rather than vicious. And at least he mentioned them: a *real* Mouldy Fig would have found a way to exclude them from his copy on the grounds that any publicity simply encourages them and their no less deluded putative listeners.[11] Elsewhere, his comments range from thoughtful agnosticism (6 and 7) through warm approval (1, 4 and 10) to frank celebration (3 and especially 2). Only 5 sounds a Draconian note – and that is levelled not at Loussier the modernist but Loussier the trifler.[12]

In sum, all the *ARD* extracts cited so far exemplify the quality of Larkin's critical ear as much as the 'poet at work'[13] mastery of his pen, thereby demolishing three important myths. First, they make it impossible to contend that Larkin hated all post-1940s jazz on principle and to distraction. Second, they render ridiculous Max Harrison's claim that 'By 1961 Larkin had no idea where jazz was.'[14] Nobody could have coined such phrases as appear in 1 to 10 above without having both a profoundly engaged knowledge of jazz and a formidable feel for its peculiar joys. Third, they expose the various 'confessions' offered in *ITAWJ* as at best artful bunkum:

I hadn't really any intention of being a jazz *critic*. In literature, I understood, there were several old whores who had grown old in the reviewing game by praising everything, and I planned to be their jazz equivalent. This isn't as venal as it sounds. Since my space was to be so limited, anything but praise would be wasteful; my readers deserved to be told of the best of all worlds, and I was the man to do it. It didn't really matter, therefore, whether I liked things at first or not, as I was going to call them all masterpieces.

But there came a hitch. When the records, in their exciting square packages, began obligingly to arrive from the companies, the eagerness with which I played them turned rapidly to astonishment, to disbelief, to alarm. I felt I was in some nightmare, in which I had gone confidently into an examination hall only to find that I couldn't make head or tail of the questions. It wasn't like listening to a kind of jazz I didn't care for – Art Tatum, say, or Jelly Roll Morton's Red Hot Peppers. It wasn't like listening to jazz at all. (pp. 18–19)

The first paragraph is facetious nonsense. *ARD* runs to nearly 300 pages and encompasses getting on for 1,000 records: perhaps two dozen are termed 'masterpieces' or praised to that kind of level. More subtly but no less telling, not only do *ARD*'s assessments evince genuine pleasure more often than not: they are models of judiciousness. In the course of a 1984 conversation with A. N. Wilson Larkin declared: 'I really did put my effort into the reviews. I mean, when I review, I really take it very seriously ... It takes me an awful long time. *And that is what I would really like to be judged by.*'[15] On that occasion he was talking about books, but the credo informs his record reviews just as much. Yes, it is usually possible to infer his reservations or dislikes, but as a professional reviewer he never loses sight of the fact that his is 'not the only ear in the world' (*ITAWJ*, p. 28) and that his prime task is to tell other ears whether a record might be worth investigating or buying. The venal duplicity he ascribed to himself in 1968 is without foundation.

The second paragraph may be less obviously dishonest, but its claims still do not begin to match the constant edification provided by the reviews themselves. There could be few more futile exercises than to trawl *ARD* searching for admissible evidence of the reviewer's 'nightmare' or the governing sense that he's reviewing an alien music. Had that been the case, he would surely either have abandoned the job or been fired; more affirmatively, he could not possibly – as late as 1967 – have written appraisals of records by modernists Peterson, Dave Brubeck, Bill Evans and Jim Hall, Clark Terry and Ed Thigpen which consistently maintain a combination of geniality and acuteness.[16]

However, as 1967's columns unfold, a change does become noticeable. One is still a long way from the exuberant bad temper that permeates *ITAWJ*, but a certain tetchiness is evident in the sudden attack on Ellington (March); the witty but conclusively weary reflections in April on the antics of Archie Shepp in particular and the New Wave in general; July's newly crabby summaries of Thelonious Monk and Cannonball Adderley, two modernists whom he had often praised earlier; and of course his remarks on John Coltrane (August especially). Palpably, 'something has gone wrong'. But with what? Larkin? Jazz? Both?

'The dance' as requiem

I would plump for the second answer on the grounds that it was the artistic, commercial and spiritual crisis in the state of jazz that best explains Larkin's 1968 mood and performance; nevertheless, the other two considerations inevitably impinge. Before exploring all that, however, it is illuminating to consider what had happened to Larkin since his *Telegraph* debut, and what he had achieved.

By the time he had completed four years of record reviewing, Larkin was newly famous. The 1964 publication of *The Whitsun Weddings* was hailed by critics and the general public alike; the next year an official imprimatur arrived in the form of the award of the Queen's Gold Medal for Poetry. Moreover, by now he had fully established himself as a bona fide jazz critic. The monthly *Telegraph* columns increasingly commanded respectful attention, he was still in demand as a book reviewer, and in February 1965 he was invited to take part in the *Melody Maker*'s Critics' Poll – something of an honour in those days.[17] And two months later the *Telegraph* commissioned an essay which is the finest extended jazz piece Larkin wrote, and whose text, ethos and implications go to the heart of my concerns.

'Requiem for Jazz' (henceforth *RFJ*) appeared in the *Telegraph*'s recently launched colour magazine on Saturday 23 April. As the title indicates, it approximates an obituary notice, not only memorializing the pre-war jazz he loved so much but also brooding on the precipitous decline into obscurity of the genre itself. While that may appear to adumbrate the contentions dramatized in *ITAWJ* three years later, the tone is markedly different. Sorrow rather than anger is the key; in addition, the analysis of bop and of New Wave jazz, though evidently that of an outsider, is more judicious, more sympathetic and (crucially) broader. He recognizes that jazz's sidelining since the advent of the Beatles and the Big Beat would very likely have happened even if the music had been in a much healthier state. But he also emphasizes that the modern jazz of Coltrane *et al.*, its possible virtues notwithstanding, was neither dance-able-to nor fun, and that its harsh earnestness had caused that drift away from jazz to become something of an avalanche. The thesis was unwelcome then, and to many it remains inviolately so. Yet there is a profusion of evidence that endorses it – from Larkin's own pen, that of others, and things that may not have been written down but which significantly altered the fabric of Western cultural life.

In his most ambitious *Telegraph* column to date, March 1962's 'After the Moderns', an already troubled Larkin reflected:

> Despite the different facets of jazz today – the veterans, the blues, trad, mainstream, hard bop, soul, free form – the two primary questions about it are, first, is modern jazz driving out the traditional; and, second, if it is, can modern jazz keep the hold on public taste that traditional jazz had?

The answer to the first is yes. Jazz is always what the young American Negro is
playing, and today he is a modernist. Armstrong and George Lewis, Ellington and
Basie, Pee Wee Russell and Buck Clayton all maintain a traditional approach, but
they are all over 50 now and not being replaced.

The answer to the second is less clear. To some extent modern jazz, like other
modern arts, is a performer's art – it began, by all accounts, as a private language:
'Something they can't steal because they can't play it.' Its revolutionaries, however,
are already elder statesmen[18] (pp. 57–8)

This is largely prescient. Britain was still in the grip of the trad boom, but
Larkin's answer to his first question shows an awareness of how temporary and
finally irrelevant was that phenomenon, though he quite enjoyed the resultant
records. The great traditionalists may still have been playing, but they were
'not being replaced'. Within ten years nearly all of them would be dead, in
common with many other jazzmen of different persuasions.

The 'private language' point raises a different concern: whether jazz could
sustain its commercial appeal and thereby its aesthetic health. It is significant
that the column's last paragraph suggests that the music's 'future may be
shaped by tenorist John Coltrane' and concludes: 'As a taste of things to come
it is a thought glacial' (p. 59). The Ice Age duly arrived – and in doing so
mercilessly exposed Larkin's incautious assertion that 'Jazz is always what the
young American Negro is playing.' Overstated anyway, it was about to become
wildly inaccurate. Within a few years, black American musicians – and listeners
too – had turned away from jazz in their droves, favouring instead soul music,
rhythm 'n' blues or the rapidly expanding worlds of rock and pop. Some have
suggested that this desertion was prompted by the Beatles' conquest of the
USA in late 1963, but major domestic changes were already afoot. Tamla
Motown, which had begun the decade as a small independent company, soon
mushroomed into a gigantic corporation; such enterprises as those led by Phil
Spector and James Brown, as well as the Stax and Atlantic labels, enjoyed a
comparable success.

It would be silly to berate the 1962 Larkin for failing to foresee the extent
and rapidity of such change. No other critic predicted the cataclysm, and when
it came, he was among the first to identify one of the root causes: the demise of
jazz as 'good-time music'. An instance is the column of May 1964, which
launches a contention that would become familiar to readers of *ITAWJ* – the
history of jazz as a study in remorseless attenuation:

Originally an integral part of all aspects of Negro communal life, jazz in [the Swing
Era] became a nocturnal art for dancers only. And one could add that [the next
decade] shows the process going a stage further, a stage memorably summarized by
Benny Green in *The Reluctant Art* as 'After Parker you had to be something of a
musician to follow the best jazz of the day'. What was all-pervading had become
occasional; what was general, special; what was popular, esoteric. (pp. 111–12)

Those ominous reflections are confirmed by Richard Williams during his retrospective on 1965 (in *Long Distance Call: Writings on Music*, pp. 79–89). Intriguingly entitled 'Annus Mirabilis',[19] it charts his teenage exposure to what he calls 'the last year of innocence in popular culture' which 'contained so much great music that it would take a year to listen to it all even now'. Among the musicians and records he celebrates are Bob Dylan, the Byrds, the first three singles by The Who, a string of Motown hits, Van Morrison, *Rubber Soul* by the Beatles ('their most satisfying album') and the Righteous Brothers' 'You've Lost That Lovin' Feelin''.[20] As a recently converted jazz fan of 18 at the time, I did not share most of those enthusiasms then and I certainly don't now; nevertheless, Williams's absorbing reminiscences mount a persuasive case for 1965 as *the* 1960s year. Paradoxically, that is what Larkin does too: not for nothing was 1965 the year of 'Requiem for Jazz'.

If there was never a time when 'the righteous jazz'[21] was exclusively the popular music of the day, for a long time the two genres enjoyed an intimate relationship. To cite just two indices, jazz would have been infinitely the poorer without the nourishment afforded it by Kern, Porter, Rodgers and other masters of the American popular song, and the subsequent force of nature that was rock 'n' roll would have been impossible without that quintessence of jazz, the 12-bar blues. By 1965, hindsight suggests, that symbiosis was no more. Separation had replaced companionship; reciprocal benefit had become mutual contempt, even hostility. That is implicit in Williams's survey and more or less explicit in 'Requiem for Jazz'; if I incline to the latter's doleful case rather than to the former's more jubilant one, that is because I share Dave Gelly's belief: 'When jazz and popular music lose all contact with one another they both degenerate into pretentiousness, chaos and absurdity.'[22]

However, jazz might have survived this schism if that had been all there was to it. Like all modernist art, it had always had an avant-garde which (by definition) the general public did not take to; moreover, there were still plenty of musicians around who refused to turn their back on the audience, on Lester Young's ultimate court of appeal 'Can you sing me a song?'[23] and, above all, on the need to keep the foot engaged as well as the brain. But suddenly it was almost impossible to get across such jazz truths in the locales it had long regarded as its own: the ballroom, the club, anywhere with a dance floor. With astonishing rapidity, such places were superseded by the discothèque.[24] And it wasn't just the location or the ambience – colossal volume, fancy lighting effects – that changed so radically. So did the very nature of social dancing: come 1965 *danse à seul(e)* to a loud and insistent beat was the new orthodoxy. No rock musician has ever swung with the lissom power of (say) Armstrong, Peterson or the Basie Orchestra, but that rhythmic élan was no longer relevant to what the young wanted to hear, groove and twitch to.

All that underscores the composition of what is, in the view of many, the most tantalizing piece that Larkin ever wrote. When he began work on 'The Dance' in June 1963, he was exploring territory that would have been familiar to the majority of his readers, if not indeed central to their lives. The British palais and its many recognizable variants had been social meccas for two generations, and their enduring quotidian magic is perfectly identified in the poem's first four words – 'Drink, sex and jazz'. The virtual conflation of the second and third of those 'sweet things' could not be more apposite. The jazz at issue is jazz-as-dance-music, whose purlieu in both America and Britain had always been the ballroom or its equivalent. Even at its hippest, dancing was a close physical partnership between a couple. (That was precisely its appeal, and why such venues had prospered for so long!) More often than not, perhaps, the jazz would not have impressed the discerning listener, but that wasn't the point: the music's aesthetic qualities were decidedly subordinate to functional properties which both reflected and were determined by the mores of the time.

So despite the speaker's awkwardness and intermittent desire to flee, 'The Dance' is on one level a celebration of jazz-as-dance-music, and in ambience and detail it is absolutely of its time. British teenagers, 20-somethings and even 50-somethings had jived together happily enough to Barber, Bilk *et al.* during the trad boom, and plenty of the same was still going on. Not for much longer, though – which is why, on another level, 'The Dance' reads more like a prophetic autopsy: within less than a year the discothèque would in effect consign the traditional dance floor to history.

On and off, 'The Dance' occupied Larkin for over a year. The 1988 *Collected Poems* records it as abandoned in May 1964, but that is not quite so. As Trevor Tolley has shown, Larkin composed a further eight lines at some subsequent date.[25] He did not include them in his typescript version, and in all conscience it's not hard to see why. They do not comprise a full stanza, nor are they grammatically complete; with one exception they add nothing to what has already been achieved, and the stirring potential of that augmentation – 'I see for the first time as something whole / What earlier seemed safely divisible' – atrophies almost instantly: what that 'What' might be remains forever unrevealed. It is not fanciful to suggest that any such reader frustration is a mere echo of what the poet himself felt. The fact that there is no punctuation point after 'divisible' prompts the inference that it was at this precise point that the poem was shelved for good.

Tolley draws attention to six other lines which did not appear in the typescript version. They end – again with no punctuation point – 'But is it acting that creates a sense / Of something snapped off short, that arches tense /And aching from the gullet to the tongue'. However, in stanzas eight and nine of the 1988 *Collected Poems* version, one reads: 'The tense elation turned / To something snapped off short, and localized //[26] Half way between the gullet and the tongue.' If most readers are likely to endorse Larkin's preferred version as superior, that matters a lot less than the definitive importance of four words common to both. For 'something snapped off short' in effect serves as a multiple epitaph for the poem itself, the milieu it chronicles, and jazz as good-time music.

Tolley dismisses the notion that the poem lost impetus through problems of technique. I largely agree, though I would repeat my hunch that the poem's ever-growing size troubled Larkin.[27] I am less convinced by Tolley's accompanying argument that 'The Dance' found Larkin 'preoccupied with too many impulses ... [and] unable to bring them to coherence'. I take this to mean emotional and intellectual 'impulses'; I think the true cause was *sociological*.[28] The root of 'Larkin's difficulties' was external, something quite – and suddenly – beyond his control: he had not been deserted by his muse but overtaken by events. By the summer of 1964, it is as if he had sensed that the poem's abandoned status was more eloquent than any resolution could be. The world he had sought to capture when embarking on it a year before had become 'something snapped off short'.

And those four words could also be read as Larkin's diagnosis of the state of jazz by the mid-1960s. A slightly less dramatic but nonetheless close paraphrase of them – 'now dissipating and will not recur' (*PLJW*, p. 142) – appears in *RFJ*'s final paragraph, the rest of which makes explicit the conclusion I have drawn from 'The Dance' and its abandonment:

> Jazz was a unique phenomenon, set off by an unprecedented balance of sociological factors – in the same way as, shall we say, the Border ballads ... The music Parker split in two is now vanishing simultaneously into the vulgarities of popular entertainment, and will soon be a historical memory, like ragtime. The world will have lost that incredible argot that in the first half of the 20th century spoke to all nations and all intelligences equally.

The last observation shows his awareness that jazz from its inception was definitively 'modern'.[29] But the whole case radiates authority, as does Larkin's 1981 reflection: 'It's a bit simplified, I suppose, but I think it's all perfectly true. I can't see how anyone could possibly deny it, any of it.'[30]

It will already be clear that in my view 'Requiem for Jazz' is superior as a text to the 'Introduction' to *AWJ*, even if it cannot compete *qua* performance. The only trouble about *RFJ* is that nobody read it, or rather nobody seems to have taken due note of it, and it quickly became as obscure as its successor remains celebrated. I first became aware of the essay as late as 1997, before which I had never seen or heard it mentioned, let alone discussed. It came to my attention as Entry C247 in Barry Bloomfield's original *Bibliography 1933–1976*; with the much appreciated help of the *Daily Telegraph*'s archivist I was able to disinter it, and it became the prime item in Part Two of *Philip Larkin: Jazz Writings*. I hoped that book would enable *RFJ* to become widely known; naively, no doubt. After all, Larkin himself had, it would seem, no such desire. He never made even an oblique reference to it anywhere in his mainstream work; moreover, it appears not to have crossed his mind to resurrect it in *Required Writing*. Perhaps he thought its sobriety would clash with the very different ethos of *ITAWJ*, which he was clearly determined to include.[31] In any event, *RFJ*'s almost instant obscurity furnishes one reason why he felt impelled to write its successor. The message had not got through and it needed to be re-sent, not least because by 1968 things had got much worse. This time ordinary mail wouldn't do. Special Delivery was required – and Larkin was now in a position to effect such high-profile action.

All What Jazz: Determined Perversity

If jazz had reached its nadir, Philip Larkin, Writer, was approaching his zenith. He had already written a third of the poems that would comprise the triumphant *High Windows*, and it is apparent that he had reached that state – felicitous but also dangerous – where anything he wrote or had written was of interest, especially to publishers. It would be unjust to suggest that come 1968 he knew he could get away with practically anything: he was the most conscientious of writers. However, he was also properly aware of his own worth, and it cannot have escaped him how eager Faber had been to reprint *The North Ship*, a collection Larkin had long since come to disdain.[32] Indeed, that anthology's re-launch demonstrated that he was now almost irresistibly marketable.

On 20 November 1968 he wrote to his original sponsor, Donald Mitchell, outlining his plan to collect his *Telegraph* reviews for private publication, asking permission to dedicate the volume to him, and inviting him 'to read the introduction, which is a *jeu d'esprit* not perhaps to be taken too seriously' (*SL*, p. 408). So far, so straightforward, confirming one fact – Larkin had already completed the 'Introduction' – and usefully identifying two corollaries: *jeu d'esprit* or otherwise, it had mattered to him to get the piece written, and from the outset he saw it as integral to the publication of *AWJ*. But in the letter's final paragraph the plot thickens: he wonders aloud if 'for instance' Faber might be prepared to distribute it and on what terms.

Andrew Motion rejects any possibility that this was 'disingenuous', pronouncing it 'perfectly sincere' (*AWL*, p. 386). He notes that Larkin had also just written to Hull Printers, asking for an estimate of what it would cost to produce *AWJ*, and considers that sufficient grounds for asserting 'Larkin had no secret hope that Faber would want to publish the book himself [*sic*].' I am surprised he can be so sure. Simple disingenuousness doesn't come into it: Larkin was exploring two options at the same time, and his enquiry to Mitchell strikes me as a far-sighted opening gambit, an innocuous-looking 'P – K4' prior to a dazzling Sicilian Defence.[33] What is beyond dispute is that almost at once Hull Printers lost any chance to play. At Mitchell's instigation,[34] Faber & Faber had, 'within a fortnight' (Motion's estimate), agreed to publish the manuscript themselves, given Larkin an advance of £200, allowed him to design the dust jacket and agreed that the introduction should stand unchanged. The terms were generous, but the speed was something else.

Arithmetic can sometimes be a telling factor in literary analysis, and the transformation of *AWJ* from private cock-shy to front-line Faber operation is a signal instance. For Motion's 'fortnight' won't do – as his text immediately, albeit unwittingly, goes on to demonstrate. Quoting from Larkin's subsequent letter to Mitchell and then from one to Charles Monteith (Faber's MD), he not only implies a false chronology but also fails to spot the significance of the dates in question. The letter to Monteith is the earlier of the two; dated 27 November 1968, it is in part a reply to Monteith's congratulations on the 'Introduction'. A bare week after Larkin's initial letter to Mitchell, therefore, Monteith had already written to Larkin expressing said enthusiasm, which in turn means that Mitchell must have posted off the manuscript of *AWJ* within 24 hours of reading Larkin's 20 November letter and enclosures. It would have taken Monteith a couple of days to absorb the manuscript, decide he wanted to publish it, write to Larkin confirming same, and so forth. That may not necessarily prove the Sicilian Defence analogy above, but it makes it even harder to believe that Larkin had no such pre-emptive strategy in some part of his mind when he first approached Mitchell.

Having, so to speak, set a new publishing lap record, Faber almost immediately took its foot off the gas pedal. *All What Jazz* eventually came out in January 1970, several months later than promised, and it might have been a good deal later but for Larkin's angry intervention (see below). The delay is significant for two reasons, aside from Larkin's justified pique. First, the lethargy with which the firm went about publishing the book paradoxically bears out my implicit contention that its primary aim was to *secure* it. And second, during the 12 months which ensued, speed was replaced by something just as dramatic – the violent pitch-and-yaw of Larkin's expressed attitudes to *AWJ*, which feature a number of assertions and *bon mots* which have not been examined anything like carefully enough.

In that 27 November letter Larkin confesses to being 'taken aback' by Monteith's enthusiasm for the 'Introduction', repeats his view of it as a *jeu d'esprit* 'in the manner of [H. L.] Mencken or someone like that' and then declares: 'to pass it off seriously will earn me the biggest critical clobbering I have ever experienced'. That is early and powerful evidence that Larkin knew he was on a collision course but was nonetheless determined to publish. There are several other observations in the same vein that are equally problematic: together they amount to an important conundrum which nobody has yet solved.

Two weeks later, there is no trace of such fearful modesty. In its place is a ludic bravado: 'I have a sneaking affection for [*ITAWJ*] ... It's about time jazz had its Enoch Powell' (to Mitchell, 9 December 1968). The PC cops who have been after Larkin ever since the appearance of *A Writer's Life* and *Selected Letters* naturally seize on that second sentence as damning evidence of his unwholesomeness; his admirers look to defend it as a self-deprecatingly winsome gag. I think both are wrong: the remark is not so much either nasty or harmless as idiotic. Its only apparent virtue, topicality, is extinguished when one recalls *why* Powell's name was on so many lips: this was a right-wing ideologue who identified rampant immigration as the British sickness and repatriation as the certain cure.[35] Whatever may have been his private views, Larkin the jazz critic was always an eloquent champion of black musicians and culture; moreover, the analogy connotes – absurdly – a connection between reductive and inflammatory populism and an art form distinguished for its courageous, enabling egalitarianism. A celebratory awareness of the latter permeates the pages of 'A Record Diary', and the Powell 'gag' seems all the more disagreeably inane when one recalls that *ARD* was the very text Larkin had written his *jeu d'esprit* to introduce. What on earth was he thinking about?

Exactly the same question needs to be asked about an even more infamous remark made five months later. In the interim Larkin – 'always a good businessman'[36] – had corresponded with Faber's Vice Chairman Peter Du Sautoy over contractual and financial details; he also suggests, with tart courtesy, that the *AWJ* be marketed as 'a book on jazz'. But on 19 June, writing to the firm's Sales Director, Peter Crawley, his advice is of a very different hue:

> I think the best line you can take is that you are promoting a freak publication: please don't put it forward as a piece of jazz scholarship, or even as any sort of contribution to the field. Treat it like a book by T.S. Eliot on all-in wrestling. (*SL*, p. 416)

I have no idea why Larkin has been so much admired for these sentences, which comprise another piece of artful bunkum, weirdly proleptic of much of *ITAWJ*'s text. Perhaps it's because the witticism is so likeably disarming that few have bothered to dwell on its utter *silliness*. Larkin may be witheringly partisan in the 'Introduction', but there is never a moment when one suspects he has no idea what he's talking about. Furthermore, the remark could not be less apposite if considering *ARD*, the work of a dedicated and deeply informed jazz scholar – which makes the first sentence either blatant false modesty or just stupid: it is a moot point which is worse.

The Crawley letter as a whole is of further interest in being a microcosm of the see-saw rhythm that characterized Larkin's attitudes to *AWJ* in preparation, on publication and thereafter. He briefly recovers his balance, citing once again the pleasure he has derived over the years from writing the columns; then he slides into a cautious advocacy far removed from that 'all-in wrestling' nonsense but still contentious: 'The thesis of the introduction ... [is something which] I don't think has actually been said before, and, while it may not be wholly defensible, I think it is sufficiently amusing to say once.' (*SL*, 417)

Similar see-saw symptoms emerge from his letter of 3 October to C. B. Cox. It makes no mention of *AWJ* or jazz itself: the focus is on poetry. A warmish reference to Douglas Dunn is followed by a decidedly spiky one to Seamus Heaney, and it ends: 'Anyway, to hell with poetry. I'm fed up with it' (*SL*, 419). One would hardly guess that in that same month he completed one of his most affecting poems, 'To The Sea', and would very soon begin work on the surpassingly beautiful 'The Explosion' (completed on 5 January 1970). As many have observed from any number of standpoints, with Larkin the Letter Writer what you see is far from what you necessarily get or what is really going on.

Larkin was by now no less 'fed up' with the snail-like progress of *AWJ*'s production, as evidenced by his 15 November letter to Judy Egerton:

> *All What Jazz* will be published in January sometime – another matter for croaking complaint. The agreement said it would be published in 'Autumn 1969' (agreement signed 21 Jan. 1969), but in fact they just bloody well forgot about it until I raised mild enquiries & found they were idly scheduling it for March 1970 – God! The howl I set up got it back dated to January, but as you say, it will miss Christmas, and since it was finished in 1968 it will seem drearily out of date … It's a pretty silly book, but might amuse you. (*SL*, 422)

A bizarre mixture once more. On one level – Faber's professional incompetence – his outraged 'howl' makes sense; yet doesn't it seem odd to fulminate so about 'a pretty silly book'? Odder still is the morose reflection on its obsoleteness: again, what was Larkin thinking about? *ARD* would be no more passé in 1970 than in 1968, and the same applies to *ITAWJ*'s attack on modernism: a couple of extra years makes no difference if you're shooting at virtually everything performed since 1940. The remark could be interpreted as a veiled reference to his weariness at the book's protracted preparation, but the only thing which then might qualify as 'drearily out of date' would be his original enthusiasm. He is, quite simply, not thinking straight.

The New Year brings little in the way of resolution. With publication imminent, Larkin indulges in his biggest dose of gallows humour yet, in a letter to Anthony Thwaite of 13 January:

> Copies of *All What Jazz* will be going out shortly, so you will see your old friend abused in the public press as never before. Try to imagine a book by Humphrey Lyttelton saying that modern poetry is no good, while at the same time charmingly admitting he's never read any since 1940, and you will get some idea of how mine will be handled. (*SL*, p. 425)

This is of course witty and engaging, and the first sentence is, sadly, all too prescient. The rest is, again, utter nonsense. Even *ITAWJ* shows that Larkin has listened to a great deal of modern jazz, and *ARD* not only bristles with knowledge but finds much contemporary fare a great deal better than 'no good'. Indeed, this analogy is *so* ridiculous – more so than even the Powell and T. S. Eliot ones – that one is moved to detect an additional, underlying, almost secret joke. Ten years before, in his review of Lyttelton's *Second Chorus*, Larkin observed with ringing approval '*he knows what he is talking about*'.[37] When it came to jazz, so did Larkin: he was much closer to the real Lyttelton than the fantasy caricature drawn for Thwaite. And he knew it.

The Price of Wit

Overall, then, the picture is dramatic, funny, poignant and absorbing. But it is not *clear*. Indeed, it portrays a Larkin who is all over the place – fiercely determined to publish his collection-plus-polemic but convinced from the outset that he'll be roundly 'clobbered' for it; alternating (sometimes within a single sentence) between self-laceration and defiant proselytizing; uncomfortably often committing to paper things as close to drivel as makes no difference. That last can also be levelled at the sentence in *ITAWJ* which precedes the 'jazz whore' confession examined above: 'When I was asked to write these [*Telegraph*] articles, I was patently unfitted to do so and should have declined' (*AWJ*, p. 18).

The remark is doubly unfortunate. First, as *ARD* demonstrates from the start, it is patently untrue; second, it gave his opponents immediate 'out of the horse's mouth' ammunition. Larkin might have heeded the words of his great friend Kingsley Amis in another context – 'That's no way to go on. [It ignores] that most elementary maxim of the writer's trade, *People take you at your own evaluation*.'[38] – but obviously he didn't, either then or later. What caused these lapses into something far beyond disingenuousness or the exquisite I-am-dumb persona exemplified by his 'Who's Jorge Luis Borges?' reply to Robert Phillips in their 1982 *Paris Review* interview?[39]

Finding an answer is very difficult for any post-*SL* reader: there is a triple problem of chronology. All the correspondence quoted and discussed pre-dates the publication of *AWJ*. On the other hand, it post-dates the *composition* of the 'Introduction'. On another hand still, nobody who read the 1970 or indeed 1985 edition of *AWJ* was remotely aware of that pre-publication correspondence – its clues, its angst, its passionate ambivalence. There was, in fact, only one person who knew the whole story: Larkin himself. And I believe that virtually everything which he wrote from his kite-flying letter to Mitchell in November 1968 onwards hinges on the 'Introduction' being at root a multiply brilliant but self-destructive jest.

To nominate 'the best' of *AWJ*'s jokes is about as difficult as choosing one's favourite Larkin poem. However, the most flagrant (and it is scarcely credible that nobody has yet pointed this out) is the fact that *ITAWJ* does not 'introduce' the main text at all: its relation to *ARD* is a subversive, even antipathetic one. The tone of the two texts is quite startlingly different; as already demonstrated in part, the judgements offered about a number of leading musicians are often unnervingly out of kilter with each other; *ITAWJ* contains several passages rife with dishonesty or at the very least crafty disinformation, whereas *ARD* is scrupulous in its disinterested honesty. Best (but also most infuriating) of all, there is only a single reference to an actual review throughout the text – a joke doubled by the fact that the column in question did not appear at the time![40]

That should be enough to start alarm bells ringing in any reader's head, and they ought to reach Nine Taylors proportions when Larkin launches his famous tirade against Modernism. That is not just because the attack on his 'infernal trilogy' of Picasso, Parker and Pound is mischievously contaminated anyway: as John Osborne has pointed out, it is flawed at both an ancillary and even deeper level.[41] *For jazz was the quintessence of Modernism from its very inception.* The developments in all other genres – literature, dance, painting, classical music – were radical, shocking and many other things, but they were not, finally, new. Their practitioners used the same means, the same media, even the same vocabulary as the artists and work from which they so self-consciously were departing.

Nothing like jazz had ever been heard, not even in its own country: field-holler and the early forms of the blues have a bearing on the genesis of jazz, but they do not sound anything like it, nor is the overall effect on the listener remotely comparable. Admittedly, jazz took its harmonic base from European classical music, but the way it used melody and form was often radically innovative. Above all, its rhythms and very concept of rhythm were *sui generis.*[42] In addition, its provenance and growth in sociopolitical terms were quite unlike any other modernist phenomenon. As Osborne says: 'The really distinguished thing about jazz is that here was a rare Modernism, a modernism with street credibility, modernism rising from the bottom up not percolating down from a cultural elite.'[43]

And Larkin knew that perfectly well. The realization implicitly permeates *ARD*, and the pages of *Larkin's Jazz* abound in similar perceptions:

> What was so exciting about jazz was the way its unique, simple gaiety instantly communicated itself to such widely differing kinds of human being – Negro porters, Japanese doctors, King George VI. (pp. 55–6)

> It is ironical that the first American music to catch world attention should have originated among the nation's most despised section – the Negroes, who well within living memory had been regarded as a species of farm animal. (p. 57)

Furthermore, in *RFJ* he celebrates 'the universality of jazz' and that it 'conquered pretty well every capital city in the world', led by his greatest hero Louis Armstrong, who 'gave jazz its speaking voice [which] was heard all over the world' (p. 140). In short, Larkin's anti-modernism-in-jazz stance was *knowingly idiotic.*

That was a joke I suspect he treasured. But until now it has remained an entirely private one – in resounding contrast to the very public jest that is the '3Ps' assault. The sheer brio of its prose is enough to show that he enjoyed this joke just as much, and his pleasure must have been increased by the astounding credulousness of his readership. To a man and woman, they seem to have found the alliteration of his 'dismissal' so beguiling as to preclude any further examination. Yet Picasso, Parker and Pound are a decidedly disparate trio. Apart from a rudimentary congruence as 'modernists' (a necessarily vague umbrella term) they have nothing in common; moreover, there is the matter of their separate artistic stature.

There can be no question that Picasso is the greatest figure of the three, beside whom the other two seem picayune – another thing Larkin knew perfectly well. When he celebrated Louis Armstrong as 'an enormously important cultural figure in our century, more important than Picasso in my opinion',[44] he was lauding the trumpeter, not denigrating the painter. Indeed, the fact that Larkin cited Picasso in championing his greatest hero is a measure of his understanding of the painter's eminence, no matter what his private opinions of Picasso's work may have been.

Jazz was more important to Larkin than visual art, but he also knew perfectly well that for every 50 people who occasionally go to an art gallery or buy a reproduction or print, just one will buy a jazz record, attend a jazz gig or be able to tell Beiderbecke from Bilk. On that basis alone, to place Parker alongside Picasso was mischievous – all the more so because he recognized from the outset the altoist's central and enduring significance as a jazz artist. As we have seen, he equates his importance with Bechet's and then with Armstrong's, and there is no hint of gloating when he later observes that Parker's music 'remains a minority taste' (*AWJ*, 63). All he is doing is reflecting that if jazz had indeed become a 'twilight art',[45] then as a modern jazzman Parker stands in a deeper dusk than Armstrong, Ellington or even the inconsequential Glenn Miller, whereas the twentieth century long ago afforded Picasso the brightest of spotlights.

And what is Pound doing in such company? Whereas Picasso and Parker were centrifugal modernist forces in their respective genres, the same cannot be said for Pound. His influence was weighty for a time; nevertheless, no one has seriously considered him the 'Father of modernist poetry' or any such thing. Innovation can be a suspect criterion anyway, but even those who disagree would have a hard time championing him on that score; moreover, by 1968 he was an almost entirely forgotten and unread figure.[46] His inclusion is decisive proof that Larkin's purposes were ludic. If he'd been more in earnest, it wouldn't have been very difficult to find another 'P' figure. Three that come quickly to mind are Proust, with whose work Larkin was certainly familiar (*SL*, p. 119), Sylvia Plath, on whom Larkin would write one of his finest essays, ('Horror Poet', *RW*) and Harold Pinter, a modernist in all significant ways.

The 'P-triumvirate' jest gets better the more one dwells on it, not least because delicious subordinate jokes emerge as a result. For a start, the Parker demonized in the 'Introduction' had acquired AM radio familiarity – wholly accessible to and accepted by the 'uncultured' in their tens of thousands.[47] By 1968 'modernism' in jazz terms meant the New Wave, and it had done so for more than a little while, as *ARD* regularly acknowledges. By that time, too, not only was Pound forgotten but Picasso had graduated to what in effect was Old Master status. In short, Larkin's 'P-triumvirate' was not only deliberately awry; it was seriously out of date. And of course he was thoroughly – gleefully – aware of both properties.

ITAWJ is predicated on and embodies a persona proud to be the only one in step. It was a mask he went to very considerable lengths to sustain, despite – or maybe because of – the fact that the reviews of *AWJ* were as hostile as he'd predicted from the outset, denouncing the essay as, *inter alia*, foolish conspiracy theory,[48] aesthetic Ludditism[49] or ivory tower isolationism.[50] Nevertheless, he continued to defend – no, *brandish* – *ITAWJ* for the rest of his life, via later interviews and comment, and by rehearsing it all over again in *RW*.

A final joke (or at any rate an anomaly that further spoofs his *ITAWJ* stance) is the fact that he went on with the *Telegraph* column for a further three years. The last item in the original *AWJ* was December 1968's 'Rabbit Jumps the Blues'. He went on to write another 33 columns,[51] reviewing over 200 further records and some dozen books. If he so hated what jazz had become by this time, *why* did he go on? In the footnote to the 1984 second edition of *AWJ* he says he 'enjoyed doing them', following that with the celebrated declaration 'listening to jazz records for an hour with a pint of gin and tonic is the best remedy for a day's work I know' (p. 29). Fine; and as always the columns *do* evince pleasure – if not at times in the music at issue, then in his wordsmith's skill in finding just the right phrase to capture his reservations or displeasure. But the whole thrust of *ITAWJ*, even at its most temperate, is that the task had started as a 'nightmare' and got worse; what is Larkin doing, prolonging his own agony?

One answer is that he was a liar. Max Harrison openly accused him of mendacity in the first swingeingly anti-Larkin piece to appear after the poet's death (see note 14), and John Osborne goes at least some way down the same path: 'Larkin loved many aspects of modernist music but lied about it.'[52] The case is uncomfortably congruent with much of what has been examined above. No less congruent, however, is an alternative which is more edifying and in my estimation more accurate. It hinges on Larkin's dualism rather than mendacity, and to elucidate it I want to consider briefly another figure noted for *jeux d'esprit*: Puck in *A Midsummer Night's Dream*.

The joyously and multiply mischievous Puck for whom 'jangling' is 'a sport' and who is 'best please[d]' by 'those things ... / That befall preposterously' (III.ii.353 and 120–1) is one side of Philip Larkin, Jazz Critic. His enjoyment of this subfusc Lord of Misrule persona not only survived the publication of *AWJ* and its critical reception but grew stronger. Realizing that nobody had got any of the underlying jokes in *ITAWJ*, he decided to play some further games, chuckling the while to himself, 'Lord, what fools these [readers] be' (III.ii.115). But just as Puck was also Robin Goodfellow, the ludic Larkin has an opposing alter ego: the writer of *RFJ*, all 66 other pieces in *LJ* and almost all of *ARD*. This is the critic who regarded jazz as high art (even jazz he disliked) and who wanted to proselytize it.[53] Clearly, by 1968 and beyond, fewer and fewer people took any notice, but that didn't mean he was yet ready to stop trying. Larkin as Robin Goodfellow remained sympathetic to musicians and readers alike, looking to advance the cause of the former and the pleasure and edification of the latter. The mixture of subversive and affirmative characterized him right up to the end.

For all his powers, though, Puck is decidedly fallible: as he (truthfully) says to Oberon at one point, 'I mistook' (III.ii.347). Analogously, and its many still-dazzling felicities notwithstanding, *ITAWJ* was a mistake from which Larkin's reputation is still recovering. It caused him to be written off by most jazz critics and aficionados as both ignorant and cloth-eared, not so much a reactionary as a dinosaur, calumnies that are only now being (slowly) redressed.

Even more unfortunate, it effectively condemned the book's main text to being unread by virtually all those not already interested in jazz. Some may have been simply lazy; others may have been intimidated by Larkin's virtuoso scorn; others still may have thought his case unanswerable and therefore complete in itself, requiring no further gloss. But all were at least implicitly encouraged by the author to believe that the effort was unlikely to be worthwhile, given that the remaining pages were to be dominated by meaningless praise meted out largely to rubbish. And if those non-readers might have stopped to reflect that it was a mite strange to introduce a book with the apparent purpose of deterring people from reading most of it, or that Larkin was not usually in the habit of allowing tails to wag dogs, the prime fault was nonetheless his. So is the additional *bêtise* that his wilfully created monster still bears the same relation to his *oeuvre* as *Lady Chatterley's Lover* does to Lawrence's or 'If' to Kipling's – i.e. well known for almost all the wrong reasons, and the fame of which is at the expense of achievements both superior and more representative.

Most unfortunate of all, it damaged his reputation and public perception of him in a much broader way. The anti-modernist stance dramatized by the 3-P attack hardened suspicions that Larkin was, *inter alia*, an anachronistic Little Englander; a closet Philistine whose preferred reading was Victorian poetry and twentieth-century thrillers and who would especially have no truck with anything foreign; a poet who for all his undoubted craftsmanship and moments of spare beauty was ultimately both a sentimentalist and a curmudgeon; someone, in short, who mainlined (in Harrison's phrase) on 'The Pleasures of Ignorance'. Later, of course, would come the teeming accusations of racism, misogyny and sexism, crypto-fascism and all the rest of the post-*SL* and post-Motion farrago. But already it would be possible for professional critics wilfully to misread his poems and get away with it partly on the basis that Larkin's 'true colours' were there for all to see in his 1968 essay.

I end this chapter by returning to Larkin's 1979 remark that is my first epigraph: 'Actually, I like to think of myself as quite funny.' Perhaps that self-image mattered sufficiently for him not to mind the consequences he so deftly identified in 1983: 'One uses humour to make people laugh ... The trouble is, it makes them think you aren't serious. That's the risk you take.'[54]

Or to put it another way and in the lap of his twenty-first-century readers: either you 'the Puck a liar call' or you hope that ultimately 'Robin shall restore amends' (V.i.421 and 424). Either you judge Philip Larkin Jazz Critic as mendacious or at any rate culpably facetious – in which case his lifelong devotion to the music will inevitably go on being regarded as an eccentricity, the phonographic equivalent of philately or trainspotting[55] – or you see him, as I do, as among the finest, most erudite and illuminating writers on jazz there have been or are likely to be. But if it is that latter conclusion to which one inclines, then the onus is on his readers to take proper detailed note of *all* his work in that field. Twenty years after his death and over a generation since most of it was written, it seems high time.

And that ushers in the centrepiece of this Jazz section: a detailed consideration of the columns which make up Larkin's 'Record Diary', and which show him to be a jazz critic of rare discernment and tough but sympathetic acumen.

Chapter 3

'Essential Beauty': Larkin's Righteous Jazz

Music, to create harmony, must investigate discord.

Plutarch

I have already pointed out that Larkin's own tastes and aversions are rarely difficult to detect in his 'Record Diary'; however, two additional observations need making. First, the overriding characteristic in all these pieces is – in sharp contrast to the 'Introduction' – *fidelity*. Larkin's genius for pinning a style or sound in a single phrase seeks to honour the musician's craft, and on the rare occasions that he cannot do so, a vestigial respect is still present. Second, his catholicity of response and range of reference are remarkable: taken as a whole, his jazz writings have the kind of comprehensiveness one looks for in a reliable encyclopedia, even though they are considerably less disinterested.

Moreover, quite unlike the 'Introduction', the 'Record Diary' does exactly what the noun is supposed to connote.[1] Chronologically logging the experience of a critical listener, it thereby charts the 1960s development of jazz – including (and perhaps primarily) what he saw as a decline into something approximating catastrophe. That view partly explains the ethos and thrust of the 'Introduction', and if hostile critics might argue that the latter compromises the overall moral integrity of *All What Jazz* as a text, they could have no such doubts about the structural integrity of the columns themselves. Larkin's rigorous investigation of discord (including his own) evolves into a unified anthology which demands – and repays – the same attention as do *The Less Deceived, The Whitsun Weddings* and *High Windows*.

'Play that thing': the musicians and their records

I want first to explore Larkin's appraisals of four musicians whom in varying degrees he did not care for – Charlie Parker, Dizzy Gillespie, Miles Davis and John Coltrane – and also the New Wave movement of the 1960s, which he not so much abhorred as considered ridiculous. The first two musicians were the founders of bop, the genre he attacks so virulently in the 'Introduction'; the second two took bop several stages further, and one would expect him to reject them even more violently. But this is often not the case; moreover, it is little short of astonishing how many times he writes about them. As I observed in the previous chapter, the kind of reactionary ideologue that is Larkin's persona in the Introduction would never have returned again and again to Coltrane in particular, whose music he liked least of the four. Even if one ascribes those many returns to mere conscientiousness, it still impresses – and given the laziness of so many assessments of *AWJ*, it might be said there's nothing 'mere' about that quality anyway.

Charlie Parker (alto saxophone)

I've already looked in detail at Larkin's first 'Record Diary' assessment of Parker,[2] commenting that in both tone and substance it is wildly at odds with the virulent 3-P antipathy of the 'Introduction'. Granted, his reservations are not difficult to discern. The parentheses round Parker's name at the end of the first paragraph hint at what he privately thinks of coupling the altoist with his beloved Bechet, and the emphasis on speed of thought and technique is ambivalent: Larkin never considered facility per se a criterion of worth. Even so, the passage is riveting about Parker's music and his very nature: the concluding aphorism – 'it would be absurd to call Parker's music a reaction. As well call leaping salmon a reaction.' – is as illuminating as elegant.

When Parker is next discussed, it is alongside Louis Armstrong. Again, there is never any doubting whose music Larkin prefers, but a true Parkerphobe would be capable of neither the sympathy nor the trenchant analysis that distinguishes this May 1962 column:

> He came to maturity just when the initial impulse of the twenties and early thirties had spent itself, and the jazz scene was dominated by the large, white, commercial swing bands. The effect of playing their music six nights a week can be imagined. Where Armstrong had accepted, Parker rejected. 'I kept thinking,' he said afterwards, 'there's bound to be something else.'
>
> That 'something else' ... was, in a word, complication. Parker found jazz chugging along in 4/4 time in the tonic and dominant, and splintered it into a thousand rhythmic and harmonic pieces. Showers of sixteenths, accented on half- and quarter-beats, exhibited a new harmonic fecundity and an originality of phrasing that had scarcely been hinted at before. Parker did not 'follow' anyone, as Armstrong followed [Joe 'King'] Oliver. He just appeared. (p. 62)

His rider, that Parker's music 'remains a minority taste', is poignant rather than partisan; indeed, it leads into the reflection that 'the decision of the BBC to ban modern jazz from its weekly "Jazz Club" ... [is] regrettable'.[3]

September 1963 sees an incisive review of Robert George Reisner's *Bird: The Legend of Charlie Parker*, where any severity is at the author's expense rather than the subject's. He then proceeds – astoundingly – to equate the first four albums in the Realm label's Parker Memorial series with Armstrong's Hot Five recordings, ending with this masterly summary:

> These recordings of 1944–8 ... exhibit a musician of unprecedented fluency and stature among colleagues not his equal. Parker's easy, flexible alto with its complete

command of a new harmonic language makes the young Miles Davis sound stiff and mechanical, and on many tracks the rhythm section stumps along unregenerately. (pp. 93–4)

The next three assessments are less laudatory but just as authoritative. Larkin finds the Parker of 1953 almost saddening: 'it is Gillespie who takes the breath away ... [he] was five years stronger and more practised while the Bird was five years deeper into self-immolation' (p. 100). Next, he considers the three-volume *Historical Masterpieces* hyperbolically titled – but only because by Parker's standards they are 'fairly run-of-the-mill' and 'not at all well recorded': he still finds time to praise the altoist's 'brisk and oddly humorous musicianship' (p. 127). And in April 1965 he challenges the hagiographical 'popular view' that Parker 'from 1945 to 1954 poured out an undifferentiated sequence of brilliant recordings'. Far from being anti-Parker, his impatience is that of the serious critic who expects 'normal critical standards' to be applied:

It would be useful to have this Birdolatry corrected occasionally ... to know whether Parker got better, or changed, and, if so, in what direction. I have never seen any mention of his clichés, which were as numerous and obtrusive as [Muggsy] Spanier's.

Yet immediately after voicing these (to some) waspish heresies he welcomes 'I Remember You', 'Confirmation' and 'Now's The Time'[4] as evidence of Parker's realization that 'plainly stated themes and fully valued notes could be as artistically satisfying as ... bop' and delights in the altoist's 'warm mellow tone reminiscent of Bechet and ... Johnny Hodges' (p. 135).

By now, I would hope, the point about Larkin on Parker during *ARD* has been established well enough. There are further reviews in the columns of December 1965 and November 1966; the altoist is also discussed when Larkin appraises Barry McRae's *The Jazz Cataclysm* (July 1967) and in the 'Wells or Gibbon?' piece of August 1970. However, two final points need to be made.

The first is that all Larkin's reviews of Parker on record pre-date the 'Introduction', most of them by several years. By the time he composed that essay, Larkin's *Telegraph* pieces were becoming increasingly despairing. It matters little whether that growing disenchantment fuelled the 'Introduction' or vice versa: the important thing is that the demonized Parker who dominates the 1968 polemic is conspicuously absent in the 'Record Diary' itself. It would be overstating the case to say that Larkin enthuses about his music; on the other hand, he annotates its skill and import in a fashion both penetrating and handsome, and his judgements have proved enduring.

The second point centres on some observations Larkin made about Parker in 'Requiem for Jazz'. That essay's disparity from its notorious successor in both tone and argument is especially noticeable in its last paragraph:

To say Parker destroyed jazz as well as himself would be the crudest of generalisations, and would imply that what has happened, the 'development', could have been averted. Very likely it couldn't. Jazz was a unique phenomenon, set off by an unprecedented balance of sociological factors ... which are now dissipating and will not recur. (*PLJW*, p. 142)

The tone is mournful, the argument terminal: this really is a Requiem. Yet no blame is attached and rancour is absent.

Only in the 'Introduction' did Larkin seek to belittle Parker. Elsewhere in *AWJ*, although his private reservations are evident, he not only controls his antipathy in the interests of briefing his readers: on one level he recognizes Parker as a force of nature – 'leaping salmon'; 'He just appeared' – whose impact transcends matters of personal taste.

Dizzy Gillespie (trumpet)

With the exception of the Dial sessions, Larkin got to review most of Parker's essential records; in Gillespie's case, he was less well served by the record companies. It is apparent that he did not receive any of the records the trumpeter made with his 'State Department' big band of the mid-1950s; nor did the two superb suites written by Lalo Schifrin, *Gillespiana* and *The New Continent*, come his way. He fared a little better with Gillespie's small group work, but not much. Important sessions with, variously, Roy Eldridge, Stan Getz, Sonny Stitt, Sonny Rollins and Stuff Smith did not reach him, and he had to make do with the potpourri compilation *The Best of the Dizzy Gillespie Small Groups*. None of this was Larkin's fault, naturally, but it does mean that his 'Record Diary' assessment of Gillespie is necessarily circumscribed.

Nevertheless, there is more than enough to edify; once again, his powers of concise exegesis can only compel admiration. A definitive example occurs when he appraises Gillespie's seminal recordings in early 1946; as with much of his Parker analysis, one needs forcibly to remind oneself that this is the kind of jazz he is supposed to have disliked:

> Listening to Gillespie, one realises how impossible it was to imagine what the next great jazz trumpet stylist would sound like, yet how unmistakable he was when he came. His solos on the 1946 small band Victors ... are still tremendous; free, rocketing phrases, each punched out powerful and precise. Beside him, the rest of the group seems hardly to have emerged from the John Kirby era. (p. 58)

It is not easy to see how that could be bettered, even by a Gillespie enthusiast.

Elsewhere, Larkin is unimprovably shrewd about the somewhat bizarre album the trumpeter cut in 1960, *A Portrait of Duke Ellington*,[5] briefly complimentary about the live quintet date now known as *An Electrifying Evening*,[6] and in his very last column (December 1971) excellent on the reissued *Ebullient Mr Gillespie* and *Have Trumpet, Will Excite*, still-undersung sessions that it is cheering to see championed. By that time, however, Gillespie's new releases were pale in the extreme (the late 1960s were his nadir, on record at any rate) and Larkin is rightly perfunctory about such feeble fare as *The Melody Lingers On* and *Jambo Caribe* – 'just another Gillespie exotic' (p. 234).

Larkin considers Gillespie largely 'an up-tempo genius' (p. 58) and is consistently less impressed by him as balladeer; he also finds him 'rather emotionless' (p. 151). I agree with neither view, though there are plenty who do; what is more significant is, again, the durability of his judgements and his ability to communicate the nature and detail of what he hears to the edification of aficionado and novice alike.

The writings on Parker and Gillespie in *AWJ* dramatize one kind of contradiction: the ideological antipathy of the 'Introduction' constantly softened – arguably subverted – by the perception and frequent warmth of individual reviews. Now for a different kind of disparity.

Miles Davis (trumpet, flugelhorn)

We know what Larkin made of Davis's tyro work with Parker – 'stiff and mechanical'[7] – but what about the mature stylist? A few *en passant* mentions apart, he is accorded just one sentence in the 'Introduction'. It does not suggest the 'Record Diary' is going to enthuse about him all that much –

> Davis had several manners: the dead muzzled slow stuff, the sour yelping fast stuff, and the sonorous theatrical arranged stuff, and I disliked them all. (p. 21)

– and these two 'Record Diary' passages would appear to confirm in full that lack of promise:

> He runs phrases to death with a calculated perversity, and spends whole blocks of bars trying to emaciate his tone to a still further degree of unpleasantness. (January 1962; p. 55)

> I freely confess that there have been times recently when almost anything – the shape of a patch on the ceiling, a recipe for rhubarb jam read upside down in the paper – has seemed to me more interesting than the passionless creep of a Miles Davis trumpet solo. (November 1965; p. 150)

Yet only a few months after that 'calculated perversity' dismissal, he hails *Miles Davis at Carnegie Hall* as 'sombre and magnificent … pouring out a succession of smoky and sonorous solos'. He applauds the music's emotional and repertorial range, deduces 'a warmth about the entire proceedings' and concludes 'this is a most enjoyable LP' (October 1962; p. 73). Further, the 'passionless creep' diatribe prefaces a welcome for the album *ESP* as

> an immense improvement. The slow Davis solos … are declaimed with enormous authority, keen and kingly … [He] is his usual bleak self, his notes wilting at the edges as if with frost, spikey at up-tempos, and while he is still not my ideal of comfortable listening his talent is clearly undiminished.

The picture beginning to develop is, if not one of inconsistency, notably chequered. Sometimes that quality surfaces in a single review, as in this November 1963 reaction to *Seven Steps to Heaven*:

> For three tracks ... his lifeless muted tone, at once hollow and unresonant, creeps along only just in tempo, the ends of notes hanging down like [Salvador] Dali watches ... [These are] musical snail races ...
>
> ... The three other tracks ... are up-tempo pieces that show Miles fully in control of his own harsh, rather unfriendly mode. His tone, clouding and clearing, scrambles stabbingly into the stratosphere without the fluffs we have somehow come to expect, and on [Victor] Feldman's 'Joshua' in particular he phrases with almost conversational ease. (pp. 96–7)

If nothing else, Larkin tellingly identifies the album's disparateness: it caught Davis at a transitional stage, and listening to it remains a markedly fragmentary experience. But there *is* something else – an intriguing mixture of outright rejection and a respect bordering on surprised enjoyment.

Perhaps Larkin was less certain about Davis than he thought. In that last extract he labels Davis's tone 'unresonant', yet four years later, during an otherwise hostile review of *Milestones*, he is at pains to add 'although I am not indifferent to Davis's resonant and dignified trumpet' (*AWJ*, p. 190). In November 1964 Larkin can find his *Blue Moods* with Charles Mingus and Britt Woodman 'a credit to all concerned', only to call him 'a master of reverberative boredom' the very next month (pp. 125 and 126). Four years later he responds to back-to-back albums in an analogously non-uniform way. *Nefertiti* gets short shrift – 'six new tracks by Miles and his usual buddies ... called by titles such as "Riot" and "Madness" and sounding about as jolly' – but *Miles In The Sky* he deems 'undoubtedly beautiful in a melancholic and fenlike way' (pp. 207–8 and 219). Indeed, he named the latter as one of his 1969 Records of the Year.[8]

Further traces of uncertainty can be detected in his May 1966 praise for *Birth of the Cool*, containing 'solos by Miles that he has never surpassed' (p. 163), and his summatory comment on the *Modern Jazz Giants* session of 1954 with Jackson, Monk and Sonny Rollins: 'I have never heard Miles play better than this' (November 1967; p. 194). The two encomia do not quite amount to a contradiction, admittedly, but a degree of indecision is nonetheless evident.

That indecision – or something like it – can be said to characterize the overall portrait of Davis that emerges from the 'Record Diary'. Larkin reviewed sixteen of his records; their 'grouping' is fascinating. Six are to a varying extent negative; another half dozen are laudatory, though the degree of warmth is similarly various; two manage to be both.[9] It would be inflationary to suggest that Larkin was ambivalent about Davis – ultimately he liked him no more than he did Parker or Gillespie. It is nonetheless intriguing that the player whose jazz he once called 'heartless and uninteresting' (May 1967; p. 180) was the same player he would later nominate, albeit in somewhat gnomic fashion, as one of his favourite trumpeters.[10]

John Coltrane (tenor and soprano saxophones)

Larkin's summary of Coltrane in the 'Introduction' immediately follows his one-sentence appraisal of Miles Davis: its antagonistic majesty is worth quoting in full.

> With John Coltrane metallic and passionless nullity gave way to exercises in gigantic absurdity, great boring excursions on not-especially-attractive themes during which all possible changes were rung, extended investigations of oriental tedium, long-winded and portentous demonstrations of religiosity. It was with Coltrane, too, that jazz started to be *ugly on purpose*: his nasty tone would become more and more exacerbated until he was fairly screeching at you like a pair of demoniacally-possessed bagpipes.[11] [Larkin's italics]

Virtually all the assessments of Coltrane offered in the 'Record Diary' are in keeping with those words; two quick examples might be the compact dismissal of *The John Coltrane Quartet* in October 1965 – 'screeching dreariness' – and the inspired coinage of 'polycacophony' in May 1970. And although he reports on some of Coltrane's work in a more positive, even complimentary fashion, his every response is in tune with the sentence he wrote after the tenorist's death – 'I still can't imagine how anyone can listen to a Coltrane record for pleasure' (p. 187). Unlike the *Telegraph* columns which address Parker, Gillespie and Davis, Larkin's reviews of Coltrane hold few surprises.

What *is* surprising is how much attention he gives him. I have briefly commented on this already,[12] and I still find it remarkable that *AWJ* reviews 21 Coltrane records; only Ellington with 24 outscores the man he defined in 1967 as 'enormously boring, massively ugly'. Those statistics are of course partly contingent on what the record companies chose to send him; they might also be seen as testifying to Larkin's formidable conscientiousness. Even so, such explanations do not satisfy. There is no doubt that Larkin found much of Coltrane's music truly painful to listen to, and to stay at his post for so long smacks of a masochism alien to his nature. Why did he not leave the records unheard in their sleeves, or just tell EMI, Atlantic and the other companies to stop sending them?

In the course of his exploration of *AWJ*, Clive James suggests that Larkin's reviews of Coltrane dramatize a shift in the reviewer's taste over time: 'in 1962 he was still in two minds, but you could already guess which mind was winning'.[13] The insight is as acute as one would expect from the author of 'one of the handful of essential discussions of Larkin's aesthetic',[14] and in advancing another explanation I intend it to be complementary rather than an alternative.

For it seems to me that it was not just Larkin who was in two minds but Coltrane as well. The discrepancy between what B. J. Leggett calls 'the fair-minded Larkin of the early [Coltrane] reviews with the vitriolic Larkin of the later ones'[15] hinges, surely, on the music: it is a very long way from *Ballads* and *Africa/Brass* (1961) to mid-1960s work such as *Ascension* and *Meditation*. The difference is not merely one of degree but of *kind*: the latter works are not only more strident, more difficult, more relentless than ever, but a signal departure from his previous style. Most crucial is the fact that they eschew swing; indeed, for all their frenetic rhythmic activity, nothing resembling a jazz pulse is detectable.[16] The absence is deliberate rather than an unlooked-for casualty, which if anything makes it worse; Larkin wasn't the only jazz enthusiast who couldn't stay this particular course.

So when one reads in August 1964's column –

> This month I found myself liking a Coltrane record: 'Coltrane Live At Birdland' (HMV) has some excellent tri-partite discussions between Coltrane, [McCoy] Tyner and [Elvin] Jones, notably on 'Afro-Blue', and there is a passage on 'Your Lady' when Jones and Coltrane exchange unaccompanied statements that are eloquent with a new kind of authority in jazz. (p. 119)

– something other is at work than the fair-minded/vitriolic contrast James and Leggett propose, even if that is also germane. I suggest that we can take this warm appraisal at face value, not least because the previous reference to Coltrane – a review of *Impressions* in December 1963 – was the notably *un*fair-minded '[he] sounds as if he is playing for an audience of cobras' (p. 102). *Live at Birdland* swings hard and abounds in melody, especially 'Alabama' and 'I Want To Talk About You', and listening to it anew while writing these words made it easy to believe that Larkin's professed affection was genuine.

Another reason for Larkin's assiduousness and stamina was that he acknowledged Coltrane's central importance, not just as the most influential tenorist around (much more so than Getz or Rollins) but as *the* key figure in 1960s jazz. He may in many fundamental respects have been an extreme musician, his music prompting commensurately extreme reactions from adulation to detestation, and all points in between; nevertheless, he had now become the most charismatic and influential jazzman of the period – more so than even Miles Davis. An exemplary index is provided by the 1965 'Readers' Poll' conducted by *Down Beat*, in which Coltrane won four separate categories; moreover, the margin of each victory – Hall of Fame, Jazzman of the Year, Tenor Saxophone and Record of the Year (*A Love Supreme*) – was enormous.

As a private person Larkin may have found that very hard to stomach, but as a professional critic he recognized a duty to chart this extraordinary musician's every move. That he was aware of Coltrane's seminal status from the outset is evident from the columns of September 1961 and June 1962, his first reviews of Coltrane's work:

> 'Stan Getz At Large' ... and 'Coltrane Jazz' make a violent contrast ... Coltrane, that relentless experimenter, intersperses the vinegary drizzle of his tone with chords (yes, two notes at once) ... Getz is the pleasanter listening ... but Coltrane is thinking harder, and is still far ahead of his fellows. (p. 46)

Personal taste is subjugated. Coltrane is the way jazz is going – a perception that also informs this appraisal of *Olé* and *Africa/Brass*:

> Coltrane's records are, paradoxically, nearly always both interesting and boring, and I certainly find myself listening to them in preference to many a less adventurous set. 'Dahomey's Dance' and 'Aisha', on the former disc, have moments of real beauty and excitement. (p. 65)

He later finds things he can compliment in Coltrane's collaboration with pianist Cecil Taylor (February 1963; pp. 80–1) and praises *Ballads* (July 1963; p. 89) for its 'commendable economy' and 'bleak beauty', a particularly incisive phrase. That last adjective is also employed to contrast Coltrane's tone with Milt Jackson's 'luscious vibraharp' (March 1962; p. 59), but although he gives *Bags and Trane* a guarded welcome as a 'unique mingling' having 'much to commend it' as 'a novelty', it is evident that some kind of crunch is fast approaching, and it arrives with Coltrane's legendary *A Love Supreme*.

The album was reviewed in July 1965's column, 'The Tenor Player With 50 Legs', a title whose studied grotesqueness matches the writer's now-cemented view of his subject. The gag is explained and developed in a paragraph where Larkin initially demolishes the 'absurd' canard that Coltrane cannot play his instrument – 'the rapidity of his fingering alone dispels that notion' – before wondering if such facility has anything to be said for it:

> It would be juster to question whether he knows what to do with it now that he can play it. His solos seem to me to bear the same relation to proper jazz as those drawings of running dogs, showing their legs in all positions so that they appear to have about fifty of them, have to real drawings. Once, they are amusing and instructive. But the whole point of drawing is choosing the right line, not drawing fifty alternatives.

About *A Love Supreme* itself Larkin is cautiously judicious here and there – '"Psalm" ... has something of the manner, if not the spirit, of the delightful "Alabama" from *Coltrane Live At Birdland*' – but the veneer is wearing thin. He calls the sleeve essay 'pretentious guff',[17] berates the tenorist for 'a degree of self-seriousness most inimical to an artist', and in all the piece is terminally eloquent: Larkin has had enough.

A Love Supreme was one of Larkin's *Telegraph* Records of the Year for 1965[18] – not (obviously) because he liked it but because, punctilious and prescient as always, he recognized its far-reaching importance – and he continued faithfully to report on every Coltrane record sent him. But the struggle was over, and a consonant sense of liberation is evident in all his subsequent reviews. Time and again one detects Philp Larkin, Writer's subfusc pleasure in finding *les mots justes* to signify his aural pain. Of *Ascension* (1966) he observes that 'Soloists appear and submerge like *Titanic* passengers'; later that year *Meditations* may have 'a wild audacity one can't help admiring' but it is also, and mainly, 'the most astounding piece of ugliness I have ever heard';[19] *Live At The Village Vanguard Again* epitomizes 'the blended insolence and ugliness known as New Wave'. In similar vein, Coltrane's solos on *Expression* (1968) resemble 'the scribblings of a subnormal child',[20] while *Cosmic Music* (1969) is simply 'the usual tumults of noise'. The best, perhaps, is left till last. The 1970 appraisal of *Selflessness* opens with a deliciously brutal paraphrase of *Macbeth*, III.iv.78–80 –

Time was, when a man had snuffed it, you heard no more of him

– further observes that Coltrane had 'two habits, bad and worse', and ends with the aforementioned neologism 'polycacophony'.

One obvious, and by no means untrenchant, reaction to all this is to say that Larkin simply got it wrong, that his ears and mind weren't up to Coltrane's innovations, that he should have acknowledged a deaf spot and left well alone. Certainly, history has not vindicated Larkin. In that 1967 column he wondered if Coltrane himself thought he was 'hearing something significant' and comments

Perhaps he was. Time will tell.

Well, Coltrane remains the greatest influence on today's jazz saxophonists, he is one of the biggest and steadiest sellers on the CD market, and many of the records that Larkin dismissed in a mixture of anguish and exuberant scorn are now regarded as classics. As Stuart Nicholson says of Coltrane, 'Thirty years on no one in jazz has filled his role of musical pathfinder so that, in a sense, he's still leading the way.'[21] To that extent Larkin *was* wrong; for all his discernment in music, literature and a number of other things, prophecy was not his métier.[22]

But then Larkin wasn't particularly interested in being right in such a fashion, and his opposition to Coltrane went beyond what he thought of the music itself. Arguably the most heartfelt moments in that quasi-obituary and his appraisals elsewhere concern Coltrane's attitude to his audience and, by extension, the saxophonist's conception of art. Those were anathema to Larkin, and they also furnish the final and most decisive reason why he dedicated so much space to Coltrane's records. Clive James has suggested that the 'Record Diary' constitutes 'the best available expression by the author himself of what he believed art to be',[23] and the Coltrane reviews are crucial to that articulation. Latter-day Coltrane embodied an idea of the artist that Larkin found alien and offensive, and that mattered so much that his visceral commitment to the Pleasure Principle was temporarily superseded. Even so conscientious a reviewer as Larkin would not have gone on facing and assimilating the 'pain barrier' that was Coltrane's music just out of duty. Doing so helped shape and deepen his idea of what he most wanted to achieve.

The first expression of that, no matter how perverse, was *ITAWJ*. That key sentence in the 1967 obituary of Coltrane –

He did not want to entertain his audience; he wanted to lecture them, even annoy them.

– coincides with the rationale and strategy for Larkin's *jeu d'esprit* a year later. If Larkin can be absolved of the first charge, there can be no doubt that the other two accusations apply: as I've argued, he knew almost from the start that he was on a collision course there too, and never wavered in his wish to pursue it.

More important, and also more edifying, I do not think it fanciful to suggest that some of the qualities of *High Windows* – not least the poems' economy – have their origins in Larkin's collisions with John Coltrane. I return to that idea, and all that stems from it, in Part Two.

I have just remarked that Larkin wasn't all that interested in being prophetically accurate. But that does not preclude the possibility that he was *aesthetically* accurate in abominating Coltrane's later work. In his 2006 *Considering Genius: Writings on Jazz*, the distinguished black American critic Stanley Crouch essays two appraisals of Coltrane. 'Titan of the Blues' is a shortish but always illuminating study of the earlier years of the Tyner–Garrison–Jones quartet, filigreed by a penetrating commentary on *Plays the Blues* (Atlantic) and underscored by an analysis of how the group's sound evolved and how Coltrane arrived at its still-unique grandeur. In contrast, 'Coltrane Derailed' is decidedly Larkinesque in both argumentative thrust and an underlying sadness at what Crouch sees as apostasy on Coltrane's part. He starts by wondering in bewilderment, 'What could have led one of the intellectual giants of jazz – one of the great bluesmen, one of the most original swingers and a master of the ballad – into an arena so emotionally narrow and so far removed from his roots and accomplishments?', and continues:

During that period of the 1960s ... much black nationalism was really about enormous self-hatred and contempt for Negro-American culture. Its vision misled certain black people into denying the depth of the indelibly rich domestic influences black and white people had had on each other, regardless of all that had been wrought by slavery and segregation. The greatest of John Coltrane's music reflects that confluence of races and influences.

A country Negro from North Carolina, Coltrane was as much an heir to all that Bach and his descendants gave the world as he was to the blues. He was an heir to all that Negroes had done with the saxophone and what he admired in Stan Getz.[24]

Elsewhere Crouch declares his unending love for jazz itself –

I have maintained my love for the unsurpassed variety of that inimitable sound, and have continued to evolve an ever-deeper feeling for what distinguishes it and how jazz became the uniquely great art form that it continues to be ... [25]

– and celebrates how

> Negroes in America through extraordinary imagination and new instrumental techniques provided a worldwide forum for the expression of the woes and wonders of human life.[26]

Both sentences are very much of a piece with Larkin's own championing of jazz as 'that incredible argot that in the first half of the 20th century spoke to all nations and all intelligences equally'.[27] Such congruence prompts two thoughts. First, maybe the Larkin–Crouch 'line' on Coltrane has more to be said for it than has yet been acknowledged in the still-esoteric world of jazz criticism. Second, one of the reasons for that continuing esotericism is that, in Crouch's words,

> Hardly any of the men who write about jazz can be considered intellectuals or very knowledgeable about aesthetics. They tend to know little about the arts at large and do not really understand much about what really makes jazz unique.[28]

Sweeping though that may be, there remains the near-irresistible converse that those who do know a great deal about aesthetics and the arts at large tend to know little or nothing about jazz. Larkin has incurred double jeopardy. As a distinguished intellectual and creative writer of the first order, he remains a living provocation to those members of the jazz fraternity who want their *sui generis* secret guarded; in addition, some of them seem incapable of reading what he actually wrote. On the other hand, many admirers of his literary work either do not or will not take seriously his passionate belief in jazz as (to re-quote Crouch) 'a uniquely great art form', regarding this fundamental credo as a strange if harmless quirk. As I observed at the end of the previous section, it is high time his readers – of all types – got Larkin right.

New Wave Jazz

Not much time need be spent on Larkin's opinion of New Wave jazz. Most of it is implicit in his appraisals of latter-day Coltrane; moreover, although he detested the music of Archie Shepp, John Tchicai, Albert Ayler and the like, he considered their work insignificant in comparison. He also sensed, correctly, that unlike bop or Coltrane himself, their cul-de-sac antics were likely to be short-lived in appeal.[29] That explains the lordly tolerance of his remarks in May 1966:

> Though once upon a time I resisted bop, I find myself letting the New Wave flow over me ... there is a rich absurdity about the present revolution that is rather appealing; furthermore, as it cannot possibly be called a travesty of jazz (at least, no more than of any other kind of music), one is freed of resentment and can afford to be tolerant. (p. 162)

To put it another way, Larkin could not take such stuff seriously, as he took Coltrane and other jazz that he disliked but which had proved durable. He is as much freed of respect as of 'resentment', which allows his sardonic gusto free rein:

> I sometimes wonder whether, despite all evolutionary claims, Negro jazz men do not constantly divide into crowd-pleasers and conservatory men – Bolden and Jelly Roll Morton, Armstrong and Ellington, Gillespie and Miles Davis. And the distinction is always cropping up, sometimes unexpectedly: take the business of hats, for instance. Wearing a funny hat is surely the essence of Uncle-Tommery, yet what else unites Dizzy, Monk and now Archie Shepp? 'You've got to dress up for it … I like hats, I change them all the time,' he says on the sleeve of 'Archie Shepp Live in San Francisco' (HMV). It gives the music a new slant: these death-to-all-white-men wails, this portentous gibberish recited in the accents of Sir Henry Irving against two bowed bassists, this semi-farcical resurrection of the [Ben] Webster breathing-down-your-neck manner – all this is suddenly seen as no more than an act for the folks, and as such is jolly enough. [30]

Then, with acute timing, he suddenly asks a question that goes to the heart of avant-garde jazz and its invariably first-class rhythm sections:

> What would happen to the New Wave, though, if its bassists and drummers played as horribly as its horn men?

In all, Larkin's view of the avant-garde in jazz is not so much jaundiced as amused. He thinks it fundamentally awry[31] and also deluded: his thoughts on Archie Shepp's aesthetic impress as a magisterial critique of *all* 'free-form' art.

> Shepp says he is trying to make order out of chaos, but it sounds more to me as if he thinks that if you look at chaos long enough, order will eventually emerge. Or so you think. (p. 211)

Monk, Rollins and Adderley

Before moving on to less musician-specific issues, I want to consider Larkin's assessments of three more modernists: pianist Thelonious Monk, tenor saxophonist Sonny Rollins and alto saxophonist Julian 'Cannonball' Adderley. The 'Introduction' grants Monk one lip-curling sentence (see below) and Rollins three parenthetical references; it does not mention Adderley at all. Yet his review-judgements confirm how thoroughly he could absorb their music, and while he ultimately stands at some distance from it, his responses are far more sympathetic than one would anticipate. They are also most illuminating: his investigations of their varying forms of 'discord' offer some important correctives to received wisdom while strengthening the the organic unity of his 'Record Diary'.

That 'Introduction' sentence on Monk reads:

> [He] seemed a not-very-successful comic, as his funny hats proclaimed: his *faux-naif* elephant-dance piano style, with its gawky intervals and absence of swing, was made doubly tedious by his limited repertoire.

Significant traces of those judgements can be detected during his 12 reviews of the pianist's albums, but the latter are both warmer and highly judicious. I must at this point declare an interest: Monk has never been a favourite of mine, so I am more likely than some to endorse Larkin's reference to his 'contrived hamfistedness and over use of descending runs' (p. 46), along with his suggestion that Fats Waller's title 'Numb Fumblin'' might have been composed with Monk in mind[32] (p. 85), his reservations about the pianist's up-tempo performances (p. 109) and his disappointment at how rarely Monk's music swings (*passim*). On the other hand, I am no less in agreement with the tribute to his harmonic sense – 'chording always rich and strange' (p. 58) – or the evident admiration for *Misterioso* (p. 158).

The question of Monk's technique has divided jazz enthusiasts for 50 years, and an observation like –

> I don't know how he gets away with a solo like 'I Love You', which sounds like your sister trying over sheet music from Woolworth's. (p. 138)

– is unlikely to prompt any kind of revaluation. The reaction will be either a pleased chuckle or a derisory snort, in either case more or less pre-ordained. But April 1965's column essays a summary that is provocative in the best sense: it demands an answer.

> However Monk's music can be described musically, emotionally it is flippant, 'nutty', surprising and never far from humorous. Now that is all right, but these qualities carry no more weight in jazz than in any other art, and despite his originality Monk remains a funny-hat man to whom it would be idle to ascribe profundity. (p. 136)

If more than a few would be eager to turn that four-barrelled shotgun ('flippant, nutty, surprising and never far from humorous') on the Larkin of the 'Introduction', that does not reduce the unsettling cogency of his appraisal. Monk's *compositions* have inspired uncommonly moving performances from musicians right across the spectrum, but listening to him *play* is for many almost entirely a dry experience. Larkin's observations also contain the stern hint that, while humour and the ability to surprise are certainly to be valued, they need to be accompanied by something else if they are to amount to very much. More than most, he knew precisely what he was talking about here: many of his finest poems are characterized by that full amalgam.

The penultimate review of Monk in the 'Record Diary' also headlines Rollins – the reissue of their 1953–4 collaboration *Work* (p. 199). Larkin made it one of his 1968 *Telegraph* Records of the Year, and his analysis of both men is arresting:

For narrowness of repertoire and sameness of treatment, Monk beats Kid Ory by several miles, but these five tracks … are full of snap, crackle and even pop, with a prelapserian Sonny Rollins tearing into 'The Way You Look Tonight' and 'I Want To Be Happy' in a manner that explains why everyone once thought he was good. His playing is gay, fruitful and energetic … Monk and [Art] Blakey blend beautifully … This is odd, idiosyncratic, quirky music, far from the killer-diller tradition, but so original it compels attention.

The enthusiasm in that last extract for Rollins's work is by no means untypical. One might imagine that the tenorist who blended the sound of Coleman Hawkins with Parker's harmonic and structural approach was unlikely to gain much favour with the author of *AWJ*, but a surprise or two is in store. Larkin extends a warm welcome to Rollins's 1962 'comeback' album *The Bridge* – 'lean, keen and uncompromising, yet often unexpectedly tender' (p. 75) – finds much of *Our Man In Jazz* invigorating, especially the 'delectable' work of drummer Billy Higgins (p. 88), and his two-word summary of the marvellous 'Three Little Words' from *On Impulse!* is definitive: 'smoothly amazing' (p. 152).

Any Rollins admirer will find such praise as pleasing as impressive; more important still is that all Larkin's observations, including the less affirmative ones, comprise a useful contribution to a matter mentioned in Chapter 2 – the tenorist's two-year sabbatical at the end of the 1950s. Larkin's choice of 'prelapserian' during the above review of Monk's work neatly implies that Rollins's pre-sabbatical work remained his best. I believe Larkin is mistaken in terming his style as 'angry' (p. 75): much sounder is his choice of 'plainer and more direct than today' (p. 143). Better still is the observation that the 'old' Rollins

pushed the limits of bop experiment further and further out to produce solos that reduced tunes to stuttering fragments which he then proceeded to reassemble. The effect was invigorating. (p. 131)

The 'new' Rollins could still do that in concert and indeed does so to this day. But it's a long, long time since he was captured on record in such exhilarating form, and Larkin's judgements of his post-furlough work are poignant, including the distressingly accurate 'sad' and 'silly' to describe the 1963 meeting with Coleman Hawkins, who 'sounds at a loss' (p. 105). Such a diminution can be seen as a microcosm of what befell jazz itself during this time – a notion to be revisited shortly.

Over a dozen albums by or featuring 'Cannonball' Adderley are reviewed during *AWJ*, and in the main Larkin's response is both positive and incisive. However, my chief reason for ending this section with the altoist is that towards the end of the book Larkin changes his tune about him. The change is as sudden as disagreeable and has nothing to do with the fact that Larkin found Adderley's late-1960s output pretty tiresome: a lot of 'Cannonball' enthusiasts would reluctantly agree. It amounts instead to apostasy.

The early reviews of Adderley are, if not quite celebratory, invariably approving. One of Larkin's 1961 Records of the Year was *Cannonball Takes Charge,* 'a satisfyingly positive album that should please most tastes' (p. 48), and *In San Francisco* is 'an exhilarating live performance' (pp. 50–1). Further and more, *Jazz Workshop Revisited* finds the altoist 'working up a fine boisterous storm' that is 'not to be missed' (p. 96) and the reissued *Bohemia* from 1955 represents the 'kind of past [that] gives hope for the future' (p. 117).

Two later reviews are admittedly less warm but still laudatory on balance, so when one comes to Larkin's May 1968 appraisal of Adderley's *74 Miles Away,* it is shocking in its unpleasantness:

> There seems to be a tendency to look down on Cannonball these days; since I never looked up to him, I can praise this as jolly, rather noisy stuff such as a Negro crowd wants on its nights out ... (p. 205)

A good deal of calumnious nonsense has been written this past decade about 'Larkin the racist', but on reading those last two clauses one can see where people get such ideas. The preceding clause is less obviously repellent, but its snootiness is seriously at odds with earlier pronouncements, especially March 1962's

> Adderley has the rare virtue of sounding neither screwball nor neurotic, yet always pushing towards excitement: I favour him for this reason. (p. 59)

It is tempting to parallel this glaring disparity with Larkin's critique of John Coltrane – a temptation that on the surface might seem one to be resisted. Coltrane's music engaged Larkin at a fundamental level: his relationship with it was a passionate experience, and tracing anew the dynamic of that relationship, rooted in pain and bewilderment, is strangely moving. The 1968 dismissal of 'Cannonball' is passionless and arbitrary. Sourly flippant in tone, it offers nothing other than grouchiness and a selective amnesia, and one might reflect that it is a shame that Adderley, that most genial and affirmative of musicians, should be a victim of Larkin at his (very rare) worst.

However, I have come to think that this was more than a regrettable aberration: it is eloquent of a fundamental discord that has overtaken Larkin the jazz enthusiast and critic, causing both his touch and judgement to be corroded. 'Cannonball' Adderley was *exactly* the kind of modernist one would think would appeal to Larkin. Full-throated, rhythmically exuberant and always melodious, he was as accessible as authoritative, an exemplary amalgam of jazz as good-time music and impassioned art. All that cut little ice with many critics: Larkin was by no means the first to be condescending. Adderley's performances on Miles Davis's seminal *Kind of Blue* (1959) are all things of beauty, even wonder; yet they were (and still are) virtually dismissed in some quarters as being shallow and inconsequential when set beside Coltrane's contributions to the album.

I believe that syndrome had in a roundabout way infected Larkin by the time he came to review *74 Miles Away*. He may have loathed Coltrane's later work, but he had been compelled to take it seriously as the way jazz was going, or indeed had gone. In the face of that profoundly dispiriting truth, Adderley's latter-day records seemed a facetious irrelevance. Nevertheless, the volte-face was as unfair on Adderley as it was revelatory of a deep-seated malaise in the critic. Only a few years before, during the review of *In San Francisco*, Larkin had hailed 'Cannonball' and his brother (cornetist Nat) for 'creating their familiar illusion that somewhere on the far side of modernism is hot jazz again' (p. 51). Those qualities were residually evident in their contemporary output, but Larkin could not hear them any more.

Adderley was an unfortunate fall guy. In 1982 Larkin would admit that *his* jazz had gone forever –

> [I]t's dead now, dead as Elizabethan Madrigal singing. We can only treasure the records. And I do. (*RW*, p. 72)

– but he couldn't quite bring himself to do that during his *Telegraph* stint. Instead, a jubilant saxophonist Larkin had praised and warmed to was transmogrified into a crowd-pleasing cat kicked in frustration and sadness. And while that lapse from his customary diligence and judiciousness *was* an aberration, it can also be seen as evidence of a febrile gloom which had gripped Larkin by that time. In exploring that, the last section of this chapter looks chiefly to consider Larkin's 'Record Diary' as a survey of what happened to jazz in the 1960s, although the spotlight will continue to fall on individual jazzmen from time to time.

'It is intensely sad': decline and fall

By the time Larkin came to write 'Wells or Gibbon?' in August 1970, the first edition of *AWJ* had appeared, and initially that column concerns itself with critical responses to the book:

> 'Every man', wrote Schopenhauer, 'mistakes the limits of his vision for the limits of the world', a quelling sentiment that came to my mind when I was pasting up a recent bunch of press-cuttings. For ... there was no doubt that this was what even the friendliest of my reviewers was saying. 'A pity he had to spoil things', one of them wrote, 'by holding back history.' (p. 259)

His implicit surprise is disingenuous in the extreme: he had expected – indeed *incited* – such a response from the moment he conceived the 'collision course' *jeu d'esprit* that became the 'Introduction'. More edifying is his admission that

there is a case to answer. Some of his defence rehearses now-familiar arguments about the properties of bop – 'dead tone, no collective improvisation
... chromatic harmonies rather than the familiar diatonic of all the lullabies,
love songs, hymns and national anthems that lie at the base of every nation's
musical consciousness' – but other reflections are less parochial. Insisting that
'jazz writers are either Wells or Gibbon, onwards and upwards or decline and
fall', he further observes

> The Wellses want to extend terms, to stretch points, to see things change. The
> Gibbons want words to keep their meanings, to be definite, to see things stay the
> same ... Duke [Ellington] is a Wells ... Louis [Armstrong] is a Gibbon. (p. 261)

'Well,' Larkin concedes, 'either camp has a pretty good leader', but it had long
been evident that he too was a Gibbon. His avowed aesthetic principle was
Eddie Condon's query, rightly included on the back-blurb to *AWJ*: 'As it enters
the ear, does it come in like broken glass or does it come in like honey?' (p.
28). And that prompts further questions. Did the shards come to dominate?
Was the 'development' that the many Wellses found so exciting actually a
regression?

In 'Requiem For Jazz' Larkin had defined jazz as 'an art that has travelled
from the Lascaux cave paintings to Picasso in 50 giddy years.'[33] He was not the
first to observe that in just over two generations jazz replicated an aesthetic
genesis and panorama that it took European classical music nearly ten times as
long to effect, but few have more succinctly drawn attention to its vertiginous
implications. From Gregorian chant to Schoenberg and serialism is 500+ years;
the parallel jazz odyssey starts in the late nineteenth century via ragtime,
spirituals and field-holler and by the late 1950s has arrived at Ornette Coleman
and 'free form' jazz. It is a staggering phenomenon, deftly contextualized by
Eric Hobsbawm:

> The extraordinary expansion of jazz ... has practically no cultural parallel for speed
> and scope except the early expansion of Mohammedanism.[34]

That is not falsely to lionize jazz; on the contrary, as Larkin's use of 'giddy' in
his Lascaux–Picasso analogy implies, such concentratedly accelerated development is far from unambiguous cause for celebration. In aesthetic matters as
in all others, nearly everyone needs time to adjust to change; jazz underwent
changes so numerous and so rapid that it is small wonder that a once-
interested public became bewildered or simply lost.

In any case, change does not necessarily mean advance. In 'Requiem for
Jazz' Larkin tartly pointed out that 'there are different kinds of development: a
hot bath can develop into a cold one',[35] and we do well to be aware of the
double-edged nature of change whatever the matter in question. Relevant
here is a gloss offered by the late Tony Tanner in his edition of *Mansfield Park*.

It hinges on Jane Austen's phrase 'his grounds laid out by *an improver*' (my italics), and Tanner comments, in part:

[The] move towards landscapes which were calculated to look more 'natural' reflects the increasing predilection for cultivating 'romantic' sentiments and responses. It is indeed an aspect of that emerging sensibility which we loosely call the Romantic movement. In her novels, Jane Austen often directs her satire at the cultivation of excessive 'sensibility' at the expense of 'sense' ... However, in *Mansfield Park* it is less important to estimate Jane Austen's own opinion of the habit of 'improving' estates than to be aware of its significance in the world of the novel. Henry Crawford is a great and enthusiastic 'improver' – and not only of gardens ... He is a man who, for his own amusement, likes to tamper – with other people's estates, with other people's wives. He cannot let things rest. (Similarly Mary [Crawford] is in favour of 'modernizing' Edmund [Bertram]'s vicarage at Thornton; just as she wishes to 'modernize' Edmund himself, so that he will abandon his old-fashioned sense of duty and vocation.) Henry and Mary are all for change, for novelty, for uprooting the old and interfering with the established. In this book, such instincts are shown to be potentially dangerous and destructive. Fanny [Price], who is in her own way something of a romantic, is not however in favour of 'improvements' when they involve any excessive depredations and disruptions of the old.[36]

Not much ingenuity is needed to apply those caveats to the world of jazz. Its '50 giddy years' have made it prey to similarly 'dangerous and destructive' critical impulses, including an obsession with 'innovation' for its own sake and an adolescently Wellsian belief that change = progress.

'A Record Diary' charts an alternative line. I have commented that when Larkin began his *Telegraph* stint 'new and exciting things seemed to be just around the corner' for jazz, and indeed they were. Thanks in part to the comprehensive reissue programmes launched in the 1990s by Columbia-Sony, RCA-Bluebird, Impulse! and above all Verve, it is now clear that the early sixties was an extraordinarily rich time for jazz. It had enormous energy and imagination, properly directed in the main; it was commercially attractive too. And all styles of jazz flourished. The MGM-Verve label sponsored notably radical projects by Gil Evans, Gary McFarland, Lalo Schifrin, Oliver Nelson, Dizzy Gillespie, and Stan Getz and Eddie Sauter; technical experiments such as pianist Bill Evans's multi-dubbed *Conversations with Myself*; what amounted to a complete refurbishment of organist Jimmy Smith's art and career; and a string of superb studio albums by the piano trios led by Oscar Peterson, Bill Evans and Wynton Kelly. The company also committed itself to ensuring that mainstream jazz – e.g. Ben Webster, Johnny Hodges and the Count Basie Orchestra – had a proper hearing. The same catholic range also characterized the catalogues of CBS, RCA and Impulse!.

Much of this richness and vibrancy is reflected in Larkin's early columns. There is an immediate jauntiness to his prose and an evident pleasure in his work. The first column happens to centre on some of his favourite music, as he reviews the four-volume *Thesaurus of Classic Jazz* and a clutch of blues records, but by May he has focused on the Modern Jazz Quartet, Goodman, Ellington, Basie, Clifford Brown and Gillespie, and column five visits Bechet and Parker. By the end of the year he has had the chance to write at some length about Armstrong, Beiderbecke and Pee Wee Russell, interspersed with warm appraisals of Adderley, hard bop trumpeter Kenny Dorham and Johnny Hodges's meeting with Gerry Mulligan, plus a deft comment on Dave Brubeck's then top ten hit, 'Take Five': 'This modest tricky-rhythmed piece seems an odd candidate for mass acclaim.'

By now Larkin is fully at home, his confidence palpable; increasingly the columns combine record-reviewing with comment both larger and broader. January 1962 includes this revealing portrait of New Orleans:

> In a way, it was a kind of Cockaigne: parades, picnics, funerals, all had their brass bands, and every citizen, shoeblack, cigarmaker, bricklayer, was half a musician. Their music has become synonymous with a particularly buoyant kind of jazz that seems to grow from a spontaneous enjoyment of living. (p. 54)

Lovely; yet the final sentence is over-prescriptive. Buoyancy and sense of 'spontaneous enjoyment of living' characterize the (modern) jazz that many other enthusiasts love most, and time and again in these early columns Larkin's prose evokes that exhilaration even if it is not one he privately shares: the aforementioned portraits of Parker and of Gillespie's 'Night in Tunisia'; further endorsements of 'Cannonball' Adderley and Milt Jackson; a concise recognition of the excitement organist Jimmy Smith can generate; a masterly description of Ornette Coleman's music and what he actually sounds like.

From around mid-1964 a subtle change becomes evident. The prose remains as graceful and muscular as ever, the opinions and judgements similarly unimpaired; yet it is as if Larkin senses the impending crisis that would transform the fortunes and popularity of jazz within three years. May 1964's column is significantly titled 'Decline of Night Music', and it includes these reflections:

> Originally an integral part of all aspects of Negro communal life, jazz in [the Swing Era] became a nocturnal art for dancers only. And one could add that [the next decade] shows the process going a stage further, a stage memorably summarized by Benny Green in *The Reluctant Art* as 'After Parker you had to be something of a musician to follow the best jazz of the day'. What was all-pervading had become occasional; what was general, special; what was popular, esoteric. (pp. 111–12)

If 'all-pervading' and the assumption that jazz and popular music were once synonymous are hyperbolic, the core of his thesis cannot seriously be questioned. The music of Coltrane and his acolytes was about to take centre-stage, but while it may have excited middle-aged white intellectuals,[37] it alienated the great majority of the young black audience – a huge, alternatively comic or hideous irony, given the 'Black Power' proselytizing of Archie Shepp in particular.

We have seen Larkin trace this process; nevertheless, despite an increasing balefulness – and to peruse his in-depth commentary on the 30th Anniversary edition of *Down Beat* (*AWJ*, pp. 119–21) is to have confirmed that many commentators and musicians shared both his alarm and his prognosis – he maintained a positive approach wherever he could, and the columns remained vigorous and incisive for some time yet. His observation that Gene Krupa's *Drummin' Man* 'demonstrates how completely the swing seam had been worked out by 1945' (p. 123) is refreshingly un-Luddite; there are discerning welcomes for *Charles Mingus Plays Piano* ('meditations ... of unexpected couthness and charm') and Coleman Hawkins's 17 majestic choruses on 'Bird of Prey Blues' (both p. 128); a wonderful mini-essay on Bud Powell (pp. 137–8) segues into trenchant summaries of the separate keyboard styles of Pete Johnson, Cecil Taylor, Bill Evans and Oscar Peterson: Larkin was always especially perceptive about pianists. During these mid-1960s years, too, there were regular reissues of his favourite musicians' work and a corrncucopia of blues records,[38] and in all there still seemed plenty of reasons to be cheerful.

It is during 1967 that perplexity and irritation give way to frequent impatience or even bad temper. The March column opens with this stinging attack:

> There are times when one wants to attack the whole Ellington mystique, to expose him as an indifferent pianist whose orchestral tastes lie in the direction of alternate vapidity and pretension and who has been carried along since the twenties by a succession of magnificent soloists and his own charm, intelligence and energy. (p. 176)

Although he immediately praises the band's ethos via the memorable aphorism 'A mixture of the Athenaeum and A. S. Neill', this is a sour piece. That is not to say that both Larkin's overall case and his parting shot – 'But when did he last make a record as good as, say, *Harlem Airshaft*?' – are uncogent, and it might be argued that his iconoclasm is healthy. But by the end of the year it is clear that he is finding far less to enthuse about and much more that seems either depressing or futile.

The exact pinpointings continue to delight right up to the end;[39] it should also be emphasized that by now the jazz record business was in a parlously depressed state, and there were far fewer issues for Larkin or anyone else to get worked up about one way or another. Nevertheless, there are two particular moments which suggest the end of Larkin's tenure could not be far off. The first is when even the blues music that he so loved has started to pall:

> I'm getting rather tired of the blues boom ... it gives me no pleasure to hear it banged out in unvarying fortissimo by an indistinguishable series of groups and individuals of both races and nations ... If we go on like this the day will come when the whole genre will be as tedious as, say, the Harry Lime theme. (p. 224)

The second occurs at the end of his review of British trumpeter Harry Beckett's *Flare Up*. After phrases indicating praise and even pleasure – 'admirably professional', 'ingenious and colourful pieces, adroit mixtures of scoring and ad lib' – he suddenly erupts:

> Of course I hate this *kind* of sound, but even so it seems good. (p. 275)

Not only are all the compliments effectively cancelled: such dismissive testiness makes one doubt, as one never does in the earlier years of his 'Record Diary', the accuracy and helpfulness on offer. And although shortly afterwards he wrote one of the finest of his 126 columns (August 1971: 'Armstrong's Last Goodnight'), he called it a day four months later.

The genesis of that decision is related in Larkin's 1984 'Footnote to the Second Edition', which has been almost entirely superseded by its larger and infamous predecessor. That is unfortunate: it is a significant little piece, much more sober in tone (perhaps because of when it was written) and in my view altogether more affecting. Looking back at his last months as the *Telegraph*'s columnist, Larkin's tone is elegiac rather than dismissive, more a threnody for what has been lost than a rejection of what remains. He dwells briefly on the then-recent deaths of the great masters of the jazz he loved, and although he still 'enjoyed doing' the reviews themselves, confesses to 'a deepening sense of depression' when he re-read them. In addition, 'the inescapable whanging world of teenaged pop' had sidelined jazz to such an extent that what he wanted to buy was becoming increasingly hard to get; moreover, 'review copies were supplied less and less willingly' while 'foreign labels abounded elusively'. The writing was very much on the wall:

> Consequently in July 1971 I wrote suggesting that the late Alasdair Clayre should review pop records every other month in place of me. Alasdair ... had liked the idea (he had already reviewed for the *Gramophone*), but all that happened was that my pieces for October and November weren't printed. In December I brought my contributions to an end.

The register approximates deadpan reportage; it could not be more removed from the pyrotechnics of the Introduction, and it is appropriate that the final sentences of *AWJ* – especially the last of all – confirm a sense of an ending characterized by the whimper rather than the bang:

> Miles Davis does the sleeve-note for Joe Zawinul's *Zawinul*, which is predictable as Joe was his pianist once and this is very much one of Miles's style. Pretty, jingly, with trumpet and flute and percussion thick on the ground; one of the tunes is 'A tone poem reminiscent of his grandfather's funeral'. Don't get too excited.

However, that is not the end of the story.

Chapter 4

Conclusion: 'The Natural Noise Of Good'

He is the ultimate jazz freak, alone in his room, tapping his foot and snapping his fingers to the music he loves. We all have such a room. But [he is also] a grown-up critic in the true sense of the word, seeing praise as a crucial area of responsibility ... big enough to change his mind, but also smart enough to sniff the crap at a hundred paces.

Alan Plater on Larkin, 1999

i

This final chapter of 'Larkin's Jazz' explores those things which make jazz such a significant twentieth-century phenomenon: unique rhythmic genius; a modernism both radical and demotic, rooted in popular culture and yet at its most profound a vital expression of the collective unconscious; an art form no less sophisticated for all its humble origins, smallness of scale and apparent simplicity. In the process I shall investigate the separate yet related worlds of Larkin the jazz listener and Larkin the jazz writer, and see how jazz impinged on and nourished Larkin the poet.

For all its centrality, there is one aspect of *All What Jazz* – and here I speak of both the 'Introduction' and the 'Record Diary' – which is problematic: it is the work of a middle-aged man. Nothing pejorative should be inferred from that observation; on the other hand, it does prompt the question, 'What know they of Larkin's Jazz that only *All What Jazz* know?' His devotion to the music pre-dated the first *Telegraph* column by 25 years and it remained undimmed long after the last one; furthermore, he continued to write on the subject in his last decade when his poetic muse had withered. Even a cursory perusal of the *Selected Letters* shows that the one area of his professional activity that Larkin never complained about or looked on with anything other than pleasure was his jazz work. Writing to Peter Crawley in 1969, he remarked, 'I have hardly ever found writing the [*Telegraph*] column a nuisance in the way I used to find writing book reviews a nuisance.' The middle years may be the most celebrated, but the early and late ones are no less important.

Especially the early ones. We recall that 'what got me was the rhythm' (*AWJ*, p. 16), and that remained first and forever foremost. It was the hook that went in and never came out – which is true for all jazz enthusiasts, regardless of their particular stylistic preferences. Larkin elaborated on this in his 1967 *Telegraph* column 'Credo':

> [Jazz] makes me tap my foot, grunt affirmative exhortations, or even get up and caper round the room. If it doesn't do this ... it isn't jazz. (p. 175)

Along with Stanley Crouch's 'swing ... [is] the pulsation of good will',[1] that is as good a *description* of jazz's unique rhythmic appeal as I have yet encountered, but it doesn't really *define* it. What are the musical properties that inspire such behaviour, which make one's feet tap, sometimes to an ankle-threatening degree? Classical music can (of course) exhilarate you with its rhythmic majesty and subtlety, and it would be as foolish as snooty to deny the pulsating force of rock music at its best or even at its most crudely energetic. But neither genre approaches, either in kind or response, the effects that the 'individual sound'[2] of jazz exerts on its initiates.

The precise concept at issue here is 'swing'. On one level it is elementary: it has been said – and truly, I think – that you know 'swing' when you hear it, and you certainly know it when you don't. Like all great jazzmen, Stan Getz can 'swing' at the most *andante* of tempi: his 1957 'It Never Entered My Mind', taken at about 12 bars a minute, is a perfect (as well as exquisitely realized) example.[3] The Glenn Miller Orchestra, on the other hand, does not swing at all despite the suavity of its scores and the dogged industriousness of its players. How come? Why is it that during their celebrity duets in the 1970s Stephane Grappelli swung effortlessly while his partner Yehudi Menuhin laboured fruitlessly to do so? There can be no doubt that, for all Grappelli's gifts and enduring grace, Menuhin was incomparably the superior violinist: he was indeed one of the great musicians of the century. So what was missing?

One recourse is to go to an expert academic. Here is distinguished composer, musicologist, jazz performer and jazz historian Gunther Schuller's definition:

> One way of describing what 'swinging' means is to say that it happens when the rhythm mass moves in a horizontal direction and is not merely a vertical coincidence of things happening together.[4]

Redoubtably accurate; however, it is unlikely to mean very much to anyone other than an experienced jazz aficionado or a practising musician! Nevertheless, it can be adequately paraphrased without losing too much of its exact authority. Schuller is talking about the presence – or the subliminal awareness – of a forward momentum that is both separate from and coincidental with the *metronomic* time the performance encompasses. It is the tension between the two time values – which are often only infinitesimally different – which creates that floating, fluid, irresistible pulse for and in the listener. Or as Brian Priestley puts it:

Music only starts to swing when there is regularity combined with complex variations of the pulse, and when the listener participates mentally in maintaining the tension between the two ... What is endlessly and delightfully variable is the amount of polyrhythmic interplay between members of a rhythm-section, and the amount that takes place between the front-line and the rhythm-section.[5]

Valuable though such academic reflections may be, it is hard to resist the thought that in this case particularly, a minute of music is worth a thousand words. Since *Such Deliberate Disguises* is not yet available as an audio-book, the best I can do here is elucidate a few examplars.

Larkin would assuredly have cited 'Nobody Knows the Way I Feel' by Sidney Bechet (see *PLJW*, p. 5), 'Tight Like This' and 'Muggles' (among so much else) by Louis Armstrong, and more or less anything by Bessie Smith or Bix Beiderbecke. My own choices would be Count Basie's 'Broadway'; 'Close Your Eyes' by Oscar Peterson (trio and big-band versions) and 'U-Dance' by Keith Jarrett. None of the four unarguably qualifies as 'great' jazz, though they are all pieces I cannot envisage not enjoying unreservedly – not a bad criterion for aesthetic worth. But the *pulse* in all four is unmistakable and definitive.

The 1960 Basie outfit in question was not necessarily his best (Larkin thought the 1937–9 band infinitely superior; see *AWJ*, p. 239), but for sheer ensemble power it takes some beating. The two Peterson choices illustrate my earlier point about a great deal of jazz being *written*.[6] One might think that the big-band chart was primarily the work of the date's arranger, Russell Garcia. Not so: the trio version pre-dates Garcia's chart by several months, and its author was Peterson himself. All Garcia did – and I'm not suggesting it was negligible, only secondary – was to transpose already-complete voicings and figures for brass and reeds. And the Jarrett illustrates the historical fact that we would not have jazz as we now know it without the prior phenomenon of *ragtime*. 'U-Dance' was recorded in 1989, and is as fresh and 'modern' as one could imagine; yet its roots lie in 1889.[7]

When originally I chose 'U-Dance' as one of my four exemplars, I had only its definitively 'swinging' properties in mind. But it is a significant piece for broader, though closely related, reasons. In *The Jazz Tradition* (1970), the late Martin Williams argued that jazz rhythm is not only *sui generis* but the foundation of everything else that informs the music:

If we examine the innovations of Armstrong and Parker, I think we see that each of them sprang from a rhythmic impetus ... Dizzy Gillespie has said that when he is improvising he thinks of a rhythmic figure or pattern and then of the notes to go with it, and I am sure that any important jazz musician from any style or period would give us a similar statement. Indeed, the musicians and fans give us the key to the changes in the music in the style-names themselves: cakewalk, ragtime, jazz, swing, bebop. Casual as they are ... these words do not indicate melodies or harmonies. They indicate rhythms.[8]

Alternatively, they indicate *dance* – a decisive link with both Larkin's own jazz induction and his most tantalizing poem, 'The Dance'.

Williams's essay 'A Question of Meaning' addresses another issue central to Larkin's visceral attachment to jazz: the collective unconscious and twentieth-century mankind's search for meaning and fulfilment.

> Jazz is the music of a people who have been told by their circumstances that they are unworthy. And in jazz, these people discover their own worthiness. They discover it in terms that mankind has not experienced before. I have deliberately borrowed a theological term in saying 'unworthy'. I think it is an apt one because the experience of feeling unworthy is fundamental to the twentieth-century man who, whether he admits it or not, is in danger of losing his old gods or has lost them already. But the music involves discovery of one's worthiness from within. And it is thus an experience that men of many races and many circumstances have responded to.
>
> Perhaps in jazz, then, the gods, in some small way, prepare for their metamorphosis.

Stirringly cogent – yet in 'The Art of Jazz' 30 years before, Larkin had at just 19 years of age articulated essentially the same ideas and sentiments.[9] He understood the unique sociological, cultural and perhaps above all *spiritual* dimension of jazz better than almost anybody one could mention, and he did so from the outset. And – a major point I revisit in Chapter 6 – that spiritual apprehension informed his poetry at a primal level, from the moment when he abandoned the strained poeticism which contaminates his early work (primarily *The North Ship*) and started to find his own real voice.

One more point needs to be made about the young Larkin's response to jazz, not least because it is congruent with many others' experience, including my own. A few years ago Patrick Garland voiced the idea that a lifelong love of jazz turns on the performances one heard *first*.[10] Something analogous could, I suppose, be said about any revelation, cultural or otherwise; yet Garland's further suggestion that it characterizes jazz more than anything else he could think of strikes me as extremely trenchant. A chance visit to an Ellington concert changed bassist and bandleader Charles Mingus's life – 'It was so exciting I nearly jumped over the balcony.' For me it was Oscar Peterson's *Night Train* and Stan Getz/Charlie Byrd's *Jazz Samba*. For Larkin the hook was, of course, Louis Armstrong. And while it does not necessarily follow that such 'firsts' remain absolute and immutable favourites, it is remarkable how often the epiphanies of youth become both medium and message. Jazz novitiates have a sudden, heady sense that 'The World [is] all before them'.[11]

Such intimations of endless promise characterize youthful fervour, and they imbue Larkin's jazz work. One particularly affecting instance can be found in his second-ever jazz piece, a portmanteau review for *Truth* of three fairly disparate books. The first, *Jazzmen*,[12] was the reissue of a 1939 work which in Larkin's judgement 'inaugurated a new era of jazz appreciation':

Till then, jazz writers had kept to the music, its folk-art status, use of polyphony, peculiar intonation and classical affiliations. Transcripts of famous solos and ensemble passages were appended. With *Jazzmen* the Jazz Legend burst – *almost the Jazz Myth, for isn't there an underlying suggestion that New Orleans was Eden, and the 1917 closing of Storyville a kind of ancestral expulsion therefrom? Jazzmen*, with its ancient, unbelievable photographs of primal figures in band uniform or tuxedo, and a frankly biographical approach that made full use of the subjects' raffish social background, created a new *vie de Bohème*, where between commercialism and starvation the twentieth century's version of the traditional artist scrambled for a living, his status compromised at every turn by bad working conditions and racial prejudice. Anyone who doubts this need only compare the approach of Louis Armstrong's *Swing That Music* (1937) with that of his *Satchmo: my Life in New Orleans* (1951).

(My emphasis)

The highlighted image is remarkable, the more so for appearing a full decade before the 'Introduction' to *AWJ* was composed. Despite the text's implication, the paradisal associations identified are Larkin's, not Ramsey and Smith's, and the witty audacity of the parallel neither disguises nor dilutes the underlying depth of feeling. In like vein, one remembers his reference to the young Sonny Rollins as 'prelapserian'[13] and the elegiac tone of 'Requiem for Jazz', which traces what the 1965 Larkin saw as an inevitable process of sundering, fragmentation and disillusionment.

Jazz is a Romantic art as well as a quintessentially modernist one. The Romantic poets were steeped in Milton, so it comes as no surprise to find the paradisal theme mournfully echoed in a Wordsworth couplet which Larkin quotes during a 1961 book review:

In a way it has been the jazzman who in this century has led 'the life of the Artist.' At a time when the established arts are generally accepted and subsidised with unenthusiastic reverence, he has had to suffer from prejudice or neglect in order to get the unique emotional language of our age recognised. And he has been enabled to do this by the intensity of his devotion to it. It is hard to think of the career of, say, Bix Beiderbecke or Charlie Parker without sensing ... something of the emotion behind Wordsworth's

We poets in our youth began in gladness,

But thereof come in the end despondency and madness.[14]

As noted at the end of the previous chapter, Larkin's 'Record Diary' dramatizes an analogous journey. But also as noted, that is neither the whole story nor the end of it: Larkin's passion for jazz remained undimmed for the rest of his life. Just as Milton's Adam and Eve find profound consolation in each other as they 'hand in hand ... / Through Eden [take] their solitary way', so Larkin continued to derive unabated pleasure from the music that in his teens 'spoke immediately to [my] understanding' and 'was something [I] had found for [myself]' (*AWJ*, p. 16). That affirmative note can be re-sounded as I turn to

Larkin's apprehension of popular culture and its symbiotic relationship to jazz.

ii

> It has proved impossible to effect a divorce between jazz and the American (popular) song. All kinds of reasons can be put forward to explain this happy state of affairs but they all boil down to roughly the same thing: there is no point in inventing the wheel, if it ain't broke don't fix it, and if you think you can do better than Irving Berlin or Duke Ellington, go ahead and try.
>
> Dave Gelly

In *The Waste Land* T. S. Eliot makes extensive use of jazz, the music hall, popular songs and folk music. But he does not do so in any celebratory fashion: on the contrary, he plays cruelly with these forms, pointing up what he sees as their sterility and uselessness beneath a veneer of vigour and charm. He can do no other: as the end of the poem reveals, Eliot is bent on *transcendence*, which he can only achieve through religion: that involves leaving behind all unfruitful distractions and irrelevant panaceas. In contrast, Larkin eschewed transcendentalism: his technique, his drive – and, it can be said, his ideology – was *transmutational*. As such poems as 'Love Songs In Age', 'Reference Back', 'Show Saturday' and 'Mr. Bleaney' demonstrate in their different ways, Larkin had an unwavering affection for popular culture, despite moments of irritation and an unblinking awareness of its decided limitations.

John Coltrane is to Eliot what Sonny Rollins is to Larkin. Coltrane, too, was after transcendence, and eventually that meant leaving behind virtually all the properties one associates with jazz: swing; formal precision and economy; melody and the concept of song; good-time music. In his last years, Coltrane also increased the size of his ensembles: two drummers, additional saxophones, chanting vocalists, all in the name of intensifying his 'sheets of sound'. Larkin was not the only listener to find the results bloated, weirdly inconsequential amidst the colossal effort, and about as far removed from the Pleasure Principle as could be envisaged.

That underlying paradox – Coltrane's unquestionably sincere 'search for God' is bleak in the extreme for virtually everyone else – also attends *The Waste Land* so far as I'm concerned. Its closing 'Shantih shantih shantih' may be (as Eliot observes in the 'Notes') an approximation to the ending of an Upanishad – 'The Peace which passeth understanding' – but that is not the effect those harsh six syllables have on this listener. Bleakness rules despite the late affirmation detectable in 'O swallow swallow': the apocalyptic connotations of 'Coriolanus', 'arid plain' and 'London Bridge is falling down … ' seem far stronger.

Sonny Rollins was – and remains – a transmutationalist. His *oeuvre* contains a string of titles which no other jazzman has recorded or probably thought of recording: a random half-dozen might include 'There's No Business Like Show Business' (1956), 'Rock-a-Bye Your Baby' and 'If You Were the Only Girl in The World' (1958), 'You Are My Lucky Star' (1964), 'We Kiss in a Shadow' (1966) and 'Swing Low, Sweet Chariot' (1974).

Several explanations have been advanced for such choices. One is that Rollins wishes to draw sneering attention to these tunes' awfulness, thereby commenting on the impoverishment of Tin Pan Alley and its devotees. That intriguingly Eliotesque idea does not square with Rollins's gentle and catholic nature; more important, it does not explain why his treatment of the material is invariably so joyous. There is a degree of affectionate lampoon present, but it is underscored by respect for the songs' musical possibilities – nowhere more evident than on *Way Out West*, where 'I'm An Old Cowhand' and 'Wagon Wheels' evince a genial humour that is on the side of the material, never contemptuous of it.

Possibly the best example of this penetratingly ludic side of Rollins's art is 'Toot Toot Tootsie', on *The Sound of Sonny*. The tune was made famous by Al Jolson, and one might imagine that his blacked-up antics offended Rollins at a fundamental level, as they arguably offend all blacks. Yet it should be remembered that Jolson was a Jew, and one can infer from his knowing humour a sardonic awareness of the prejudice and hatred which minorities of all kinds could attract. All that would have appealed to Rollins's angular wit, and his reading of the tune is notable for its virile good spirits. Indeed, his enjoyment is as immense as it is obvious: one can almost see him grinning at the outrage or earnest puzzlement the choice of tune might occasion in some circles as he drolly clips the melody round the ear and wades into its potential with delighted gusto.

Writ large, that is what Larkin valued so much about jazz: its genius for transmuting and thereby ennobling apparently unpromising or mediocre material. The history of 'popular' music from the mid-nineteenth century to the end of the twentieth is one of largely unalleviated sentimentality; jazz transmuted that governing quality into a music that was ostensibly simple but actually highly complex. Intense in feeling, it was also tough, rich in humour of all kinds (mirthful, sardonic, wry, witty), and tonally sophisticated to the highest degree: witness the double-edged nature of the blues, for instance, whose apparent focus on hardship, misery and tragedy so often transmutes into ineluctably tough, even joyous affirmation. And when we look closely at Larkin and jazz, we see that the overarching theme is not just a matter of happy congruences and specific illustrations, but one of deeper structural correspondences, issues of masking and revealing, of paradox, multi-valency and contradiction. All these aspects jazz has handled perhaps better than any other music;[15] they are also – and nothing could be less accidental – central to the work of Philip Larkin, Poet.

One final aspect of 'Larkin's Jazz' requires exploration; important anyway, it carries the major bonus of rendering absurd the accusations of racism that are still levelled at him.

iii

Jazz is America's true Classical Music.

Max Roach

Jazz is too good for Americans.

Dizzy Gillespie

In May 1893, during a visit to the United States, Antonin Dvorak completed his *Symphony No. 9 in E minor* – dedicated, of course, to America itself. In the same year he made these remarks about his hosts' endemic culture:

> I am now satisfied that the future music of this country must be founded on what are called the negro melodies. This must be the real foundation of any serious and original school of composition to be developed in the United States.[16]

Dvorak had the eventually tragic figure of Scott Joplin centrally in mind. Chiefly renowned for his pioneering ragtime compositions,[17] Joplin had ambitions on a grander musical scale. While he believed passionately in 'good-time music', he hated to think of his pieces as party baubles, and he was driven to write ballets and operas – good ones too. They were commercial failures, and their rejection drove him into the mental home where he died. The origins of that terminal breakdown lay in two ailments which in Joplin's America were incurable: he was black, and he took his art seriously.

The land of the brave and the home of the free could not countenance either phenomenon – which is as unsurprising as unedifying. There are a whole lot of reasons why a music engendered in slavery, created and then refined by blacks was going to bother many Americans from the start.[18] Two of the more significant were the rapidly established and frequent equation of jazz with sex (in other words 'dirtiness') and the unease, even alarm, of not only those one might term 'neutral' to blacks but also professed liberals. One such was the historian Arnold Toynbee, who in the mid-1930s declaimed:

> When we classify mankind by colour, the only one of the primary races ... which has not made a single creative contribution to any of our 21 civilisations is the black race.

Those looking to exert a maximum of charity might plead in Toynbee's defence that he was not notably musical, that he certainly wasn't a connoisseur of jazz, and that his ignorance of figures like Armstrong, Ellington and Fats Waller was hardly unique among white academics; it is worth recalling that what are now known as 'African-American Studies' did not get off the ground as an academic discipline until the 1960s. It should also be noted that even those whites who were sympathetic to blacks and liked jazz were prone to 'explain' things by recourse to that insulting and asinine tag, 'All God's

Chillun' Got Rhythm'. It is nonetheless a nasty shock to find a highly regarded sage writing such things.

There was an unconscious racism in Toynbee's words, no less palpable for being innocent, and if a deeply cultivated European academic felt sufficiently confident to declaim thus, things were likely to be both more aggressive and more sinister the closer one got to home. My earlier description of jazz as 'the twilight art' is partly contingent on its being also 'the betrayed art', and sure enough the noes came to have it – as these reflections from three of the music's leading figures sadly suggest.

> I'm hardly surprised that my kind of music is still without, let us say, official honour at home. Most Americans still take it for granted that European music – classical music, if you will – is the only really respectable kind. *[Angrily]* What we do, what other black musicians do, has always been like the kind of man you wouldn't want your daughter to associate with.
>
> Duke Ellington[19]

> America did invent *an entire musical form* – jazz; it seems to me that almost from the outset it was suppressed by the racist American white who would have no part of this 'jungle music'. Such aesthetic sabotage has proved a more complex matter than mere fascist censorship, however: it has also been effected through commercial dilution and exploitation. Even more remarkable – and distressing – has been Western blacks' acquiescence in this process.
>
> Oscar Peterson[20]

> Jazz has always been a music of integration. There were lines where blacks would be and where whites would begin to mix a bit. I mean, jazz was not just a music: it was a social force in this country, and it was talking about freedom and people enjoying things for what they are and not having to worry about whether they were supposed to be black, white and all this stuff. Jazz has always been a music with that kind of spirit. Now I believe that for that reason the people who could push jazz have *not* pushed jazz because that's what jazz means. A lot of times, jazz means no barriers.
>
> Sonny Rollins[21]

There seem to me only two possibilities here. Either we have a trio of bitter paranoiacs, or their judgements are essentially true. All three men, in addition to their musical genius, are/were notably articulate, well adjusted and, for want of a better phrase, largely happy or fulfilled individuals (compared to casualties like Bud Powell, Billie Holiday and Charlie Parker). If in their mature years they voice those conclusions, one has to go along with them – not least because all are/were *black*. The situation may have altered a little since Joplin's death, but not that much. As the work of Wynton Marsalis at New York's Lincoln Center for the Performing Arts indicates, America is now able to countenance the idea of a serious black artist in jazz. However, it remains to be seen to what extent the culture as a whole can or will be able to accept the idea that this music formed the nation's greatest contribution to twentieth-century art.

There is an additional consideration, one which Larkin raised over 40 years ago. His *Telegraph* column of June 1963 begins with some reflections on black American history:

> The American negro is trying to take a step forward that can be compared only to the ending of slavery in the nineteenth century. And despite the dogs, the hosepipes and the burnings, advances have already been made towards giving the Negro his civil rights that would have been inconceivable when Louis Armstrong was a young man. These advances will doubtless continue. They will end only when the Negro is as well-housed, educated and medically cared for as the white man. (*AWJ*, p. 87)

It will, I trust, be seen that among all else those four sentences expose all the post-Motion and post-*Letters* furore about Larkin's 'racism' as the nonsense it is. A true racist would either be incapable of having such thoughts in the first place or wouldn't dream of proclaiming them so eloquently.

Larkin then squarely faces two possible aesthetic consequences of such a prospect:

> One is that if in the course of desegregation the enclosed, strongly-characterized pattern of Negro life is broken up, its traditional cultures such as jazz will be diluted. The Negro did not have the blues because he was naturally melancholy. He had them because he was cheated and bullied and starved. End this, and the blues may end too.
>
> Secondly, the contemporary Negro jazz musician is caught up by two impulses: the desire to disclaim the old entertainment, down-home, give-the-folks-a-great-big-smile side of his profession that seems today to have humiliating associations with slavery's Congo Square; and the desire for the status of musical literacy, for sophistication, for the techniques and instrumentation of straight music ... the Negro is in a para-doxical position: he is looking for the jazz that isn't jazz. Either he will find it, or – and I say this in all seriousness – jazz will become an extinct form of music as the ballad is an extinct form of literature, because the society that produced it has gone. (*AWJ*, p. 87)

Taken overall, Larkin's observations conflate the two matters with which I have been centrally concerned throughout. One is the harsh truth that jazz's origins lie in exploitation, maltreatment and the struggle to survive; the second is the no less harsh corollary that such a shameful genesis was hardly likely to be nationally acknowledged, let alone honoured and rewarded, and that even the most successful jazz musicians can feel disenfranchised in their own land.

That is something else that, to revisit my oft-repeated clause in Chapter 2, 'Larkin knew perfectly well'. For 50-plus years he was aware that jazz was the music of 'a subject people', that its achievements were a triumphant kick in the teeth to injustice, prejudice and idiotic attitudinizing. He has been pilloried – and one can see why – for his incautious and at times frankly disagreeable comments in the *Letters* and his private papers. But real racism grants no honour or dignity to its targets: it distorts basic truths, ignores primary facts and mainlines on inadequacy-compensation. Larkin's jazz criticism and all his other reflections on the music do not just clear him, absolutely, of all such charges: they prompt the thought that a considerable number of right-on liberals are nothing like so discerning about – or viscerally sympathetic to – the folk and the values they are ostensibly championing.

In brief conclusion, I return to that most defining Larkin impetus, the Pleasure Principle, in the light of which I offer some eloquent arithmetic. *All What Jazz* preserves Larkin's *Daily Telegraph* columns written between 11 February 1961 and 11 December 1971. That encompasses

- 11 years of monthly columns – 126 in all.
- 900+ record reviews, plus some 30 book and periodical reviews.

On a comparative note: I've been reviewing for *Jazz Journal International* for nearly 30 years, in which time I've done 1,200-plus record reviews and over 80 book reviews. Unlike Larkin, I am not paid for those, though I am for any essays or columns I write. That does not matter to me – and it didn't matter to Larkin either: he did not review jazz records for the money. As Kingsley Amis once pointed out, writing solely for money is

A uniquely, odiously painful activity: not really worth the money, in fact.[22]

Pace the frequent disingenuousness of the 'Introduction' to *AWJ*, Larkin wrote those columns because he *wanted very much* to do so. Jazz for Philip Larkin was an image of the world, of being at home in that world. It was both the part (specific records and artists, the copious reviews themselves) and the whole: it was his nourishment, even his *blood*. As in all Larkin's post-war writing, the register is never grandiose or pulpit-like, as characterizes T. S. Eliot; intimately resonant, even chatty, it is, however, every bit as profound as Eliot's, and constantly expert and illuminating.

Jazz was also the key to the affirmation which I hold to be the ultimate ethos of his *oeuvre*. Nobody could have spent 11 years writing 126 columns on over 900 records, if not primarily motivated by love and deep interest. Nobody could have written poetry for 40 years, or been a top-class librarian for 35, without the same id-driven compulsion based on *pleasure*. And that ushers in the next two parts of *Such Deliberate Disguises*.

Part Two

Arrival: Larkin's Mature Verse

Chapter 5

Departures and Arrivals

False start

I was until the age of twenty-four abnormally unpromising.

That epigraph adorned the biographical blurb prefacing the early Penguin editions of Kingsley Amis's *Lucky Jim*. Not having researched Amis's juvenilia, I have no way of knowing if that remark was an honest confession or beguiling false modesty;[1] what I can say is that it applies in full measure to the prentice work of his great friend. For until the late 1940s Larkin's poetry and prose fiction are almost entirely without distinction. That view will be challenged by more than a few, and others in less obvious disagreement might still wish to point out that the early efforts of many writers are inchoate when re-examined in the light of their mature work. Quite so; what is extremely unusual – possibly unique – about Larkin's early work is not just its mediocrity but the fact that it does not remotely telegraph the poetry that would ensue, either in quality or in the specifics of style, tone, choices of form, governing preoccupations and subject matter. I can think of no other writer of the first rank of whom something analogous could be said.

Such early shortcomings have nothing to do with a shortage of talent: they stem instead from mistakes or misjudgements in approach and execution. After all, Larkin took a First at Oxford – and whatever Motion implies (twice) in *A Writer's Life*,[2] the University didn't throw those around then any more than it does now. And while, naturally, such an achievement does not automatically indicate particular creativity, it certainly does suggest a penetrating intellect: that was already evident in 'The Art of Jazz' and also shines out of Larkin's many contemporaneous letters to Jim Sutton.

Yet with the exception of certain aspects of *A Girl In Winter*, I find it impossible to summon any congruent response to Larkin's work up to 1946. I shall devote a single paragraph to the Brunette Coleman juvenilia published in 2002. I have the greatest respect for James Booth as critic, editor and exhumer, and all Larkin acolytes owe Booth a debt of gratitude for unearthing these early manuscripts and annotating them with such skill. But in all conscience, the Coleman stuff is feeble. One can therein see certain latent talents and preoccupations: Larkin's feel for a sentence; his craftily ludic mischievousness (which, albeit in prodigiously more edifying – and utterly different – form attends a good deal of his mature poetry and prose); his ambivalent attitude to sex; and the kind of cynicism that marks out the unworldly, which again in different and acutely self-aware fashion he mobilized so beautifully later on. However, his Brunette Coleman mask also suggests (all too ominously) that prose fiction was not his métier, a sad truth that his two bona fide novels would soon woundingly confirm. The Coleman narratives lack pace, point and purpose. Reading and re-reading all the mature poetry and prose brings increasing delight; *Trouble At Willow Gables* remains very hard work. And unrewardingly so: nobody would read such ephemera were it not for the 'laundry-list syndrome', i.e. the compulsion to devour every last thing composed by a man who went on to become one of the twentieth century's greatest writers.[3]

I have to be equally censorious about *Jill*. Despite some incidental felicities, it works neither as a Keatsian dream nor as socio-realism; after a promising start, the figure of Kemp is merely irritating, inspiring neither sympathy nor indeed interest, and despite its occasional slapstick moments the novel is unremittingly humourless. It strikes me, especially early on, as the young Larkin's attempt to compose a variant of Evelyn Waugh's *Decline and Fall*. Kemp is a revamped Paul Pennyfeather, and the tawdry bullies (of both genders) who give him such a hard time are similarly Waugh-like in intention and import. But, to repeat, none of it is funny, whereas *Decline and Fall* is gloriously so. The people who surround Pennyfeather (Grimes especially, but also Prendergast, the lugubrious Dr Fagan, Philbrick and Margot Beste-Chetwynde) are richly and deeply entertaining. In addition, notwithstanding Waugh's disavowal of anything psychologically trenchant about his work –

> I regard writing not as investigation of character, but as an exercise in the use of language, and with this I am obsessed. I have no technical psychological interest.[4]

– they are memorably illuminating creations. No such claims can be made for *Jill*.[5] While undeniably the work of a clever and imaginative writer, it won't do; after several close readings, I continue to find much of it unconvincing, especially concerning consistency of characterization. And to echo my assessment of *Trouble at Willow Gables*, had not *Jill* been written by one who went on to become one of England's premier poets, nobody, surely, would bother to read it again or indeed at all.

A Girl in Winter is altogether a different matter, and I remain surprised at the number of Larkin critics who consider the two novels comparable as aesthetic achievements. It is not fully successful by any means, but it has moments of distinct beauty, power and topographical skill: there are several passages which prefigure Larkin the mature poet's feel for place and landscape as enshrined in (for example) 'Here' or 'The Whitsun Weddings'. In addition, the figure of Katherine Lind is often haunting, enacted with insight and quiet delicacy: all those who peddle in Larkin-as-Sexist please note. Indeed, it is the *male* characters who fail to satisfy. I am less impressed than some by Anstey: the name is clever, not only approximating an anagram of 'nasty' but in its very sound implying something bleakly repellent. But the delayed revelation of his (potentially touching) liaison with Veronica Parbury fails to ring true; more disappointing still is Katherine's final demolition of him at the end of Part Three's Chapter 4. It is nothing like as satisfying as one would want: the come-uppance one has been anticipating is not so much the 'depth charge' signalled in the text as a damp squib.

Robin Fennel is in some respects a fetching portrait of a part-charming, part-messed-up late adolescent; however, most of his dialogue with Katherine is stilted or otherwise inauthentic, and although the ending deftly underlines the fragility and confusion we have noted all along, his portrayal is ultimately a fragmentary one. And Jack Stormalong is as absurd as his name and about as convincing: he may briefly satisfy as a sub-*Three Men in a Boat* comic turn, but his marriage to Jane is farcically improbable.

In all three characterizations, plausibility is made subservient to narrative preoccupation – in Anstey and Stormalong's cases, sacrificed to it. That may also be because the relationship Larkin became most interested in is Katherine's with Jane. There is nothing of the raffish lesbian nudging to be found in Larkin's juvenilia, but its female focus is undoubtedly central – their dialogue has a vibrancy rarely evident elsewhere – and for a tantalizing while it looks as if it might emerge as both climax and axis.

Sadly, Larkin allows it to peter out, and in a clumsy way. Jane marries the ridiculous Stormalong: why? No reason is given, and the move makes no thematic or narrative sense. She and Jack have a child in India which dies, and we're left with a sense of Jane as exhausted, broken and just waiting to die herself. Katherine emotes very little about this, which again is disagreeably odd, and in all the final denouement is as unsatisfying as untidy (appropriately reflected by Katherine's messy sexual encounter with the returned Robin).

'Faith Healing' is not among my preferred Larkin poems; however, it contains one of his most devastating poetic moments: the third stanza's opening 'What's wrong?'. Less dramatic but no less consequential is the corresponding question, 'What was wrong with Philip Larkin, Novelist?'. By 1940 Larkin had already served notice that he had an intellect both incisive and radical, evinced by 'The Art of Jazz' and these remarks written the year before:

> When will people learn that you can't teach children what they don't know already? Education should consist of helping a child to know its own faculty – its ability, rather. Each man (generally) has one talent. Education should help him find it – should make the child say 'of course' as it recognizes with delight what it has always potentially known.[6]

Larkin was just 19 when he wrote that – as decisive an insight as anything I have read on educational theory and practice[7] in over four decades engaged in that world. Nor can there be any doubting Larkin's early talent, industry and perception: *Jill* and *A Girl In Winter* may be variously unsatisfactory, but they are hardly unimaginative or plodding or shallow. So what was the problem for the man who as late as 1979 told Miriam Gross, 'You must realize I didn't want to write poems at all, I wanted to write novels'?[8]

Waugh's remarks quoted above offer a vital clue. Larkin's approach to prose fiction may differ a little from Waugh's in betraying *some* 'technical psychological interest', but he is similar in being much more concerned with 'the use of language' than with 'an investigation of character'. The unfortunate fact is that whereas Waugh's 'obsessive' (and at his best totally successful) premium on the use of language also leads, as noted, to characterization not just convincing but on occasion profound, Larkin's interest in language is often to the direct detriment of other elements.

The whole question of the relationship between an author's interest in language and reliance on, or development of, earlier models of narrative and characterization would soon come to something of a crisis point. Central here are the theories of Roland Barthes and the parallel emergence of the *nouveau roman* of Alain Robbe-Grillet among others. While Barthes's ideas about what he called 'the death of the author' and the interplay of texts that make up a book are stimulating, at this juncture I wish to propose a different perspective on Larkin's own crisis by exploring what may seem to some an unlikely pairing: Larkin and Vincent Van Gogh.

Neither was in his element when it came to standard portraiture – to borrow Larkin's words in *AWJ*, 'a large claim, but I'll stick to it'.[9] The power of Van Gogh's brushwork and the profusion of richly realized details notwithstanding, his *oeuvre* is a celebration of the general, not the particular. And that distinction characterizes all that is best in Philip Larkin's writing. Both as a man and as a mature poet, he was essentially – and wonderfully – demotic. What he was very rarely good at was 'people' in the conventional portrait sense.

If that is a tenable judgement, it amounts to an unfortunate fate for someone who once opined

> I've said somewhere that novels are about other people and poems are about yourself.[10]

The second clause is highly contentious, and I return to it later. But the remark can be coupled with a declaration made three years later:

> I think a novel should follow the fortunes of more than one character.
> (*Paris Review* interview; *RW*, p. 63)

In both his novels and the Brunette Coleman juvenilia, Larkin certainly obeys that dictum; it's just that by and large he doesn't bring it off. And the key to *that* is something he said to Gross just after the remarks quoted:

> I didn't know enough about other people, I didn't like them enough.

That isn't quite disingenuous: the reflective modesty impresses as genuine. But it surely is not true of the man who later could write 'The Whitsun Weddings', 'An Arundel Tomb', 'The Explosion', 'To the Sea', 'The Building' and a host of other poems brimming with affectionate and detailed understanding of 'other people'. Nobody could have conceived, let alone written, those stanzas – filled to the brim as they are with the most acute and tender–tough insights – without having a deep-rooted understanding of ordinary life and a near-infallible observer's acumen.

No: a dearth of knowledge or affection is not the problem. What is missing in his fiction is *caring* enough about that psychological, character-investigation side of a novel as opposed to its formal and imagistic properties. Moreover, there is an additional and entirely different reason why the young Larkin was out of his element and away from his 'proper ground'.

That is *size*. As a writer Larkin was not temperamentally suited to the large canvas. In Part One's *Prologue* I explored Larkin's championing of jazz as a miniaturist art, making specific mention of his appraisal of Duke Ellington, whose longer works he considered perceptibly inferior to the three- or four-minute pieces composed during the 1930s and 40s. Larkin resembled Ellington in that respect. The difference is, Ellington happened upon the ideal setting for his genius almost at once, and only later was seduced into forms that suited him less. With Larkin it was the other way round. Whatever he might have thought and wanted, the novel was not his métier. It is now time to trace the journey that led him to discover what was.

'Begin afresh, afresh, afresh'

I have already during Part One made clear my opinion of *The North Ship*. I shall be considering it further in due course, but here I want to go forward to the point where, despite being a by-now prolific author (masses of juvenilia, two novels and his first book of verse), Larkin was nonetheless in crisis. He came through it in the end; however, the process was not just tortuous but to my knowledge has never been adequately accounted for. My attempt to do so hinges on a fundamental question: *How and why did Larkin's poetic style change so crucially during the mid-1940s?* Much has been made of his *soi-disant* revelation that he 'switched allegiance' from Yeats to Hardy. He dated this conversion very precisely in his 1965 'Introduction' to the republished *The North Ship*:

> In early 1946 I had some new digs in which the bedroom faced east, so that the sun woke me inconveniently early. I used to read. One book I had at my bedside was the little blue *Chosen Poems of Thomas Hardy*. Hardy I knew as a novelist, but as regards his verse I shared Lytton Strachey's verdict that 'the gloom is not even relieved by a little elegance of diction.'[11] This opinion did not last long; if I were asked to date its disappearance, I should guess it was the morning I first read 'Thoughts of Phena at News of her Death'.

He elaborated three years later:

> I was beginning to find out what life was about, and that's precisely what I found in
> Hardy ... [W]hat I like about him primarily is his temperament and the way he sees
> life. He's not a transcendental writer, he's not a Yeats, he's not an Eliot; his subjects
> are men, the life of men, time and the passing of time, love and the fading of love.[12]

Andrew Motion is right to suggest that in some important respects this
reflection 'misrepresents the poetry [Larkin] wrote for the next forty years'
and that if he had 'abandoned Yeats as completely as he tells us he did, he
would be strictly half the poet he is'.[13] I would add that any attempt to trace a
significant pattern of similarity between Hardy and Larkin, either in style or
content, would be a forlorn one. Many of Hardy's poems are intensely personal, obsessively so at times; it would be a superficial and precipitate reader
who suggested anything similar about Larkin.

So there are two things amiss with Larkin's account and with those who have
accepted it unquestioningly: the alleged speed of his conversion to Hardy and
the influence one must assume Yeats continued to exert. A question arises:
which Yeats? It is reasonable to parallel the quality of tragic romance in Yeats's
early work with Larkin's juvenilia; equally, the pared-down Larkin of later years
is surely analogous to the piquant muscularity of Yeats's final period. There's a
further similarity in both poets' preoccupation with madness, exemplified in
Yeats by the 'Crazy Jane' poems and the identification with King Lear ('Why
should not old men be mad?').[14]

Larkin's poetics clearly *did* undergo a profound transformation, and I
believe that two decisive clues as to how and why are to be found in 'The
Literary World',[15] along with some closely related reflections he made to
Robert Philips in 1982.

Part I of 'The Literary World' runs thus:

> 'Finally, after five months of my life during which I could write nothing that would
> have satisfied me, and for which no power will compensate me ... '

> My dear Kafka,

> When you've had five years of it, not five months,
> Five years of an irresistible force meeting an
>   Immoveable object right in your belly,
> Then you'll know about depression.

From the outset I have emphasized the need to be highly circumspect about
Larkin's *obiter dicta*. They are frequently unreliable, or at any rate a great deal
more slippery than they seem; sometimes they are simply not to be trusted.
Like so many writers, he was a formidable theoretician of his own work, and he
additionally affected a public mask of timidity, cultural ignorance and witty
self-deprecation. He may have been timid in certain public milieux, but there

was nothing timorous about him as a writer, thinker or sensibility: he knew what he valued, and he was also prodigiously more erudite than he pretended.

Hence the reference in my Preface to his *sprezzatura* persona: a self-presentation much simpler, lighter and amateur, much less engaged and committed than is actually the case. Larkin was a very bright man, and he always knew it: three years before his death, when he was wise as well as clever, he looked back on *A Girl In Winter* and commented:

> I do think it's remarkably ... I suppose the word is *knowing* ... not really mature, or wise, *just incredibly clever ... considering I was only twenty-two.* (*RW*, p. 63; my emphasis)

He was also artistically ambitious to the highest degree: one of the shrewdest insights logged in *A Writer's Life* is Monica Jones's *aperçu*, '[Philip] wanted to be a great man' (p. 169). As an artist seeking to be forever hallowed, he saw it as a primary requisite to (appear to) be unconcerned about that very thing: his own reputation and one's legacy to posterity. Moreover, he was extremely funny, and as I observe during Part One, many of his jokes were simultaneously at his own expense and at that of those credulous souls who believe as gospel anything in print.[16]

All this means that it's a gullible or simply lazy reader who takes at face value a great deal of what Larkin said in his interviews or (in this case) a squib not published in his lifetime. Indeed, it is frankly impossible to square that waspish response to Kafka with what is known about Larkin's publishing history. Here he is reflecting on his mid-1940s crisis 32 years after writing that Kafka fragment:

> After finishing my first books, say by 1945, I thought I had come to an end. I couldn't write another novel, I published nothing. My personal life was rather harassing. Then in 1950 I went to Belfast, and things reawoke somehow ... I felt for the first time I was speaking for myself. (*RW*, p. 68)

The last sentence persuades: by 1950 Larkin *had* found his own voice. But overall the account is bewildering. When he cites 'published nothing', is he suffering from selective amnesia, prevaricating or – most probably – being literally but very craftily truthful? In 1946 he wrote 'Going' (completed February 1946), 'Come then to prayers' (13 May), 'The Dedicated' (18 September), 'Wedding Wind' (26 September) and 'To a Very Slow Air' (29 September). Five notable poems composed within a span of just over six months; it surely matters not, or only a little, that they were not 'published' until later. Larkin was writing all right – and with a new, radical vigour.

While the five poems are variable in quality – 'Going' and 'Wedding Wind' are significantly superior to the other three – they are congruent in two ways. First, that inconsistency notwithstanding, they are quite different in both achievement and kind from anything he had written thus far.[17] Second, all five are drenched in religious/biblical/ecclesiastical language. I address that in

Chapter 6;[18] all I will suggest here is that it is possible that Larkin 'forgot' these poems in the above recollection to Phillips because it was convenient to do so. As always, he was anxious not to give any of his games away – and his most serious and passionate game, his own 'irresistible force', was the desire to *shape* his own myth amidst an all-consuming drive to accomplish something of outstanding literary craftsmanship and enduring aesthetic value.

Moreover, by the time he was talking to Robert Phillips in 1982, he had long known that there is just enough mystery and (deliberate) contradiction in his writings to keep people arguing about him for decades to come. He may well have learned that trick from T. S. Eliot, and it is yet another way in which he has ensured his own immortality. And is it not also possible that herein lies the *real* reason for his proclaimed dissatisfaction with what he had written before 1950? Had he not come to recognize that a few 'notable' poems do not a permanent reputation make?

Weighing all the evidence – including all that Larkin did not mention or about which he was cunningly obscurantist – the middle and late 1940s saw him engaged on a profound rethink about what he wanted to do with his life and his writing. And the 'instant conversion' to Hardy notwithstanding, it was necessarily a slow, gradual and often highly frustrating experience, exacerbated by dealing with an unsatisfactory publisher and embarking on a new (and for a while largely joyless) career as a librarian.

That said, I cannot agree with Andrew Motion that Larkin's transitional work mainlines in misery. There is palpable joy in 'Wedding Wind', and if 'Come then to prayers' and 'Going' have a forbidding, even fearful air, there is a vibrancy to their diction and vision quite different from anything in the novels or *The North Ship*. And by the time he moved to Belfast in 1950 the process was cemented: on one level, 'Arrival' is Larkin celebrating (in the famous words of his admired D. H. Lawrence) having 'come through'.

> I land to stay here;
> ... this ignorance of me
> Seems a kind of innocence.
> Let me breathe till then
> Its milk-aired Eden.

Those clauses are full of newly convinced hope. They signal a writer who is suddenly confident that he has not only his found own voice and governing aesthetic temperament but is about to become truly original. Many years later he remarked:

> One reason for writing, of course, is that no one's written what you want to read. (*RW*, p. 76)

And that ability to write on subjects that, in his maturity, had become simultaneously ordinary and utterly remarkable hardly ever left him until his Muse dried up after *High Windows*.

Larkin was by no means an aesthetic democrat, and he was never comfortable with commissions; on the other hand, both his subjects and his voice reach out and touch people at a profoundly simple level, his virtuosity of craft, tone and lexis notwithstanding. 'He spoke to me,' Jonathan Smith remarks of his first reading of *High Windows* when an adult;[19] I have found that kind of instant rapport also characterizes much younger readers.[20] Larkin's genius, like Hardy's, may not be 'transcendental'; it is, however, sublimely *transmutational*: he will take something ordinary – a journey, a glass of gin and tonic, a cocktail-party invitation, a room to let – and endow it with extraordinary definition, resonance and power.

And that leads me back to the 'unlikely pairing' telegraphed earlier: Vincent Van Gogh's genius had an analogously transformatory quality. Like Larkin, though, he took some time to find its most appropriate and enabling expression – as is evidenced by one of his most renowned yet flawed works, 'The Potato Eaters'. Van Gogh finished the painting in 1886, after a characteristic profusion of preliminary studies and drawings.[21] The Van Gogh Museum in Amsterdam terms it 'his most ambitious composition', and he was never to attempt its like again. It was severely and widely criticized; obviously enough, that wounded Van Gogh, but eventually he just got fed up with it all – exhaustion as much as the pain of critical rejection may explain why he went in a different direction thenceforth.

I think the agnostics were and remain right: there's something distinctly awry about 'The Potato Eaters'. On one – perhaps the most profound – level, it is a political statement. The harsh darkness of the scene is designed to reflect the monochrome bleakness of these peasants' lives and work. As Van Gogh describes it, they 'have dug the earth with the self-same hands they are now putting into the dish, and it thus suggests manual labour and a meal honestly earned.'[22] The perception is affecting, yet its chief effect is to increase one's unease about the composition and its underlying purpose. And it compels the thought (logged earlier) that Van Gogh's métier was not people-painting.

What he did do, supremely, was portray *peasant life*. He did it with affection, even reverence, but also with utterly unblinking accuracy. A painting such as 'Old Shoes' is resonant to the highest degree of the man who lived in and worked in them. And the amazing 'Wheatfield with Reaper', arguably among Van Gogh's bravest as well as most sumptuous works, evokes the tough truths of peasant life even though (or maybe because) the human figure is cumulatively dwarfed by field, hills and blazing sky.

To a Marxist, those tough truths would suggest the idea of an historical 'type', as made famous by the writings of Georg Lukács. However, as with any cultural achievement, the question must arise as to whether or not the categories of historical thinking necessarily account for the full depth and resonance of that achievement. If above and beyond the more spectacular aspects of his art, Van Gogh was a realist, he was one in a very special sense of the word. That is something which Michael Tucker has captured with rare cogency:

> For all the visionary power of his work, Van Gogh saw himself as a realist painter. He was suspicious of purely imaginary painting, and once warned the painter Émile Bernard of the 'stone wall' waiting at the far end of the enchanted grounds of any Gauguin-like abstraction from nature ... In his greatest work, such as the 1889 *Wheatfield with Cypress*, he sees with the rhythmic integrity, the transfiguring magic, of a dancing seer. As Karl Jaspers says: 'He simply wants to paint present actuality; in return he conceives this presence as a mythos; by emphasizing the reality he sees it transcendentally.'[23]

That transcendental – what I prefer to call transmutational – realism is in all likelihood the reason why Van Gogh has become the most popular artist in the world (in terms of postcard sales and other such indices).

Tucker further points to the painter's healing dimension:

> Van Gogh's life was one long struggle to develop and express an impulse to exalt life ... [T]he painter's personal sense of religious awe involved his conviction that one needed 'a certain dash of inspiration, a ray from on high' in order to create art that might inspire people. Beauty was to serve the soul: [he hoped] that his art might offer spiritual comfort 'as music is comforting'.[24]

There was nothing sentimental about these impulses. Van Gogh was steeped in tradition: he knew his art history (spending, for example, many hours in front of Rembrandt's 'The Jewish Bride' in Amsterdam), and he sought to make all such impulses new. There is a musicality of rhythm and colour in all his mature work: he gathers up history, replenishes and distils it with fundamentally simple landscapes and contexts, creating a remedy for all those, as he put it, 'sick of the boredom of civilization'. At root Van Gogh celebrates and defines 'mythic reality': it was that, and the fact that he anticipated – even made possible – so much that twentieth-century art would address and achieve, which prompted Pablo Picasso late in life to call Van Gogh 'the greatest of them all'.

All that may seem a very long way from the ethos and method of Philip Larkin the 'Parnassian Ron Glum', and perhaps prompt the thought that Larkin might more profitably be compared to L. S. Lowry rather than Van Gogh. But as I now look to show, the affinities are many and profound. These words of Van Gogh have a notable resonance in terms of Larkin's mature work –

> It is true you can see [such things] daily, but there are moments when the common everyday things make an extraordinary expression and have a deep significance and a different aspect.[25]

– and so do these observations made in 1878:

Nothing less than the infinite and miraculous is necessary, and man does well not to be contented with anything less, and not to feel at home as long as he has not acquired it.

Van Gogh remained devout throughout his short tortured life despite abandoning the ecclesiastical career his father so wanted him to pursue; Larkin lived and died an atheist. Yet as I have started to show in my account of those 1946–7 poems above, the poet was almost from the start preoccupied with matters spiritual. No matter that he was always on the outside looking in: he understood that longing for the 'infinite'. He constantly dwelt on his own state of uncertainty, even 'Ignorance' – a state which he well knew characterized innumerable millions of others. That sense of the 'infinite and the miraculous' informs several of his greatest poems: 'High Windows', 'The Explosion', 'Church Going', 'Livings #2', and 'The Card Players', to be considered in a moment.

To return to my portraiture theme: the 100-plus poems that belong to Larkin's mature greatness are hardly ever lexic portrayals of specific individuals. Needless to say, exceptions or partial exceptions can readily be found. 'Lines on a Young Lady's Photograph Album' (1953) is one obvious instance. Appraisal of it has often involved the identity of the subject: we now know it was Winifred Arnott (later Bradshaw), with whom Larkin had a close friendship for a while. Precisely what was the nature of that friendship is still mildly controversial or uncertain. James Booth discusses it under the heading of 'Flirtations' in *The Poet's Plight*, but also records that Arnott fervently denied that she and Larkin had indulged in any such thing.[26] All that may be interesting, but it blurs what should be a sharp focus on the poem itself: as Larkin remarked tartly, 'I think a poet should be judged by what he does with his subjects, not by what his subjects are.'[27]

One could cite other poems which are, or seem to be, specific portrayals. Three that immediately come to mind are 'The Card Players', 'Wild Oats' and 'Mr. Bleaney'. But in their varying ways, all are far less portraits than statements about life in general, be it celebratorily pagan, ironic or desperately forlorn.

In an albeit oblique way, 'The Card Players' has Van Gogh written all over and through it. The mildly obscene, spoofed Dutch names form a simple congruence; more telling, and rich, is the evocation of both the imperatives and pleasures of peasant life. The harshness of the elements contrasts with the tough cosiness of the inn, apotheosized in the last, stand-alone line of this most unusually constructed sonnet, where 'Rain, wind and fire!'[28] are countered by 'The secret, bestial peace!' that is applauded and relished. The ethos is closely analogous to Van Gogh's 'The Cottage' and even 'View of Arles': the power of the elements and the firmament are contrasted with the ordinary truths of mortal life and harmoniously underscore them.

'Wild Oats' is a very different poem: funny in a sardonic way, sometimes bitter ('Well, useful to get that learned') and with a decidedly gnomic ending.

On the surface, it is in part a portrait of two girls, 'bosomy English rose' and 'her friend in specs'. But closer exploration reveals it to be more of a *self-portrait* and a narrative of amorous failure, self-deprecating and defiant at one and the same time. The title's vinegarish irony sets up the prevailing tone; the poem emerges as not so much an exercise in portraiture as a wry commentary on ordinary human life and love at their least prepossessing.

Something very similar applies to 'Mr. Bleaney', though it is a much more considerable piece. The speaker avers, 'I know his habits', but of course he *doesn't*: the superbly judged catalogue which follows is one of cliché inspired by prejudice. And by forlorn envy. In the midst of his apparent contempt for Frinton, Stoke, 'the jabbering set' and 'the four aways', there is a hankering for a 'yearly frame' that would comfort and regulate a life which is characterized by emptily grinning shivers at the realization that 'one hired box' is all that he is worth.

'Mr. Bleaney' is arguably Larkin's most dismal, despairing poem. It is unremittingly bleak – more so, I would say, than 'Aubade'. That brooding personal elegy has a tough stoicism that calms, even cheers; the flinty purposefulness of 'Work has to be done' is not that of a man 'just waiting for the end'. Indeed, the poem is amongst all else remarkable for its *complete absence of horror or terror*. Fear is implicit, yes, but it is controlled and understated: there is nothing here of the emotions evoked and explored in 'The Old Fools' or even the 1946 'Going'. But there is real 'dread' in 'Mr. Bleaney', hinging on the ferociously honest perception that 'how we live measures our own nature'. This is the misery of life, not the approach of death; it is more terrible as a result.

Because Larkin is a great artist, he can inspire even at his bleakest. As John Bayley has observed, 'If I am feeling really low I often read "Aubade" or "The Building", and they have an immediate and bracing tonic effect: however perverse the process might seem, they at once raise my spirits.'[29] That insight testifies to a healing power; in addition, it dramatizes Martin Amis's conviction that 'Good literature is incapable of depressing anyone,'[30] with which I concur: the reader cannot but respond in exhilaration to what Hopkins in 'The Windhover' called 'the achieve of, the mastery of the thing!'.

That is also how Van Gogh affects not only this writer but millions who gaze upon his pictures. For all their colour, effects of light and extraordinary perspective, his subjects are not infrequently bleak or at any rate redolent of hardship, toil and vulnerability. One responds with awe and even something approaching joy, not just out of that pleasure in the mastery of genius but because the paintings focus on life as it is for ordinary people – which, in the end, means all of us.

Exactly that can be said of Larkin's mature poems. Furthermore, he has very much a painter's eye. Even in the callow attitudinizing which predominates in *The North Ship*, there are striking images of light and space, and just to flick through the *Collected Poems* (2003 edition) is to become aware time and again of his painterly intuition: 'Coming', 'Reasons for Attendance', 'Next, Please',

'Water',[31] 'Days', 'Reference Back', 'An Arundel Tomb', 'The Trees' ... the list may not be endless, but it is certainly prodigious; in all those poems (and more), the concrete precision and evocative power of lexic detail are mobilized by Larkin's desire to deal with ritual and affirmation,[32] as also characterizes Van Gogh. Even more important, both men understood such ritual as a matter of modesty and demotic grace. It was nothing to do with public display but with what they really needed to do, both privately and as a form of reaching out to others of like sensibility.

It is surely significant that Larkin hated poetry readings – and not just those when he was compelled to perform himself. When I fully discovered Larkin's work at the age of about 30, he was the first poet I had encountered who challenged a truism which had been drummed into me since early sixth-form days: that poetry is before all else a *public* medium. Larkin thought that nonsense: whether quietly recited or boomingly declaimed, much in the poems, whether his or anyone's of any merit, is automatically lost. One needs to read as well as hear, and at one's own pace, not the speaker's. Larkin referred to himself as 'timid' more than once, but it was not shyness or introversion that made him champion the private experience over the instant public one: it was a hard-nosed aesthetic awareness of what high art is and how it works. He would have approved, I think, of Kierkegaard's observation that only in Science can one demonstrate: in all other areas you can only hint, intimate, suggest. Publicly to recite a poem is a form of false or deluded demonstration: the experience is almost bound to be less rewarding than exploring one's own intimations at one's own speed and rhythm.

'Something to think about'

The more one studies his *obiter dicta*, the more disingenuous, deceptive or even perverse Larkin can appear. There follow three prime exemplars.

> Form holds little interest for me. Content is everything.

James Booth finds that 'either the most misleading judgement any artist has made on his own work, or ... startling proof of the truism that form is content'.[33] If I favour the former explanation, that is partly because Larkin is one of the most meticulous formal craftsmen poetry has seen: not for nothing did Kingsley Amis call him 'our finest metrist since Tennyson'.[34] But I also incline to Booth's first reading because it can be coupled with this second instance, arguably *the* most disingenuous assertion Larkin made in his entire career:

> There's not much to say about my work. When you've read a poem, that's it, it's quite clear what it all means.[35]

Anyone who believes that to be true does not know how to read properly. Much more apposite are these observations by T. S. Eliot which, though wittily mischievous, carry much weight and can be applied to Larkin's work as much as his own:

> A poem should give you something to think about. When I read a poem and understand it first time, then I know it isn't much good.

The third exemplar returns us to

> I've said somewhere that novels are about other people and poems are about yourself.

As a *bon mot* round a chattering-classes dinner table this may have its virtues, but I can't find any other ones. It is prescriptively narrow, even shallow, reducing poetry to an exercise in self-exploration and self-advertisement. There are great poets who largely qualify – Wordsworth 'the egotistical sublime', D. H. Lawrence (in his novels, too, not to say in every other genre he essayed), Sylvia Plath (whom Larkin, amidst his admiration for her originality and skill, dubbed 'Horror Poet') and, perhaps, the Tennyson of *In Memoriam*. But it is not remotely adequate as a descriptor of *inter alia* Milton, Pope, Blake, Browning, Eliot himself or Larkin's beloved Hardy, whose dictum 'the emotion of all the ages and the thought of his own' he once quoted so admiringly.[36]

Nor is it, of course, remotely adequate in Larkin's own case. Moreover – not unlike those (deliberately silly) démarches Larkin essayed in *ITAWJ* – it takes on an almost self-destructive quality, encouraging readers to regard the many speakers in his poems as always and only Philip Larkin. As a result, he risked – and goodness knows the consequences of that risk have been abundantly evident, from *A Writer's Life* onwards – rendering

> his poetry single-person-bound, forever reduced to an ephemeral historical moment in one (relatively insignificant) twentieth century life. This [is] a horrible injustice as his poetry is both deeper and has far wider application than his own little span.[37]

Precisely. In the poems already discussed, the speaker in 'Mr. Bleaney' is not Larkin any more than those in 'The Card Players' or 'Wild Oats' are, no matter what biographical congruences can be notionally established. Larkin once said, 'Don't confuse me with the poems: I'm bigger than they are.' Maybe so, but the assertion is palindromic: as works of art whose appeal is timeless, the poems are immeasurably more important.

Consider, further, three more seemingly disparate poems: 'Sunny Prestatyn', 'To the Sea' and 'Annus Mirabilis'. The first has attracted a considerable variety of interpretations; mine hinges on the controlling belief that Larkin is invariably on the side of the ordinary people – in this case symbolized by the pathetic yet defiant 'Titch Thomas'. 'Sunny Prestatyn' is driven by an angry hatred of lying that curiously recalls Marlow in Joseph Conrad's *Heart of Darkness*. The sneering that many have accurately identified as the poem's governing tone is prompted by the lies that inform the poster for a (fairly dismal) Welsh resort, adorned by absurd palms and a plastic sub-porn bimbo. 'She was too good for this life' is a superbly judged inverted cliché: what the poem irresistibly shows is that this meretricious image has nothing to do with 'this life' as lived by actual people in Prestatyn (or anywhere remotely analogous) and that her being 'too good' reduces to a kind of tawdry Platonic ideal whose mendacity rightly inspires obscene vandalism. The closing 'Now *Fight Cancer* is there' shows Larkin at his sharpest, tearing into the world of commercialism and phoney-dream-peddling which not only wastes money that should be spent in better ways but can be said to cause the very things to whose cure that money should be devoted.[38] Larkin rarely 'did' anger: he was exceptionally good at it when the occasion demanded – and it is a demotic anger inspired by an empathetic respect for the unglamorous, often dreary existence of those whose fate ought to be better, even 'too good'.

In total contrast, 'To the Sea' is as gentle as affirmative. Doubling as ode and mild injunction, the poem conjures up a succession of vivid images which alternatively belong to history ('red bathing caps', 'frilled in white', 'Famous Cricketers') or are timeless; in doing so it quietly celebrates the mundane truths of life – 'half an annual pleasure, half a rite' – and the warming simplicity that underscores them:

> Teaching their children by a sort
> Of clowning; helping the old, too, as they ought.

Those final words lack all pulpitry: instead they bear out what Larkin told Robert Philips he also had learnt from Hardy:

> not to be afraid of the obvious. All those wonderful dicta about poetry: 'the poet should touch our hearts by showing his own', 'the poet takes note of nothing that he cannot feel' ... Hardy knew what it was all about. (*RW*, p. 67)

'Annus Mirabilis' is an equally demotic piece. I do not number it among Larkin's finest, but it has been tiresomely misunderstood: one still encounters readings which take at face value the speaker's Grumpy Old Man persona and his sour jealousy of the sexually liberated young. The poem's true thrust is almost the reverse of that.

Larkin wrote the poem in 1967: the title is 'borrowed' from John Dryden's piece of exactly 300 years before, written to celebrate England's victory over the Dutch and her handling the twin catastrophes of the Plague and the Great Fire of London. It is a pleasing paradox that, although Dryden was of course famed as a satirist, this particular piece is not a satire, while Larkin's is, for all that he rarely employed that genre.[39]

I find it incredible that anyone can or ever did take literally the first three lines of Larkin's 'Annus Mirabilis'. For a start, 'sexual intercourse' began for Philip Larkin in 1948, with a lady named Ruth Bowman; but while that biographical snippet is a useful corrective to the literal-minded, one doesn't really need it to explode the opening proposition as a whole. What Larkin is up to in this poem is partly historical analysis (stanza two) and partly contemptuous spoof of facile claptrap masquerading as sociological commentary (the other three stanzas). That second stanza recalls the 'not-until-we're-engaged' orthodoxy of his own youth and the 1950s; it was still going on in the 1960s and beyond, and Larkin knew that perfectly well. Like anyone with any understanding of humanity and life, he knew that, for all the impact of class and religion, fundamentally sexual behaviour and mores have changed very little over the centuries. What *does* change, almost as fast as any other kind of fashion, is how such things are discussed and publicly viewed.

Further, the idea that *any* date – 1963 or whatever – can be identified as a seismic moment in 'sexual intercourse' is joyously absurd; less joyous – indeed, one detects a note of sympathetic anger – but no less absurd is the notion that life for the fortunate 1960s young became 'A quite unlosable game'. Most ridiculous of all, of course, is the idea that 'Everyone felt the same'. The deliberately stilted diction (including the *apparently* feeble near-verbatim duplication that is the final stanza) satirizes the kind of shallow journalism that not only distorts the local truths of the phenomenon in question, but whose simplistic formulae are at total variance with the way life is lived and how people think and conduct themselves. Those formulas remain insistent nonetheless – which is why Larkin makes the poem virtually circular at the end: the repetition is deliberately inane, underlining the idiocy of the speaker's take on the world. And if 'Annus Mirabilis' lacks the stunning transmutation that climaxes 'High Windows', the poems are alike both in incidental subject matter and the crucial nature of their tone: hear it wrong and their true meanings vanish.

Finding 'My proper ground'

Larkin's dissatisfaction with *The North Ship* was in the first place largely a matter of its pitiful fate in terms of both kudos and remuneration. Many years later he denounced nearly all of its poems:

> These poems are such complete rubbish, for the most part, that I am just twice as unwilling to have two editions in print as one ... When I came to read the poems they seemed so abysmally *bad* to me that I felt the Introduction should have a much more apologetic tone ... There are some pieces in it I hate very much indeed.[40]

But long before that he had come to realize that the overheated imagistic attitudinizing was not his métier, not what he wanted to do.

So I think it wisest to look on this mid-1940s time as not so much one of 'Writer's Block' as advertised by his 1982 remarks, but as a much more productive taking stock. Or, more exactly, a quiet but drastic revision of his entire aesthetic and literary ambition. He may well have learnt something else from Hardy implicit in some earlier remarks of mine – to avoid any over-personal obsessiveness, creating instead not only a significantly changed lexis but a multi-personae-ed enigma which it might never be possible entirely to unravel. A telling example of that is his renowned declaration:

I didn't choose poetry: poetry chose me.[41]

Once again, that epigrammatic sally is not to be trusted. Larkin *did* choose poetry – and poetry of an entirely different diction, preoccupation, form, ethos and kind from what he had so far essayed. The discovery of Hardy may be the 'simple' explanation, but the truth is that during this time – and I would hazard aided by Yeats – he gradually found a way to see, feel and write 'afresh, afresh, afresh'.

Frustrated at not seeing what he wanted to, Van Gogh provided it himself. So did Larkin: 'One reason for writing, of course, is that no one's written what you want to read.' And – a final congruence, and perhaps the most important of all – both men were motivated by *love*: a love for what really matters in one's own life and in life in general. These words written by Van Gogh to his brother Theo in April 1878 may be rather more effusive than one associates with Larkin, but in reading them one does well to remember that the last line of 'An Arundel Tomb' – 'What will survive of us is love' – was something Larkin did believe, as he told Maeve Brennan many years later.

Love is the best and noblest thing in the human heart, especially when it is tested by life as gold is tested by fire. Happy is he who has loved much, and is sure of himself, and although he may have wavered and doubted, he has kept that divine spark alive and returned to what was in the beginning and ever shall be. If only one keeps loving faithfully what is truly worth loving and does not squander one's love on trivial and insignificant and meaningless things, then one will gradually obtain more light and grow stronger.

The sooner one tries to become accomplished in a certain position in life and a certain field and adopts a relatively independent way of thinking and acting, and the more one keeps to set rules, the stronger in character one will grow, and that does not mean becoming narrow-minded. It is a wise thing to do this, because life is short and time passes quickly.[42]

Chapter 6

Larkin and Religion

The treasure buried[1]

> ... for we must pass
> Beneath the huge decapitated cross ...
>   Philip Larkin, 'Träumerei', 1946

As long ago as 1975, J. R. Watson observed:

> One of Larkin's greatest strengths as a poet is his position as *homo religiosus*, with an intuitive awareness of the tenuous sacred in the midst of the profane.[2]

To those whose sense of Larkin the man and poet derives chiefly from *A Writer's Life*, that remark will prompt either bewilderment or derision. And even for those whose knowledge of Larkin is more extensive and discerning, it does not fit at all easily with the picture of him that has been built up over the years since the publication of Motion's biography, the *Selected Letters* and myriad gossipy pieces in various media. In what follows, I shall draw upon the fundamental truth of Watson's insight. However, I shall also seek to identify Larkin as a poet whose central concerns are spiritual rather than religious, concerns that can often be illuminated by reference to the idea of the *numinous*, as used by Rudolf Otto in his classic work *The Idea of the Holy* to summarize the experiential qualities of the human perception or apprehension of the holy in life.

In the Identikit portrait often furnished of Larkin, he emerges as the definitive card-carrying atheist who is also a misanthrope, a racist, a reader of soft and (occasionally) hard porn, and in whom the fires of genuine spirituality would seem to have burned low, if at all. This is the man whose last great poem, 'Aubade', witheringly rejects religion, any such and all of it, and who having complied – in full – with his friend A. N. Wilson's request that he read the Bible, said to Motion:

> It's absolutely bloody amazing to think that anyone ever believed any of that. Really, it's absolute balls. Beautiful, of course. But balls.[3]

Three things need immediately to be said about that apparently conclusive judgement. The first is the mention of 'beautiful' – a matter of profound

importance to both the poet and the man. The second is that it is a signal
instance of Larkin the mask-wearer, the masterly trafficker in 'such deliberate
disguises'. I would not suggest that his dismissal of the Bible's theology was
dishonest or even partially prevaricative; I do say, however, that Motion's blithe
acceptance of the idea that Larkin absorbed the Bible for the first time in 1981
just a few years before his death is *absurd*. For a start, I doubt it was possible to
get an Oxford First in 1943 without some conversance with Milton and a
concomitant knowledge of the Bible, which was utterly central to seventeenth-
century life and literature, and remained so long beyond that time. Moreover,
Larkin's poetry is often drenched in biblical language, or at any rate very much
more than sprinkled with it; time and again, too, his cadences and rhythms are
biblical in their quiet momentum and majestic beauty.

The third point is to register that it is beyond dispute that Larkin did not
regard religion, whether biblically based or otherwise, as a necessary concomitant of spirituality: it is probable that in many respects he believed the
opposite. He would also in all likelihood have applauded these remarks by
James Booth concerning the 'Identikit portrait' I sketch above:

> [The implication is] that the categories of misanthropy, racism and pornography
> naturally go together with atheism. It would seem to me that St. Paul is the greatest of
> misanthropes (certainly of misogynists), the greatest promoter of racism over the
> centuries has been religion, while pornography in the modern sense is born out of
> Baroque Catholic art. Atheism on the other hand, from Epicurus and Lucretius to
> Housman and Hardy, has been the great promoter of spiritual sublimity and respect
> for human dignity. George Eliot, Bertrand Russell, Guiseppe Verdi (and Linda
> Smith) were atheists.[4]

That 'implication' was by no means intended, but Booth's words are nonetheless trenchant and, I would say, 'right'. However, it does not alter my
conviction that despite ostensible evidence to the contrary, Larkin was steeped
in matters ecclesiastical and deeply engaged by the eschatological, the transcendental and the transmutational, even if his stance was in all those things
always that of outsider. That last emerges from Watson's 1975 essay, which
should be much better known than it appears to be, as should R. N. Parkinson's 1971 'To Keep Our Metaphysics Warm: A Study of "Church Going"'.[5]
These articles draw proper attention to Larkin's interest in the spiritual, the
tension between surface and underlying reality, the desire to know things that
may finally be unknowable but which still command our deepest
consideration.

Finally in this preamble, a simple question: given 'Aubade' and the cited
reaction to the Bible as 'absolute balls', isn't it extremely odd that Larkin
should have written any poems about religion *at all?* If you don't believe in
something, or (its negative converse) you don't hate or resent it, the natural
inference to make is that you are also unlikely to be interested in it. That which
fails to engage our belief, pleasure or rage is unlikely to concern us – certainly

not to the extent of devoting to it the kind of fierce and meticulous labour which fashioning a poem requires. Yet Larkin wrote *well over 50* poems that address religion, the numinous or the epistemological and the whole business of 'What are days for?'.

It seems to me distinctly possible that one of the reasons why this area of Larkin's work and thinking has been bypassed is that there is hardly any sign of it in his prentice work – and it is not just Motion whose approach to Larkin is a linear, chronological one. On one level that is fair and natural enough, especially for a biographer: it is reasonable to expect the seeds of both the life and the art to be palpably sown early on. And certainly in the early verse and the prose fiction there is hardly anything of the spiritually uplifting or even the spiritually engaged; exceptions might be argued in the form of 'A Stone Church Damaged by a Bomb' and 'Night Music', but exceptions they would undoubtedly remain. *The North Ship* is dreary, permeated by images of winter and wintriness,[6] and often characterized by an unattractive self-conscious angst and melancholy; the work is poetical but seldom poetic, and it is truly astonishing that its author would within two years write 'Going', 'Come then to prayers', 'The Dedicated', 'Wedding Wind' and 'To a Very Slow Air'. It is not just that those poems are decisively *better*: as I argued in the previous chapter, they evince a sudden new depth of thought, sensibility and lexis in Larkin's work.

While I consider 'Wedding Wind' to be the finest of the five, the other four deserve and repay close attention too. There are those who see 'Going' as analogous in sensibility and ethos to *The North Ship*, but I am not among them. Even if read in an entirely secular way, the diction has a concentrated precision absent in that volume; the opening image of an unknown, doom-laden 'evening' stealing across 'the fields' is instantly sinister,[7] and the frightened bewilderment of the concluding 'What loads my hands down?' is a long way removed from the self-indulgent attitudinizing of the earlier collection. And there is an extra – and major – dimension embedded in the poem. The 'tree ... that locked / Earth to the sky' can readily be heard as a reference to the cross which reconciles man to God as the former faces the certainty of death. The 'earth' is what we are made of, and what 'loads my hands down' is, perhaps, the sense of unatoned-for sin that haunts one as life comes to an end.

That last suggestion might not seem to sit well with the fact that Larkin was just 24 when he wrote 'Going'. Why would a young man with a burgeoning literary career be preoccupied with future sins and their possible non-expiation? There are two answers to that. First, Larkin the man was preoccupied throughout his life with our inevitable end.[8] Just four years later, still only 28, he opens and closes the first stanza of 'Wants' with 'Beyond all this, the wish to be alone', and in the second does the same with 'Beneath it all, desire of oblivion runs'. And if the tone and thrust of 'Wants' is Darwinesque (and/or Freudian) as opposed to crypto-religious, each poem dramatizes a sensibility which, though still youthful, is drawn to the mysteries of life and death, much like the angels who 'long to look into these things' (1 Peter

1.12). As Watson further points out, Larkin had a profound, highly active imagination which he used to explore 'the complex and sensitive disturbance' that characterizes all human inner life.[9]

Larkin thought highly enough of 'Going' to include it in *The Less Deceived.* He did not do the same for 'Come then to prayers', 'The Dedicated' and 'To a Very Slow Air'. Perhaps that's because he thought they might give his game away, something he was always anxious to avoid.[10] For they are *awash* with Christian imagery that even an agnostic reasonably schooled in the Bible, let alone a believer, will recognize. 'Come then to prayers' hinges on the tension between the terrors of the awareness of darkness and the need for and fear of the dawn, which brings both light and judgement. The 'hearts' which beat 'towards the east' (symbol of Jesus and new life); the 'sword' which will 'execute or crown' (punishments or rewards in eternity for actions carried out on earth); the 'all-capable flood' (suggesting both baptism and the Holy Spirit carrying us safe to the shores of heaven); and the concluding 'arouse us noble' (a prayer for resurrection): the mythological thrust is inescapable.

It is no less so in 'The Dedicated'. I find it an uncomfortably hectoring poem despite the charm of some of its phraseology, but its biblical import could hardly be clearer. One might instance the use of 'scythe' and 'grasses'; 'locks' being kept 'in repair', signifying the preachers who unlock the doors to heaven for the 'visitors' to God's inner sanctuary; the martyr's sacrifice – 'sign away life' and the hapless soul ('bird') who flies into the Devil's ('fowler's': a superb pun) snare against its own desire; or the third stanza's beautiful echo of Hopkins's curtal sonnet, 'Peace' (apostrophized as a wood-dove) in which appears the 'contentment' that comes via 'the feet of the dove / Perch[ed]' on the looming scythe.[11] Then, life's work done, humans await with faith the 'colder advent' of 'the quenching of candles'.

'The Dedicated' is a much grimmer poem than 'Come then to prayers' or even 'Going', but in that respect it is eloquently proleptic. Throughout his poetry, Larkin investigates his own and all others' terror of illness, decline and death; this 1946 dwelling on last things is very different in its contextualization, and that sets up the intriguing possibility that those later poems have a resonance additional to their predicated surface. [12]

Before I address 'Wedding Wind', a few observations about 'To a Very Slow Air'. The religious imagery is not so much compact as compact*ed*: not a line passes without at least one conspicuous biblical usage or specifically Christian vocabulary – 'sheep'; 'feeding'; 'contentment'; 'praises'; 'scourged'; 'joyous'; 'cloven hills' (unclean beasts that also symbolize unsaved Gentiles, with a semi-pun on 'hills'/'heels' to indicate the Devil); the 'sun' (another pun, on 'son'); 'anointment / Upon the forehead, hands and feet' (performed in the ordaining of Jewish and Christian priests[13]); 'candid clothing' (referring to our nakedness when born and when we leave this world). In addition, the title's 'Air' has a distinct musical dimension, in this case (irresistibly) a celestial one.

After all that, it is perhaps anticlimactic if not curmudgeonly to say that the poem is less than the sum of its parts: it crosses one's mind that Larkin wrote it as an *exercise* in how much religiously redolent diction he could pack into one short poem! The phrases analysed in the previous paragraph all make immediate sense to a believer or to anyone versed in ecclesiastical writing; yet the poem as a whole is incoherent.

That sense of taking on the cloth comes to a climax in 'Wedding Wind', the finest of the five early poems under discussion and a significant milestone in Larkin's career. I have a clergyman friend whom I first encountered in the mid-1980s when he took the Open University Arts Foundation Course (A101) under my tutelage.[14] That year 'Wedding Wind' was the 'set poem' for the Literature component, and, in the tutorial dedicated to it, he suddenly said, 'I think this is about the Annunciation, though of course like all good-or-better "symbolic" poems, it functions beautifully as the reflections of a young bride too.' At the time I thought this an arresting possibility, but it was not really explored, either in class or in his own assignment. But, obviously, I remembered it – and reconsidering the poem with it in mind has proved not only an endorsement but a revelation.

The first stanza and the opening three lines of the second have an Old Testament resonance to them – even, occasionally, a touch of Apocalypse. Such phrases as 'night of the high wind', 'horses were restless', 'twisted candlestick / Yet seeing nothing' are, if not exactly terminal, violently unsettled and eerie. Nevertheless, the reference to 'happiness' at the end of the stanza sets up a potentially transformed mood redolent of the New Testament. In those first lines of stanza two, 'All's ravelled under the sun by the wind's blowing' is resonant of something more tempestuous than a mere storm. There is a kind of biblical anger or disturbance at work, and it is therefore hard not to infer from the next line's 'floods' an association with Genesis chapters 6–9. However, as noted when appraising 'Come then to prayers', the word 'flood' also suggests the Holy Spirit and the promise inherent in baptism – which, hand in hand with the previous line's telegraphing pun 'under the sun', ushers in a transcendental finale.

'Chipped pail' is, in Angelo's words in *Measure For Measure*, 'very pregnant': pails and buckets are standard metaphors for the womb. No less pertinent is 'the wind … / thrashing / My apron': aprons are associated with pregnancy, hiding and protecting the burgeoning child. As a result, the earlier 'All is the wind / Hunting … ' can be heard as the wind of change or even the wind of God in his manifestation as the Holy Spirit.

It builds and goes on. The phrase 'the hanging cloths' carries three unmistakable reverberations:

1. The cloths in the tent (cf. Solomon; cf. even the 'seven veils');
2. The 'swaddling bands' in the Bethlehem manger;
3. The executed Christ's clothes apportioned to whomever after the Crucifixion.

And immediately afterwards, the speaker's 'Can it be borne, this bodying forth by wind / Of joy ... ?' may be on one (and delightfully sensitive) level a question asked by every anxious mother-to-be; on another, it is sublimely suggestive of Advent and the ensuing Redemption.

The biblical/Christian resonances are now in full cry: 'like a thread / Carrying beads' has unmistakable rosary associations; 'perpetual morning' is no less forceful, additionally mobilizing a superb pun on 'mourning': Christ as simultaneously the tragic victim and the Life. And by the time one reaches the last three lines of the poem, the momentum of the exercise is inexorable.

> Can even death dry up
> These new delighted lakes, conclude
> Our kneeling as cattle by all-generous waters?

This posits the transcending of death, reinforced by the Psalmist resonance of 'delighted lakes' and 'all-generous waters' (Psalm 23), the prayerful implications of 'kneeling' and the additional notion that such genuflection will prevent death from being able to 'conclude [us]', capped by the Bethlehem link in 'cattle'.

While it is feasible for an agnostic (in either theist or literary-critical guise) to gainsay some of the individual interpretations put forward here, I do not think the cumulative aggregate of connotation and indeed direct reference can be sidestepped. It adds a stirring dimension to 'Wedding Wind', also adumbrating a number of Larkin's later thematic, lexical and conceptual preoccupations. However – and importantly – I also think the over-generous cut of the cloth in this poem cannot be ignored. My admiration notwithstanding, 'Wedding Wind' is portentous, even bloated, at times. It reveals a poet who is deliberately experimenting, trying out new lexical forms and new thematic foci, involving the adoption of new personae – including, fundamentally, religiously centred ones. 'Wedding Wind' exemplifies a Larkin in transition, aware of 'other voices' and getting close to finding his own voice as a result, but not quite there yet.

Yeats's 1914 collection *Responsibilities* included 'A Coat', where the poet speaks in the persona of a poet who had once fashioned a coat for his song, covered from heel to throat with 'embroideries out of old mythologies'. However, the fools of the world had caught hold of this coat, wearing it as though they had wrought it. The poem concludes, 'Song let them take it, / For there's more enterprise / In walking naked.'[15] It is difficult, if not impossible, not to sense a similar poetic logic at work in Larkin.

That is why the post-1950 poems are different, even if the original, sudden preoccupation with the biblical, the numinous and the self-abnegatingly spiritual continues to resurface right up to the end, albeit in a different register. In Chapter 5, I drew attention to the crucially distilled nature of Larkin's finest work, and that can apply as much to specific images as the finished poems themselves. Those portentous 'lakes' in 'Wedding Wind' give

way, nearly 20 years later, to a glass of H_2O in 'Water'. The reductive transformation is wonderful, and as expansive as economic. Depending upon one's
point of view, it can conjure echoes of Shintoism as much as Christian baptism,
the *Tao-te ching* of Lao-tzu as much as *The Prophet* of Kahlil Gibran.

Surprising seriousness and serious surprises

As an anthologist Larkin is chiefly known for his 1973 *Oxford Book of Twentieth
Century Verse*. Not all readers will take to the observations Alan Bennett made:

> It's full of poets I've never heard of and rather than organising little trips to Larkin's
> parents' grave and any other spots the poet may have known or visited, the Larkin
> Society would do better putting together a companion to this particular Oxford
> book. It would tell you more about Larkin and about these out-of-the-way poets he
> discovered and would, I think, commend itself to him far more than their brackish
> trips down memory lane.[16]

However, that waspish reflection identifies how revealing were Larkin's editorial choices. The same holds true for his activity as a self-anthologizer, which
amounts to yet another study in disguise. When asked about how he
sequenced his collections, Larkin replied with the deprecatory

> I treat them like a music-hall bill: you know, contrast, difference in length, the comic,
> the Irish tenor, bring on the girls.[17]

That is facetious – which was one of Larkin the critic's most damning epithets.
It subverts the immediately foregoing declaration that he took 'great care' over
sequencing, suggesting instead something of a party turn. The truth is that he
plotted the 'geography' of his collections with masterly devotion. It is no
accident that 'Church Going' lies at the heart of *The Less Deceived*, nor is it
anything but deliberate that each of his three mature collections ends with a
poem that is spiritually affirmative.

'At Grass', completed in January 1950 but chosen to conclude the 1955 *The
Less Deceived*, is a quietly joyous poem. The adjective might not strike some as
the most obvious descriptor to employ, and early on in the poem it doesn't
seem all that pertinent to 'cold shade', 'distresses' and 'anonymous', or the
later discordant implications of 'heat, / And littered grass' and 'long cry /
Hanging unhushed'. But then comes the almost wonder-struck epiphany

> ... they
> Have slipped their names, and stand at ease,
> Or gallop for what must be joy.

and the lovely concluding image of

... the groom, and the groom's boy,
With bridles in the evening come

whose marriage-puns connote a final harmony, peace and a sense of the rightness of things. And while there are no ostensibly religious resonances in 'At Grass', its final serenity has an undeniably spiritual dimension in that it both consoles and edifies – which two things Larkin believed all significant art should look to do.

Much has been made of the fact that the 1950 'Arrival' more or less coincides with Larkin's move to Belfast, where he lived and worked for five years. That biographical congruence is indisputable; however, the poem has a greater resonance and depth than that of a single nervous initiant in a 'new city'. Once again the biblical lexis is tellingly frequent: 'curtains', 'doves', 'innocence' and, above all, 'milk-aired Eden'. The poem seems to reject all such potential with its last line, 'A style of dying only'. Yet what a curious – and very *difficult* – line that is. It reverberates without one being quite aware of what those reverberations signify. It might communicate a resigned awareness that all the promise telegraphed by the opening 'Morning' and all the other enabling portents will come to 'grey-veil[ed]' nothing; that seems congruent with the starkly rueful 'Fast enough I shall wound it', signalling an awareness of sin or at any rate the capacity to damage 'innocence'. Yet it is also possible to detect a troubled residual quest for the 'wood-dove of peace' I cited above when looking at 'The Dedicated'. 'Arrival' hinges on the tension between the need for and fear of the dawn and the terrors of the awareness of darkness. If those words seem familiar, they should be: they are a slightly recast version of an earlier observation about 'Come then to prayers'.

'Next Please' (which appears immediately after 'Arrival' in the *Collected Poems*) continues the momentum in question. The first stanza speaks of being 'too eager for the future' and of 'bad habits of expectancy', while its successor further captures the notion of febrile, perhaps already-deluded hope in the superb 'Sparkling armada of promises'. But the poem turns out to be more subtle and complex than such telegraphing might seem to indicate.

The prayerful penultimate stanza

We think each one[18] will heave to and unload
All good into our lives, all we owed
For waiting so devoutly and so long.

is apparently subverted, even cancelled, by the final stanza's baleful 'But we are wrong', setting up the declaration that the only 'ship ... seeking us' is 'a black-sailed unfamiliar' whose import is that of entropy: 'In her wake / No waters breed or break.'

Yet – to localize a generic point I made earlier – why should Larkin go to such sophisticated aesthetic trouble to arrive at a conclusion that is, for all its grimness, decidedly banal? The answer is that the poem's power lies in its tension, not its conclusion: the penultimate stanza has as much potency to uplift as its successor does to engloom. In that respect it is akin to one of Larkin's finest achievements, 'Dockery and Son' (see below) and to 'Ignorance'.[19]

The last (and crucial) three words of 'Mr. Bleaney' are 'I don't know,' and it is that admission which both drives 'Ignorance' and makes it more enchanting than dispiriting – notwithstanding the fact that, as often is the case with Larkin, the poem's initial impact is cheerless. Negatives or indeterminate 'hedging' phrases abound from the outset: 'to know nothing'; 'never to be sure'; 'so I feel'; 'it does seem so'; 'Someone must know'; 'ignorant'; 'strange' (three times); 'imprecisions'; 'die'; 'no idea why'. Quite a formidable list for so short a piece. Yet the tone is interestedly perplexed, not cynically aloof: once again a quietly universal resonance obtains. On this occasion Larkin draws attention, unfussily and understatedly, to the basic truth that *none* of us can ever absolutely 'know' or 'be sure of' all the most sacred and profoundly important things in our lives – at least not in the sense of demonstrating them as absolute fact.

What I have long felt to be the subtext of Tom Stoppard's *Jumpers* (which centres on philosophy) might be expressed thus:

> You cannot prove those things which you most trust, and you cannot altogether trust those things which you can prove.

'Ignorance' posits something analogous. That triple repetition of 'strange' does not signify 'odd and highly disconcerting' so much as 'wonderful', in the prime sense of 'full of wonder'. Larkin's stance is very much that of the speaker in stanza three of 'Rabbi Ben Ezra' by Robert Browning:

> Rather I prize the doubt
> Low kinds exist without
> Finished and finite clods, untroubled by a spark.

Our final 'ignorance' should not be a cause for anxiety or complaint: it should instead be cherished. There's something lovely about it, and there's something noble about the fact that we have 'no idea why'. We just *do* it: that is not only all right by Larkin but at root a governing credo. That can be confirmed by an in-depth look at 'Dockery and Son', whose second half is as tonally ambiguous as anything Larkin wrote.

Its first half is sombre (though funny also), abounding in images of death and solemnity; it is also characteristically uncertain, hedged by vagueness. Who *was/is* Dockery? Is he still alive? Or has he gone the same, premature way as 'Cartwright who was killed', and has Larkin been attending his Oxford funeral? Appropriately, we don't know. Larkin 'escapes', falls asleep – and then follow in quick succession two utterances central to not only this poem but Larkin's very method: 'I changed' and 'joining and parting lines'. The tone indeed *changes* – radically; and those 'joining and parting lines' become a magnificent metaphor for the complex and never-quite-certain 'tracks' down which our lives run. It may be very different from the sardonic reflections of 'Self's the Man', but it does find Larkin wondering anew what spurs a man to make a late-teenage choice to become husband and father. The enquiry is genuine: once again, he really does not know. He may know enough to know it's not for him, but he is still compelled to ask 'Why did he think adding meant increase? / To me it was dilution.'

At the end of the poem, Larkin suddenly switches from fascinated bewilderment to something decisive, even didactic. Its most quoted line – among the most renowned in Larkin's *oeuvre* – is 'Life is first boredom, then fear',[22] whose numbing power tempts one to take it at face value and also as the poem's final vision or judgement. But in an obvious sense it *isn't* its conclusion: there are three more lines.

To my ears the most subtle and important of these is 'Whether or not we use it, it goes'. The fact of death/human transience is inescapable: it is the one certainty in life. Therefore, as 'Ignorance' and 'Days' (see below) suggest, why bother to agonize about such a fact? Better, surely, to 'use it' (i.e. 'life'). In short, for all its sombre hues and perplexity, the poem is much more affirmative than not – not least because the speaker is still alive while Cartwright and (I infer) Dockery aren't.

The penultimate line has been largely ignored in the many critical exegeses the poem has inspired. Perhaps that is because the surrounding lines have so much impact that it seems unnecessary to gloss it. But it *is* necessary: the line is both very difficult and, once decoded, highly problematic, altering both the mood and the thrust of the poem's vision. 'And leaves what something hidden from us chose' signifies, firstly, the subconscious decision-making mechanism which drives us to major destinations: after all, how many of us actually *choose* our careers, partners, lifestyles? As in its different way 'Money' observes, we seem to be governed either by unconscious or subconscious forces until 'age' arrives; moreover, before that time comes retirement and, with it, regret as well as fulfilment, and more often than not ill-health.[23]

Second, to any Christian or theist reader, that 'what' could indicate God Himself – as 'hidden from us', choosing and willing our destinies for us and working through circumstances in life to bring us to a certain place ('works which He prepared in advance for us to do') that we sometimes manage to understand towards the end of our lives. Either way, the 'something' is not *left*: it is that which does the *choosing* for us. Larkin may not have been a seeker after God, but he struggled in the same way as do many men and women with the notion of predestination versus free will.

And that further means that the last line – 'And age, and then the only end of age' – cannot properly be heard as the nihilistic reflection so many take it to be. The noun 'age' is grammatically dependent on 'leaves'. In this context, that verb has nothing to do with cessation or being abandoned: it can only signify 'legacy' or 'fruition'. The gift may be a forbidding one, but the idea is entirely congruent with the 'desire of oblivion' that 'runs' deep in the human psyche. 'Dockery and Son' is, all immediate appearances and virtually all critical commentary to the contrary, a poem that modulates into an uncommonly moving tough serenity.

Such *de profundis* tough-mindedness also characterizes a piece Larkin had written a decade earlier: 'Days', a ten-line poem of rare and complex audacity. Its first stanza seems to hover dangerously over Patience Strong territory, its diction one notch up from a greetings card or some such. Any incipient lip-curling vanishes after the white space which follows 'Where can we live but days?'. As soon as one hits the second stanza, one realizes that break is not so much a pregnant pause as a caesura worthy of Milton. 'Ah, solving that question ... ' (for myself I hear a heavy stress on *that*) ushers in an image that is certainly disturbing, even nightmarish. *Why* does that solution (or attempted solution) cause the long-coated priest and doctor to rush over the fields? There are several possible answers or interpretations.

One is that the determined desire to know why we are here, what our purpose in life might be, and what else there might be beyond is a recipe for becoming so distressed, mad, ill or all three that both these ministering figures are in a hurry to tend to the questioner before it's too late. Alternatively, perhaps the (successful) solution 'brings' them rushing to find out the secret so far denied them despite all their learning and dedication. But that does not altogether account for the singular 'In their long coats'. This could conjure thoughts of the gowns worn by the Inquisition, in view of which a more sinister take becomes compelling. The priest and the doctor (the latter in the original sense of 'teacher') are jealous of their 'power of the keys' and do not wish anybody to trespass on their territory: they are 'running' in order to shut the questioner up as quickly as possible.

And even if one eschews all those readings, be they benevolent or sinister, the poem still evinces a concerned menace. Yet another interpretation is that Larkin is warning the reader not to dwell too long on the unknowable: 'that way madness lies'. Days are indeed 'where we live' and (if possible) 'to be happy in': they should be accepted as fact and *used*. To ponder at length any grander dimension, either on the basis of 'How did we get here?/What are we here for?/What is the point of all this?' or to look beyond the 'Days' of our earthly life to some other state, is not healthy for either mind or body. Such a stern injunction may seem at odds with the spiritual questioning and investigation to be found in many of Larkin's poems, but it is not a contradiction: insofar as he is ever a didactic or patent moralist (which is not often), Larkin is committed to celebrating life, warts and all, and looking to help his readers 'down Cemetery Road'.

'Ignorance', 'Dockery and Son', 'Days' and 'High Windows' may abound in the spiritual and the implicitly numinous, but they have only an oblique religious dimension. Now for three poems where that element is fundamental: 'Water', 'The Explosion' and 'Solar'.

Larkin was endlessly interested in 'ordinary' life and in 'ordinary' people:

for example, it is illuminating how many of his poems feature some sort of *journey,* that unique amalgam of the mundane and the magical. He was also properly aware of the uniqueness of every individual, no matter how humdrum: better than most he understood the full force of the fact that every one of us has 'an *only* life' ('Aubade'; my italics) – 'only' in the Gore Vidalian sense of 'This is it: there's nothing else',[24] and also in the sense of uncloneable, DNA-unique. And his interest in religion stems from his awareness, at once bewildered and impressed, that myriad unique individuals *do* 'gravitate' to religion, to churches, to anything that might heal or explain.

So in the 1954 'Water' we find a debunking wit not just rubbing shoulders with lyricism and joy but symbiotically joined to them. And that wit is, additionally, wonderfully cavalier: everything he proposes as a putative consultant 'called in/To construct a religion' has of course been done, over and over again! Every image or idea resonates with long established religious practice, Christian or otherwise. Larkin has a lot of fun with such phrases as 'construct a religion' (implying in a Voltairean way that the whole God-thing was dreamed up by man anyway) and 'sousing', which has connotations of alcohol and therefore escape.[25] There is even a sly reference to organized religion's delight in wealth in the easily missed pun 'a fording'.[26] But throughout, the poem evinces enormous gusto and a sense of innocent play – and then such life-enhancing things are elevated into pure celebration and beauty:

> I should raise in the east
> A glass of water
> Where any-angled light
> Would congregate endlessly.

I have already drawn attention to the coincidental congruity between these lines and an exhibit in the Tate Gallery a decade or so ago.[27] Poem and exhibit alike enshrine the unarguable and celebratory perception that every human sees things in a unique way. *That* is what Larkin values and respects about spirituality, and though he cannot take part in the 'furious devout drench' of religion, he is sensitive to the ecumenical core within the institutional casing. And he does all this with an artistry which see-saws between the rationalism of 'construct' and the juice of 'sousing' with an aplomb as visceral as masterly.

Completed in January 1970, 'The Explosion' is a tender, virtuoso performance in which Larkin operates as scribe or reporter, albeit a most eloquent one: there is no sense of self at all. That is not to say the poem lacks emotion. It invokes grief, anger, even horror; it also inspires compassion and a strong feeling of transcendence, religious or otherwise. But all those emotions and responses are for us to infer and decide upon: we are given little or no guidance by the speaker/poet, whose personality is absent, invisible, almost impenetrable.

Significant enough anyway in view of the portraits painted by Motion and others of Larkin as selfish and narrowly ambitious, this deliberate negation of self in the face of wider tragedy and loss is additionally important for being the volume's concluding piece. Its very last words – 'the eggs unbroken' – are not just evidence of something lovely and fragile having survived the carnage, and the concomitant sense of life going on: they confirm and complete the poem's governing transmutationalism.

For 'The Explosion' is imbued with supernatural and spiritual lexis from the second line, where the 'shadows' which point 'towards the pithead' seem, in retrospect, to be a kind of ghastly hex: the mine has been targeted. Later – and again, perhaps, only in retrospect – 'the tall gates' become redolent of the Gates of Heaven rather than those at the pithead. Moreover, the central stanza ends with an unmistakable echo of the eclipse at the moment of Christ's death recorded in St John's Gospel, and its italicized successor has an other-worldliness as comforting as it is strange (which might serve as a definition of the Holy Ghost). And '*they / Are sitting in God's house in comfort, We shall see them face to face –*' has a certainty of promise that is more than hope, endorsed by the fact that the women are referred to not as 'widows' but as 'wives'.

Whatever their religious stance, alert readers even vaguely conversant with biblical and ecclesiastical language surely cannot fail to see what the poem is at the very least implicitly addressing: not just life going on, but *new* life, the promise of newness that Easter celebrates. The poem carefully chooses 'rabbits' and 'eggs', both definitive symbols of that Festival, and the phrases 'Larger than in life' and 'walking / Somehow from the sun' (with its obvious pun) decisively multiply such resonance.

Perhaps more than any other Larkin poem, 'The Explosion' illustrates the irrelevance, on one level, of personal belief. The poem palpably admits a Christian reading, and it is required of any agnostic reader to recognize that in full just as much as any Christian one. Indeed, that last line reminds me of the 'Shantih, shantih, shantih' which concludes *The Waste Land*. Both poems hinge on religious awareness, and both look to offer a peace that the intellect cannot on its own apprehend.

In Chapter 5, I likened 'High Windows' to 'Annus Mirabilis' in its adoption of an apparently defeated and envious speaker. I also declared the former to be much the superior piece; the chief reason for that is the quite astonishing transformation, in both form and content, dramatized in a mere 20 lines.

The initial sour envy is accompanied by choices of vocabulary which, of course, look to shock in the way that so displeased certain critics of 'A Study of Reading Habits' and 'Vers de Société'. But 'High Windows' reveals its true stance more quickly and more clearly than does 'Annus Mirabilis'. By the time one reaches the end of the phrase 'everyone young going down the long slide / To happiness', it is evident that the perception is ironic, debunking both the old-misery persona assumed at the outset and the young themselves, or rather any young people dumb enough to think that sexual permissiveness really is an automatic passport to 'paradise'.

The persona then switches from sarcasm to a more sober reflection on whether and how one's own life and opportunities when young might have been viewed by the middle-aged. The diction is immensely clever – and difficult. The imaginary older speaker repeats the use of 'down the long slide', adding 'Like free bloody birds'. The profanity signals jealousy; it also communicates to the reader a sense of violence and damage. That is the dark side of freedom, and at this point the true force of the earlier, ostensibly celebratory 'Bonds and gestures pushed to one side / Like an outdated combine harvester' becomes clear: such eventualities do not happen, and 'the long slide to happiness, endlessly' is just a mirage, whatever generation is in question.

And then – partly set up by that 'endlessly' – the poem suddenly transmutes into something sublime. I don't think it important where those 'high windows' might actually have been (Larkin's flat, the Hull Library, so forth), or at any rate that is far less important than the awed contemplation of the firmament with which the poem ends. There is, again, something Van Gogh-like about it, quotidian detail merging with infiniteness, moving and consoling at once.

The extraordinary 'Solar' is both further crucial evidence of Larkin's fascination with the religious, and unique: it is, finally, quite unlike anything else he wrote.

The earliest-composed (November 1964) of the poems collected in *High Windows*, it appears late on in the volume, sandwiched between the equally though differently deceptive 'Sad Steps'[28] and 'Annus Mirabilis'. There is nothing deceptive about 'Solar': it is arguably and in several ways the purest poem in his *oeuvre*. Remarkably spare, it is at once simple and complex, immediate and profound. Those combinations attend Blake's *Songs of Innocence and Experience*, and 'Solar' is appropriately Blakean in its cadences and its diction: the latter, stark but tender, is reminiscent of 'Sunflower'. Larkin's lines, lean and unrhymed, abound in plangent images which generate formidable power, no matter whether the import strikes as (again) a Van Gogh-like celebration of the sun as our planet's life-giving force, a pagan celebration of that bounty, or a Christian allegory.

Despite the impact of the opening 'Suspended lion face' and that first stanza's citing of 'stalkless flower', 'Solar' anthropomorphizes the sun, acknowledging its generosity in terms of not only currency ('your Gold / Coined there ... ') but those of human love, especially *agape*: 'You pour unrecompensed'; 'Unclosing like a hand, / You give for ever.' That grateful affection is accompanied by awe:

> Your petalled head of flames
> Continuously exploding.

The combination of the intimate and the infinite, of lyricism and scientific literacy (Larkin the *sprezzatura* yet once more) creates a transmutational grandeur. The preceding 'Our needs hourly / Climb and return like angels' and the earlier 'Unfurnished sky' are reminiscent of 'the deep blue air' which 'shows / Nothing ... and is endless' which closes 'High Windows'. Indeed, the poems' spiritual destinations are virtually identical, even if the routes they take could hardly be more dissimilar.

But 'Solar' offers an entirely different vision as well. Whether denotatively or in its (vast) reverberations, the poem's every line conveys a Christian reference of one sort or another. The opening 'lion' can connote any number of things, but amongst them must number 'the lion of Judah'. 'You pour unrecompensed' is redolent of both Jesus's redemptive sacrifice and the Holy Ghost, while the latter's place in the Trinity is confirmed by the second stanza's 'Heat is the echo of your / Gold'. That is followed up by the poem's final line, 'You give forever'. Yes, the sun serves Planet Earth in just such a way; so, to all believers, does the Holy Spirit. Larkin may not have embraced that belief, but he certainly understood it.

As with the prentice 'Wedding Wind', the more one dwells on 'Solar' as a multivalent text, the more the Christian redolences proliferate. Stanza two's

> The eye sees you
> Simplified by distance
> Into an origin.

can be read as a secular observation. But to a Christian – or indeed a biblically literate agnostic – it also evokes a reflection on the life and import of Jesus Christ; in that context, 'origin' points to 'In the beginning was the Word'. Further, if I now requote the lines –

> Your petalled head of flames
> Continuously exploding.

– that is because they echo The Book of Revelation and also the fundamental Christian mantra, 'The Light of the World'. In the same way, the sentence which follows –

> Heat is the echo of your
> Gold.

– apostrophizes the Holy Spirit.[29] Moreover, 'You pour unrecompensed' (His sacrifice) and the closing 'You give for ever' irresistibly call Jesus to mind, and God the Father is addressed with similar directness in 'You exist openly' (cf. 'I AM' and 'I am what I am').

Human worship is also evidenced. 'Our needs hourly / Climb ... ' obviously indicates prayer(s), and if that seems a curiously exact reference, one need only remember the precise schedule church services embody. In addition, Larkin evokes Jacob's ladder and his vision of angels ascending and descending with the immediately sequent ' ... Climb and return like angels.'[30]

It would of course be a mistake to limit the religious resonances of 'Solar' to

Christian ones. The mytho-poetic use of the sun as image and symbol is as old as poetry itself, and has always been pan-cultural (including the pagan).[31] But one of the sun's properties is peculiarly germane to the specific readings I'm offering here. Nobody can look at the sun directly; the same applies to the human perception of God (in this earthly life, that is). And artists are required to use a panoply of masks and oblique approaches when addressing those things which are of primary spiritual consequence but do not admit of any final definition.[32]

In 'Solar', Larkin's mask is distinguished for its graceful economy, a property which attends the entire poem. Its text comprises just 72 words, a minimalism whose significance increases when one notes that each stanza has seven lines and 24 words; in addition, the poem's characters, including the title, number 365. Such symmetry of design is not only (of course) deliberate: it is controllingly mimetic. Three equal stanzas: just like the the light/heat/fire 'codes' (elucidated in note 30), the poem's very structure is predicated on the Holy Trinity, where all three components are equal and interlockingly consubstantial. Indeed, 'Solar' finds Larkin at his most distilled, his purest. Its exquisite ending –

Unclosing like a hand,
You give for ever.

– is, at every possible level, an even more powerful tribute to the power of love than the last line of 'An Arundel Tomb'. Whatever one's 'take' on 'Solar', anything more remote from 'Dreary Phil of Hull' would be hard to imagine.[33]

And so, finally in this chapter, to 'Church Going', which I hold to be one of Larkin's supreme accomplishments. It encapsulates almost all of what makes him a great poet: ludicity; multi-layered deceptiveness; unceremonious *gravitas*; impeccable craftsmanship; doubting-but-utterly engaged truth-seeking; compassionate awareness of that which binds us all as mortal beings.

Following the punning title ('Going' signifies both attendance and disappearance, an ambiguity often not realized by the reader until later), the first two stanzas are a joyous orgy of adolescent nose-thumbing and arrogantly studied aloof ignorance. The first line itself can be heard on one level as a tumultuous dismissal of any claim to significance that religion may have, rather than a surreptitious check to make sure he is alone. Thereafter denigration of all things ecclesiastical proliferates. My own favourites are 'little books'; 'Up at the holy end'; the 'Here endeth' spoof lesson reading; and 'Someone would know; I don't', which is not only withering in its unspoken addition – 'And I don't care' – but also disingenuously *untrue*, a crucial point to which I'll return in a moment.

'Church Going' would be an impressive little satire if it closed on 'not worth stopping for'. The point of course is that it doesn't end there: there are five more stanzas of vigorous yet humble enquiry, doubt, wistfulness, warmth, wonder and surpassing *seriousness*. It is also a masterpiece of feinting, narrative subversion and 'deliberate disguise', and it is those properties I address first.

It is improbable that any reader other than a devout Christian or architectural historian would know what 'pyx' and 'rood-lofts' mean. I had to look them up; I was also unaware until recently of the full denotations of 'plate' (see below). But make no mistake: Larkin knew. He was authoritatively conversant with the technical terms defining the little box in which are kept the wafers for Communion and the place in which are stored the gigantic crucifixes used only a few times a year for the most sacred times (and accompanying ceremonies) in the Christian calendar. So these moments in the poem emerge as much more than a merely surprised realization that Larkin is, beneath that disaffected, dilettante mask, entirely au fait with matters and terminology ecclesiastical: it subverts, in devastating fashion, the callow lampoon of the first two stanzas. Suddenly, retrospectively, one sees that he *did* know whether the roof was 'Cleaned or restored', that he is drawn to that 'unignorable silence', that he invariably feels that 'the place' *was* 'worth stopping for'. The sneering vandal manqué has not just been replaced by a figure who has learnt 'proper(ly) to grow wise': the speaker was that figure all along.

There is more quietly *bouleversé* magic to come. Stanza five seems to have a lot of mischievous fun at the expense of the undevout eccentrics who frequent churches – the tappers and jotters, the 'ruin-bibber[s]', the Christmas exclusivists annually addicted to a 'whiff' of pageant and myth. But, again retrospectively, once one has reached the lovely 'A serious house on serious earth it is', one can detect real contempt in those descriptions, a scorn for those who are *not* properly 'serious'. Moreover, the speculative 'I wonder who / Will be the last, the very last to seek' churches for what they once represented is an unimprovably mordant (and very easily missed) joke: the sentiment is demolished by the last stanza's recognition that the need for somewhere offering the chance for 'our compulsions' to 'meet' and be 'recognised' is deeply enduring, not to say timeless. Were that not so, the poem would now be an embarrassment, on the basis of having proved a foolish, quasi-adolescent prophecy that turned out to be 'balls'. Larkin was much cleverer than that; he also had a 'hunger in himself to be more serious', a phrase which is both universal and utterly personal.

But the best feint-trick of the lot is when he turns back to his own self rather than the characters glossed in stanzas three to five. He wonders if that 'very last' visitor will be his 'representative' who is 'Bored' and 'uninformed'. Those two words are *lies* – lies which are at once ludic and in a brilliantly perverse way decisively corrective. Just as one gradually realizes as the poem unfolds that Larkin is anything but uninformed about church architecture and accoutrements, by now one should be fully aware that 'bored' is just about the last thing he is: the whole thing compels him. And that 'compulsion' has both a yearning quality and a mode of expression which all theists will recognize as the language of divine symbology.

I hope I'm not alone in my refusal to buy the idea, advanced by Maeve Brennan and others, that Larkin bought copies of the *Church Times* and asked friends to supply him with certain ecclesiastical terms in the quest for technical authenticity and appropriate *gravitas*. I don't believe it for two reasons. First, 'Church Going' is perfectly wrought, and had he 'grafted' such casual research into and onto it, the strain would have showed, in the form of clumsiness, archness or inappropriateness. The second, more important, is that one way or another Larkin *did* know what 'rood-lofts are' and all the rest of it: another instance of his *sprezzatura* side.[34]

In addition to all that multiple trickery, which is both playful and fundamental to the poem's narrative texture, the poem grows and grows in both *gravitas*, direct religious referencing and, most notable of all, a signal awareness that the Church has jettisoned its original Gospel message. The 'plate' kept in locked cases is grimly eloquent: such silverware used to be used to collect alms for the needy; now it's sequestered as an asset.[35] The use of 'sheep' is even more resonant for being so simple and definitively biblical – and fiercely ironic: ignored by the church, these sheep (whether literal or metaphorical) are only succoured by what they can graze for themselves.

In view of such baleful appraisal of ecclesiastical betrayal, it is small wonder that the speaker then employs the quietly menacing phrase 'unlucky places': no longer places of consolation or hope, churches now instead resemble hospitals as bleak reminders of our mortal fate. Lest that seem fanciful, Larkin makes exactly that conflation in 'The Building'.

In the next stanza, Larkin observes that 'Power of some sort or other will go on / In games … ' The observation has a pregnancy which so far as I'm aware has not been dwelt on by any commentator. On one level it is a world-weary, functionally cynical remark, indicating impatience with the delusions endemic to all plentipotentiarism, be that secular or ecclesiastical. On another, it is both more stringent and more wistful, reflecting that what before was perceived as a Gospel gift of God has degenerated into a squalid game – exactly the kind of unedifying frivolity which the first two stanzas of 'Church Going' exemplify!

To focus now on the final stanza: our 'compulsions' are our 'destinies' precisely because our choices in life are not and never can be completely comprehensible. Moreover, 'robed' suggests priests, and thereby Christ and His role in enabling us to identify with Him and become all He intended us to be; at the same time (Larkin having it both or several ways yet again), it also tartly conveys the idea of mere dressing-up and inherent pretence or self-deception. Even so, Larkin is addressing a recurring cycle of human life, aspiration and primal inquisitiveness which will indeed never be 'obsolete', since the life-defining desires to connect, commit, love, marry, have children, and recover from the ineluctable necessity one day to mourn loved ones who die are intrinsic to all human life. The 'hunger' to find meaning in (though not necessarily an answer to) all those things will never be sated. Indeed, the 'hunger to be more serious' is a majestically simple expression of all sentient humans' impulsion to find spiritual meaning.

Finally, that last line. It is multivalent, almost gnomic. One ear may hear it as a last sardonic joke, a partial return to the nose-thumbing of the first two stanzas. To another it may impress as a forlorn reflection that this 'dead' church has no power or meaning any more. To yet another it might suggest that the 'dead who lie around' are all witnesses to the truth and faith of people awaiting resurrection from their graves: the fact that Larkin the man didn't credit that himself does not mean he was unaware that others do or might wish to. Henry James once observed 'Great books read *you*': this 1954 poem is a signal instance of the liberating wisdom of that remark.

It can therefore be claimed that 'Church Going' identifies a spiritual vacuum which may well be filled with other 'dubious' alternatives.[36] And it is surely no accident – or else it is a serendipitously resonant one – that in the very next poem he wrote, 'Places, Loved Ones' (completed three months later), there is the reference to '*My proper ground*'. It is not just that Philip Larkin the man can be seen to have a 'hunger' to find that place throughout his life; Philip Larkin the poet is profoundly aware that such a search is almost universal to men and women. In *Four Quartets* Eliot reflects, 'I have knelt / Where prayer is valid.' Larkin may not have 'knelt', but his 'serious' exploration of a primary quest is perhaps one of the most telling reasons why his work remains so absorbing and much-loved.

I have devoted several pages to analysing a poem which has already attracted so much fine commentary, not out of self-indulgence but in the twin belief that the poem's multiple voices have not been entirely understood, and that 'Church Going' is in several respects definitive of Larkin's poetic strategies and lexical genius. It is also *seminal*: while not the first great poem he wrote, it establishes a series of preoccupations to which he would return again and again until his muse dried up in the mid-1970s.

In James Joyce's *Portrait of the Artist as a Young Man*, Stephen Dedalus's growth into an appreciation of natural beauty, and indeed beauty per se instead of the harsh repressive truths of taught religion, bears a striking similarity to not only the middle stanzas of 'High Windows' but Larkin's own aesthetic imperatives, intellectual tenets and spiritual concerns. At the start of this enquiry I stressed how important was Larkin's tribute of 'beautiful' in the midst of his apparent rejection of the Bible as 'balls'. To find beauty in everyday things was one of his most durable poetic strengths. I also think it was also something that drove him, at a primal level, as a *being*.

At no time during this enquiry have I sought to suggest that Larkin was anything other than a profound agnostic. But it's worth recalling that he once quipped that he was an '*Anglican* agnostic, of course' (my emphasis). Again, the joke is deceptive. Because of 'Aubade', the 'Bible-as-balls' rant and a host of other remarks both in his poetry and near-ubiquitously elsewhere, not only has Larkin the *homo religiosus* not been taken 'seriously': he hasn't even been recognized. That is a large and indeed 'serious' mistake, as even his early post-

North Ship verse reveals. In an interview, Larkin once quoted Lawrence's famous dictum, 'Never trust the teller, trust the tale.' The reference was, it must be said, caustic and dissociative. But then, given Larkin's delight in the mask – a delight both ludic and utterly serious, the fount of his genius – it would be, wouldn't it? Such deliberate disguises indeed.

Chapter 7

Fears, Antipathies and Aversions

'We shall find out.'

Not the least puzzling aspect of Larkin's career is that he dried up as a poet during the last ten years of his life. He continued to write both regularly and to great effect: in its less momentous way, Larkin's prose was always as exquisite as his verse, and that gift never left him. The interviews he gave during this period are as elegant as illuminating, and more than a few of his book reviews are minor masterpieces.[1] But the appearance of *High Windows* in 1974 not only marked Larkin's supreme achievement as a poet: it was also his swansong, as a private exchange in 1978 demonstrates.

As the then Literary Editor of the *New Statesman*, Martin Amis favoured Larkin as a reviewer whenever he could, and after one commission had been completed with customary promptness, Amis added at the end of his hand-written note of thanks:

> May I just say, too, how increasingly and near-unconditionally I admire *High Windows*. I read it entire at least once a fortnight and know most of it by heart – the Seaside poem, the Trees poem, Livings, Going Going, Sad Steps, Money and the Show poem are among my favourites. I can't think of a book published in my lifetime that has given me more pleasure.

To which Larkin replied on 17 May:

> Thank you for your very kind words about *High Windows*, but it all seems another life now. Long ago he was one of the singers, etc.[2]

Those words (which amount to a wry epitaph) were written several months after the publication of 'Aubade'. That is indisputably a major Larkin piece, but one which would appear to be the exception proving the 'departed Muse' rule. The tendency is to see the poem as not only a definitive culmination of an obsession that haunted him, but also, paradoxically, clinching proof that his muse had indeed become exhausted. No wonder, one might conclude, that it was his last significant poetic accomplishment: after it there surely remained 'Nothing to be said'.

Death

Many commentators have identified a governing moroseness in Larkin's work and attitudes that arises from 'a hopeless and inflexible pessimis[m]' (Andrew Motion, 1988), 'a tenderly nursed sense of defeat' (Charles Tomlinson, 1957), 'a central dread of satisfaction' (Geoffrey Thurley, 1974) and the curse of being 'the saddest heart in the post-war supermarket' (Eric Homberger, 1977). The dates are important, for they encompass almost all of Larkin's life as a mature poet; moreover, the case seems additionally proven when one considers 'Aubade', written in the same year as Homberger's elegiac flick.

In Chapter 5, I spoke of that poem's absence of horror; further to that, I concur with this observation by Peter Ackroyd:

> There is no despair or agony in the movement of the poem – only a calm and considered vision of its own emptiness.

But Ackroyd wasn't commenting on 'Aubade', but on T. S. Eliot's 'Gerontion'[3] – which is where the plot thickens, and enrichingly.

On one level Eliot's poem is a spoof of, or at any rate a knowing departure from, Cardinal Newman's *The Dream of Gerontius*. Larkin takes that several steps further, but they are steps on the same road. In a talk given in 2000,[4] Maeve Brennan revealed that Larkin used her as a sounding-board for 'Aubade': he was looking to pit his agnosticism against her Roman Catholicism, but no debate ensued: she was simply stunned by its bleakness. However, she also saw it as the atheistic equivalent of *The Dream of Gerontius*, which they had read together. That is a most telling insight, for it endows 'Aubade' with a properly spiritual dimension: the poem articulates a tough alternative to hopes of after-life which the reader may reject but cannot sidestep. The dualism in question is one with which all sentient humans must at some time engage, be they devoutly theistic or otherwise.

Mention 'Aubade' to any group of people conversant with it, and sooner rather than later the word 'negative' will crop up. I do not agree with that either. It would, of course, be wrong to call the poem affirmative: it is about personal extinction. But it is nonetheless 'positive', and for three reasons. The first draws on an observation Larkin made in 1967 – which among all else superbly counters the lugubrious summaries of his art offered by Motion *et al.* above.

> The impulse for producing a poem is never negative; the most negative poem in the world is a very positive thing to have done.

Amen anyway, and in this particular instance additionally cogent: 'Aubade' does, to adapt Ackroyd's words slightly, offer 'a calm and considered vision of [eventual and inevitable] emptiness', and the effect is consoling rather than depressing or fear-inducing. That is partly because 'Aubade' is accomplished with such grace and quiet power: it is impossible not to be absorbed by its sheer craft. But I also think that positive effect has to do with its lambent sense of common humanity.

There are two more reasons for proposing a revisionist reading of 'Aubade' as something quite other than determinedly morbid reflection. One is that it is not the ruminations of an invalid or anyone expecting shortly to become one: the only real illness Larkin ever had was the (shortish) one which killed him, and at its time of writing he still had eight years left to live. That may not be anything like as many as he – and his admirers – would have liked, but in 1977 he was hale, highly successful on a variety of fronts, and very busy ('Work has to be done'). The poem is much more a measured philosophical statement than an agonized emotional one.

The second is that from a remarkably early stage in his life, Larkin was in a fundamental way aware of the *attractiveness* of death, of its welcome delivery from all the difficulties, failures and terrors of life. As noted in Chapter 6, 'Beneath it all, desire of oblivion runs' are not the words of a man terrified of death: they are the thoughts of a man still young who is perplexed, but fascinatedly so, by what it is that keeps us going, what is that makes us 'use' our life as productively as possible even if that life simultaneously seems to be a matter of 'first boredom, then fear'.

Both as poet and man Larkin was treading a familiar path – and well he knew it, his disingenuous protestations in interviews and elsewhere notwithstanding. As I've commented, nobody got a First in English at Oxford in the early 1940s without being familiar with the Bible, the works of Shakespeare and Milton, and indeed acquiring the kind of scholastic depth and expertise that 30 years later was seamlessly transferred to Larkin's work editing the *Oxford Book of Twentieth Century Verse*. It is therefore probable that he was familiar with these lines from *Paradise Lost*:

> That dust I am, and shall to dust return:
> O welcome hour whenever! ...
>   ... Why do I overlive,
> Why am I mocked with death, and lengthened out
> To deathless pain? How gladly would I meet
> Mortality my sentence, and be earth
> Insensible, how glad would lay me down
> As in my mother's lap? There I should rest
> And sleep secure.[5]

If only as a disinterested scholar, the young Larkin would have been impressed by Adam's agonized 'O welcome hour whenever!' and 'lay me down/As in my mother's lap'. But even more tellingly, Milton's lines are of a piece with Larkin's 1950 'desire' for 'oblivion'. I shall return later to the magnificent neologism 'overlive'; for now, it is enough to say that Adam's words dramatize an attitude to death – or rather *life* – that is observably approximate to that which permeates so much of Larkin's poetry from 'Going' to 'Aubade'.

The Oxford English course in the 1940s did not take in the post-Romantics, so the undergraduate Larkin would not have read Tennyson 'in the way of business'. However, there can be little doubt that he knew that poet's work, and knew it well. Tennyson is the subject of his delightful early 'squib', 'The Literary World', Part II; more significant is that Kingsley Amis tribute to his great friend as 'one of our finest metrists since Tennyson'. You do not acquire such grace and feel without being schooled in that precursor's work, even if your concerns and style are otherwise largely different. And in the case of Tennyson's 'Tithonus', the preoccupation is not different at all: it is of a piece with Larkin's own take on life:

> The woods decay, the woods decay and fall,
> The vapours weep their burthen to the ground,
> Man comes and tills the fields and lies beneath.
> And after many a summer dies the swan.
> Me only cruel immortality
> Consumes ...

> ... Let me go: take back thy gift:
> Why should a man desire in any way
> To vary from the kindly race of men,
> Or pass beyond the goal of ordinance
> Where all should pause, as is most meet for all?
> ... Coldly thy rosy shadows bathe me, cold
> Are all the lights, and cold my wrinkled feet
> Upon thy glimmering thresholds, when the steam
> Floats up from those dim fields about the homes
> Of happy men that have the power to die,
> And grassy barrows of the happier dead.
> Release me, and restore me to the ground.[6]

Larkin opens his 1954 'Places, Loved Ones' with

> No, I have never found
> The place where I could say
> *This is my proper ground*
> *Here I shall stay ...*

That poem was written immediately after 'Church Going', whose final lines make reference to 'this ground / Which ... [is] proper to grow wise in' and, just beforehand, to 'A serious house on serious earth'. The last line of the Tennyson extract quoted is readily conflatable with the thrust of 'Places, Loved Ones' and 'Church Going'. If Tithonus is in agony whereas Larkin is ruefully wistful, they share a sense of the *rightness* of death, the 'proper ground' that is mortal life. Larkin is, beneath all the inevitable and continual angst of living, serene about his 'goal of ordinance' (i.e. appointed limit). Though he could never become a believer, the *idea* of belief compelled his profound respect.

In his four-volume study *The Masks of God,* Joseph Campbell examines the unfortunate tendency for the metaphors of mythology to become literalized at a local level. Just as Stephen Dedalus in *Portrait of the Artist as a Young Man* speaks of history as a nightmare from which he is trying to awake,[7] so do all of us wish in some ways to *tame* our nightmares, to domesticate them into bromides. That is understandable, and, probably, beneficial on an immediate basis. But it is also mistaken and shallow. Myth is a metaphor and mask that should open up levels within us rather than impose 'legends' from without. The notion of emptiness – paradoxically so richly evident in Larkin's poetry – engenders compassion: that insight is that of the eleventh-century Tibetan monk Milarepa, and it perfectly fits Larkin. The poet works through the masks and reaches, simultaneously, both emptiness and plenitude, out of which emerges the synthesis of compassion – a 'third stage' which is timeless.[8]

That growth towards compassion and sober affirmation can be seen as epitomized by two Larkin poems written 18 years apart: 'Ambulances' (1961) and 'The Mower' (1979). The former is almost sinister at times, and for all its fierce insight – '*Poor soul,* / They whisper at their own distress' – it is unrelievedly mournful in a way which does not characterize 'Aubade'. There is a foreshadowing of that later poem's 'An only life' in 'unique random blend', but here the emphasis is on an immediate 'shut of loss' and a demise 'Far / From the exchange of love'. The entire poem operates as a *memento mori*, and no consolations are offered.

'The Mower', one of the last poems Larkin wrote, is very different. A spare and moving account of the accidental death of a hedgehog (the matter-of-factness of 'Next morning I got up and it did not' is uncommonly poignant), it is nonetheless much less a brooding on death than – once again – a renewed invocation to use *life* as well as we can:

... we should be careful

Of each other, we should be kind
While there is still time.

As Larkin matures – or indeed just grows older – compassion illumines, even transforms the apparent gloom. Those last lines of 'The Mower' exemplify an affirmative pulse that beats beneath seemingly baleful reflections on futility and chance. In my view 'The Mower' was the last significant Larkin poem, so it is pleasing that its title irresistibly recalls the sequence of poems written by the other major 'Bard of Humberside', Andrew Marvell. I am confident that Larkin intended that resonance.

The very term 'Mower' has such ineluctable associations with the Grim Reaper that a brief final look at the religious resonances in Larkin's poetry is in order – specifically, this time, 'Cut Grass'. Even those readers still wishing to resist the Christian reverberations traced so far would be hard pressed to deny the poem's congruence with these long-archetypal lines from Psalm 103:

> As for man, his days are as grass:
> As a flower of the field, so he flourisheth.
> For the wind passeth over it, and it is gone;
> And the place thereof shall know it no more.[9]

One might ask, then, why should Larkin *not* have been preoccupied by the thought of death? The real question, however, is how and why he was able to transform that preoccupation into something positive and enabling rather than morbid and enervating.

Now to something which he abominated almost from the start, and which has been the cause of more silly calumny about him as a man than any single other issue. Philip Larkin was emphatically not a *misogynist*, and anyone who still levels that charge at him knows nothing about him, the meaning of words, or indeed women. However, he was undoubtedly a *misogamist*.

Marriage

Among all else, Larkin's mature verse operates as a chronicle of his time. Sometimes this is explicit, as in 'The Dance' (analysed in Chapter 2), 'Show Saturday', 'To The Sea' and of course The Whitsun Weddings'. But just as significant are those poems which implicitly hinge on contemporary mores, and nowhere more so than when they chart or reflect prevailing sexual attitudes, especially the centrality of marriage as a conformist desideratum.

One does well to remember that in the 1950s, when Larkin arrived at that misogamist certainty, the expectation that adults would marry unless they were eccentric or homosexual ran deep. That may have changed somewhat during the next decade (hence, in a way, the speakers' apparent envy in 'Annus Mirabilis' and 'High Windows'), but what might be termed 'the marriage culture' was still prevalent to a degree almost spectacularly different from our own time. At the time *High Windows* was published, 'single parent' was still a term of abuse rather than a demographical description; girls who got pregnant before wedlock 'put the street and family to shame'; 'living together' was still considered either daring or sinful (or both); and despite the 1968 Divorce Act, sundering a marriage was still considered shocking: I remember hearing Lady Gaitskell in 1973 describing that Act as 'A Casanova's Charter, as I always knew it would be.'

Those observations might seem to be random anecdotal reminiscences, but solid chapter and verse is provided by 'The Facts of Contemporary Life', a sociological report published in the *Guardian* on 27 March 2000. The summary of its findings included these startling statistics:

- Almost 38 per cent of babies are born outside wedlock; the 1964 figure was 7.2 per cent
- The number of children living in one-parent families has nearly trebled in 25 years to 1998, from 1m to 2.8m
- More than 40 per cent of all marriages are second marriages, compared with 20 per cent in 1971
- 150,000 children live in families of divorced couples, nearly double the 1971 figure
- Nearly 25 per cent of women born in 1973 are expected to be still childless at age 45.

That last prompts the thought that maybe Larkin wasn't *entirely* speaking for himself when he declared 'And don't have any kids yourself'. But all five items show that there has been a radical change in marital/non-marital behaviour – one both caused by and mirrored in publicly professed attitudes.

Which lengthy but germane preamble ushers in the observation that, considering how much critical-biographical attention has been devoted to Larkin's attitudes to marriage, the number of his poems that focus on the topic is stunningly few. It is possible to hear the final lines of 'No Road' (1950) –

Not to prevent is my will's fulfilment
Willing it, my ailment.

– as early proof that he had forsworn marriage, but the poem is more to do with the end of an affair (not necessarily Larkin's own) than any conceptual rejection. Marriage and children are implicitly pertinent in 'Lines on a Young Lady's Photograph Album', 'Toads', 'Money', 'If, My Darling', 'Talking in Bed' and possibly a few others. However, they are fundamental to only three of Larkin's mature poems: 'Dockery and Son', 'Self's the Man' and 'This be the Verse'.

In Chapter 6, I called attention to the bewildered question voiced by the speaker in 'Dockery and Son', 'Why did he think adding meant increase? / To me it was dilution.' To that call-and-response I would couple these thoughts on marriage, almost exactly coincidental with the anthological time-span of *The Whitsun Weddings*:

For two people in a hundred (marriage) is wonderful. The rest just work at it.[10]

Most marriages don't add two people together. They subtract one from the other.[11]

The style may not be Larkinesque; the marital agnosticism undoubtedly is. Yet Larkin is uncertain enough to transmute their assertiveness into puzzled questions. It is once again a case of 'I don't know'. The whole thing is a mystery which no one quite understands, be it Dockery, Larkin himself or the imagined co-protagonist of 'Self's the Man'.

That 1958 poem may not be among Larkin's finest pieces, but it has a significance belied by its apparent light-heartedness. For the majority of its eight stanzas the poem's tone is playful almost unto flippancy, as Larkin looks with a kind of aghast relief at the imagined life 'Arnold' has as a result of marrying. The language is harsh and unlovely – 'wasting his life on work', 'perk', 'kiddies' clobber', *'Put a screw in this wall'*, 'nippers', 'old trousers'[12] – and the ambience evoked is joyless, reductive and palpably devoid of love.

Repeating the self-beration with which the poem opens – 'Oh, no one can deny / That Arnold is less selfish than I' – Larkin then abruptly turns the argument on its head, reflecting with unblinking incisiveness on Arnold's equally selfish motives in 'Playing his own game'. The final stanza is markedly philosophical, its slang notwithstanding:

> Only I'm a better hand
> > At knowing what I can stand
> Without them sending a van –
> > Or I suppose I can.

– where the 'van' is an ambulance that would carry him to a mental institution were he to marry, a conviction which the rather endearing qualification in the last line does nothing to dispel.

'Self's the Man' also epitomizes Larkin's formal acumen. In its first, Arnold-focused half, the rhyme scheme is erratic and at times deliberately sloppy, and the length of the lines is also deliberately uneven – a mimetic combination signalling messy unharmoniousness. Equally mimetic is the second half's sudden neatness and control: rhyme scheme and line-length are ordered, compact and 'right'. The structure and diction bear out, and strengthen, the controlling notion of 'appropriate selfishness'.

Another form of mimesis is at work too – nomenclature. Unlike some of the incautious choices essayed in his fiction, Larkin's use of names in his mature verse is invariably cogent (think of 'The Card Players', 'Mr. Bleaney', 'Naturally the Foundation Will Bear Your Expenses') and the ghostly co-protagonist of 'Self's The Man' is one of his most cogent. A member of the *Monty Python's Flying Circus* team once declared the name 'Brian' to be 'wonderfully but absolutely *wrong*'.[13] Analogously, on reading 'Self's the Man', one starts to smile even before any aspect of Arnold's purgatorial life is itemized: his name may not tell the whole story, but it makes you at least half-expect it.

Throughout my analysis of this poem I have referred to 'Larkin' rather than 'persona', 'speaker' or other soubriquets. That is because I believe the poem *is* a personal testament. Its ludic properties finally emerge as aggressive, or at least stoutly self-defensive. Unusually, he is not just writing as a poet, as an observer of life, as one who looked to supply (in Hardy's words quoted earlier) 'the emotion of all the ages and the thought of his own'. He is writing as Larkin the Man and Lover, furnishing an apologia to all those who are or might become involved with him as to why he will never be 'the marrying kind'.

'This be the Verse' is – almost tragically, but beyond question *wrongly* – Larkin's most renowned poem, both among the cognescenti and those whose interest in poems is limited to National Poetry Day and other such trivia. It is by some distance the least impressive of the 24 poems which comprise *High Windows*. I enjoy it; nevertheless, unlike the title poem of that collection, its beginning bears no relation to its ending or indeed its narrative development: it is a random assemblage of attitudinizing flicks. Those may smart and cause readers concern, but the whole is smaller than the sum of its parts.

As with all finally inadequate literature, one needs to go 'outside' to make sense of the piece in question. In what follows, I owe a major debt to the aforementioned 'That Poem' in Jonathan Smith's *The Learning Game*, even though I have come to disagree with him at least in part.

The words 'This be the verse' were on Robert Louis Stephenson's tombstone. He – very much like Larkin – chose to go in a direction other than his father wanted. Father Stephenson's wish was for Robert Louis to follow in the family's footsteps: not unreasonable, since grandfather Stephenson had invented the *Rocket* and made all rail travel hence possible. Yet even that admittedly revelatory explanation which Smith furnishes doesn't entirely explain that infamous first stanza – nor, come to that, the second one, which simply repeats the scenario one generation earlier (and presumably stretching back ad infinitum). All of that leads to the decisive – and, unusually for Larkin, wholly unambiguous – 'Man hands on misery to man.' That is followed by the haunting but not entirely satisfactory 'It deepens like a coastal shelf': it is far from clear what that ostensibly profound image signifies in terms of what Larkin is talking about – family behaviour.

And then the poem curtly abandons its quasi-philosophical attitudinizing and ends with an almost savage personal testament:

Get out as early as you can,
    And don't have any kids yourself.

'Get out' of what? The marriage game? Life itself? Here the ambiguity is unhelpful, unenriching. And the last line impresses only as a personal credo: anyone who believes Larkin is offering it as an injunction or solution to the human race is not thinking straight, or indeed at all.

What frightened Larkin most was the prospect of going mad. It was that as much as the well-publicized other reasons which made him forswear marriage. The decision caused him much angst throughout his adult life, both in how it affected his personal relationships (Motion records Monica Jones as saying, 'He lied to me, the bugger, but I loved him'[14]) and as a general principle. '*Virtue is social*' may be a waspish flick in its precise poetic context ('Vers de Société'), but the notion clearly exercised him at a deep level.

All of which explains, I think, the paucity of Larkin poems which focus on marriage. It was too intimate and problematic a matter for him to write about with a serene sense of judgement and confident wisdom. That might explain the linguistic brutality of 'This be the Verse': it *hurt* him to write about families and the 'misery' they can cause, and that also explains the near-silliness of the poem's concluding lines. It is not unimportant to my overall thesis in this book that those three 'marriage poems' are naked personal testaments: elsewhere 'Philip Larkin' is far less easy, if not virtually impossible, to detect in any nailed-down way.

Decrepitude, madness and age

It is possible to detect neurosis or worse in some of Larkin's earlier work (one poem is called 'Neurotics', and there are plenty of episodes bordering on the unhinged in both his novels), but it was not until 1953 that he addressed madness in any direct fashion – 'Days', analysed in Chapter 6. But a lot more was to come.

'Born Yesterday', written six months after 'Days' (for Kingsley Amis's new-born child Sally), is in one way an oblique variant of Yeats's 'A Prayer for my Daughter'. Initially off-hand and sour – 'the usual stuff / About being beautiful ... Well, you're a lucky girl' – it modulates into a lovely prayer for ordinariness. Before that, Larkin seeks to bestow on her an equally important blessing:

Nothing uncustomary
To pull you off your balance,
That, unworkable itself,
Stops all the rest from working.

– a deceptively undramatic definition of the madness Larkin feared and was so determinedly anxious to avoid.

The poem's ending also deals in blessing. 'In fact, may you be dull' (it is hard not to hear that last word as italicized, so formidable is its metrical stress) sounds withering but of course is not: Larkin is wishing normalcy and 'happiness' on the infant, and in the process revealing something of his own wishes and strategies. He took some pains to appear dull himself – in interviews, broadcasts, even in daily life and work. He rarely if ever succeeded in that, but the very attempt says something about what he treasured – and envied – about ordinary people and quotidian life.

Completed in January 1972, 'Vers de Société' is, on the surface, *exactly* the kind of poem to cite when looking to identify disillusionment or harshness in Larkin's work. Moreover, those looking to dislike him point to what they see as the gratuitous self-congratulatory offensiveness of 'crowd of craps', 'in a pig's arse' and 'the drivel of some bitch / Who's read nothing but *Which?*' in very much the same way as they deplore the infamous lines in 'This be the Verse' and 'High Windows'. My own view is that it is one of Larkin's most moving and quietly dazzling performances.

The second half of poem VI in *The North Ship*, written a full quarter of a century before, runs:

> ... Yet when the guest
> Has stepped into the windy street, and gone,
> Who can confront
> The instantaneous grief of being alone?
> Or watch the sad increase
> Across the mind of this prolific plant,
> Dumb idleness.

Despite a couple of telling moments, the chief value of those lines is to signal how much better – and different – Larkin's diction would soon become. There is something suspect (i.e. 'unearned' and merely rhetorical) about 'the instantaneous grief of being alone'; moreover, it is very odd to find a conscientious, ambitious and prolific young poet accusing himself of 'dumb idleness' and centring his poem on same.

The world of 'Vers de Société', superficially similar to that earlier effort, is in fact surpassingly different; so too is Larkin's poetic technique, especially his mastery of *voice*. What disagreeably approximated an adolescent whine in 1944 has by 1971 become virtuoso ventriloquism. The Warlock-Williams invitation is one voice; Larkin's sardonic recoding of it another; the voices of the '*Which?* bitch', the now-defunct hermit 'Talking to God' and the 'ass' with 'his fool research' are three others he invites our imaginations to conjure up, however fleetingly; the solemn intonation of those quasi-sacred mottos '*All solitude is selfish*' and '*Virtue is social*' is yet another. And then there is the speaker's own voice, veering from near-obscenity to the troubled, pitiless honesty of 'Too subtle, that. Too decent, too.'

The combined effect of these plural voices is as initially bewildering as eventually invigorating, and about as far from the monochrome solemnity of its 1944 precursor as it is possible to imagine. Most important of all, the poem describes a remarkable progression, not just of tone but resultant mood and ultimate meaning. It begins with what I'd term exuberant contempt – not exactly happy, but displaying the confident gusto of someone who has learned that life is much too short to waste any of it on occasions you used to think might be fun but never are. But hardly is one into the abruptly sober second stanza – 'Funny how hard it is to be alone' – when one apprehends that disillusionment is not the point at all. This is not a poem about having expected things and been let down, about having travelled hopefully only to find arrival a singular disappointment, about realizing that the world is a nastier place than one thought, or just different.

It is instead a poem about a man who is no longer young and who finds solitude increasingly uncomfortable, even unmanageable. That isn't disillusion: that is *fear*. It is a fear that the poem/poet controls – through humour, anger and other resources, including the very writing of the poem – but it is fear all the same: the steely perfection of 'the moon thinned / To an air sharpened blade' has intimations of the Grim Reaper and his scythe. But while that might seem to suggest that beneath it all Larkin was most troubled by the thought of death, once again that is not really so: it is *life* that troubles this speaker. The young poet who pompously intoned about 'the instantaneous grief of being alone' has become one who now sees that 'Only the young can be alone freely' – one of those many moments in Larkin's work when an apparently casual observation emerges as a profound insight. That, and the unspecified dread that the brilliant vagueness of 'other things' inspires, gives 'Vers de Société' a final dimension of *horror* that the raffish humour of its first lines does not begin to prepare us for. The poem enacts a subterranean narrative which is a complex variant of and advance on the simpler but still powerful thrust of 'A Study of Reading Habits', written 11 years before when he was approaching 40 – that age at which, as a wise friend observes, one may not be old, but one is certainly no longer young.

The poem does indeed show Larkin's age, in the best possible way. It hinges on an awareness of the trials of no longer being young, no longer able to cast off angst in the belief that better things lie ahead. Not that Larkin is or was ever sentimental about youth: he disliked children almost on principle, and he was witheringly aware of the delusions that successive generations of the young embrace, only to be disabused. But the tough realism he exhibits in his middle age is one of his greatest strengths as a poet (and, I would suggest, as a man). 'Vers de Société' focuses on two kinds of solitude: that of wasteful social nothingness and the nothingness that is awesome, frightening yet finally strengthening, and which he has the guts to face unblinkingly.

Larkin's definitive 'fear' piece has to be 'The Old Fools'. Initially it seems to be fuelled by disgust, but that soon modulates into compassion and considerable self-identification. Yet it is not, as many have supposed, primarily about death, despite the crushing ominousness of its final words. It is much more about the miseries of decrepitude, as is the poem which could almost be called its companion piece, 'The Card Players' (though as I have argued in Chapter 5, that has a degree of pagan celebration as well which decisively lightens both mood and effect). The horror in 'The Old Fools' – and there is horror aplenty – is not about death. It is about life – a life that no longer seems worth living, a life which, to return to Milton's neologism, has been 'overlived'. And all that is why, despite its reductive opening, 'The Old Fools' is so moving: the poem is driven as much by a profound fellow-feeling as personal terror.

By now I have referred frequently to the 'prayerful' element in Larkin's work; 'The Old Fools' is, ultimately, another prayer – that such last days as characterize the titular characters do not befall *him*: oblivion will be preferable to 'baffled absence'. If that is right, perhaps we should reflect with some gladness that it did not befall him. Larkin may have died too early, but he was at least spared an existence to which the only response could be 'screaming'.

'Money' was completed in February 1973, immediately following 'The Old Fools'. It is a remarkably tricky poem, or so it would seem from the number of people who have seemed bent on misunderstanding it. Two well-known Larkin critics, Motion and James Fenton, lead that platoon. They get it wrong literally from the start: both misinterpret the first word, 'Quarterly'. Motion thinks it alludes to Larkin's bills; Fenton, in the course of a vitriolic attack on Larkin's perversity, thought it culpably weird that a sophisticated human being could react in such a way to the receipt of a salary cheque. Well, Fenton is himself perverse here, or rather careless to the point of rank silliness: salary cheques arrive *monthly*, not *quarterly*, and have done so within all living memory.

Motion's idea is less obviously ridiculous, but it is no less wrong. In her masterly essay 'Larkin's Money', first published in 1997, Barbara Everett unanswerably observes that 'Quarterly' can only refer to a Building Society statement or the like, and that the poem is all about *saving* money.[15] She makes two trenchant connections with earlier poets: Wordsworth's contemptuous-but-worried reference to 'getting and spending' and how that 'lays waste our powers', and the analogous perceptions of William Shakespeare in Sonnet 129, 'Th'expense of spirit in a waste of shame'. Shakespeare was talking there about another form of currency – sex – but so (among other things) is Larkin. And in a sentence that goes to the heart of the poem, Everett then writes:

> Money is a measure of value of no value in itself; it becomes real only by a process of conversion.

That is why the poem broods on the 'goods and sex' he might still get by 'writing a few cheques',[16] only to reject such a plan when he looks at how 'others' have gone about such things, acquiring 'a second house and car and wife'. Which is why it is, in the last analysis, useless: all it will buy you is 'a shave'. That line is quintessentially deceptive. One might assume that it refers simply to the ever-increasing depreciation of money, concluding that Larkin's point is to ridicule the notion of long-term husbandry, on the basis that by the time you cash your savings you've only got enough in real terms to buy a packet of razor blades or pay for a customized shave.

Well, yes and no – or rather, *no*. It makes sufficient surface sense, I admit; but it's an uncomfortably imprecise insight. Larkin could have chosen, say, a chocolate bar, or a newspaper, or a packet of cigarettes, or anything everyday and inexpensive: they all have the same status/thrust as 'shave' in that everyday sense.[17] In fact, the word is immeasurably more baleful and exact: the reference is to the rites that attend the preparation of a corpse for burial. Just as the finger- and toenails grow after death, so does the beard, and it is still common practice to clean-shave the cadaver's face. So 'The money you save / Won't in the end buy you more than a shave' is Larkin's genius at its most mordant, reminding us all that 'you can't take it with you'. And that is why it is 'intensely sad': something which seems so meaningful, something that drives all of us at least to some degree (and Larkin was a city treasurer's son) should in the end reveal itself as meaningless.

There is no evidence – in his life, in his poetry or indeed in this particular poem – that Larkin ever expected money to be enabling and liberating (though he was, rightly, keen to be paid properly for everything he did). This is confirmed, I suggest, by the poem's most striking image: 'I listen to money singing.' On the surface, it seems affirmative, even lovely; yet just three-and-a-half lines later he will conclude by dwelling on its quintessential sadness. The 'singing' is not affirmative: it is both illusory and dangerous. Dangerous – Everett's excellent point – in the way in which a Siren's song is dangerous: promising everything and delivering only ruin. And illusory in the way already dealt with: it has no value in itself, and whatever you do with it, all it will finally ensure is a kind of posthumous manicure as meaningless as money itself.[18]

Larkin the Little Englander and Philistine

I don't want to go around pretending to be me.[19]

Larkin has long been renowned, or notorious (according to one's agenda), for his use of, first, risqué slang or what these days is called 'inappropriate language', and later something altogether more raunchy. Still his two most renowned lines are 'Books are a load of crap' and 'They fuck you up, your mum and dad'.

As always with anything notable, there is more than one reason for this, more than one motivation. At a basic level, Larkin used such diction as an *épater le bourgeois* shock-tactic; equally elementary, though mischievously cunning, was the awareness that such moments insert 'the hook'. Readers may have spluttered with rage on encountering the first line of 'This be the Verse', but you can bet they went on reading.[20] However, the full-bore obscenity that is to found in several poems collected in *High Windows* has a subtler provenance as well. Larkin may occasionally have indulged in scatology on a 'naughty adolescent' basis in his letters to close friends, but his reasons for doing so in his published verse were entirely, and radically, adult.

In Part One I examined Larkin's increasingly tortured yet astonishingly steadfast relationship with the music of John Coltrane, observing that while he may have hated a great deal of the saxophonist's work, he always took it seriously. He had no doubt that Coltrane was a master of his instrument, was sincere in his spiritual questing-through-music, and could play with bleak tenderness and beauty when he chose to. He was also fully aware that Coltrane's way was the way jazz itself was going, or indeed by the late 1960s had gone. And it was Coltrane above all other figures surveyed in *All What Jazz: A Record Diary* who was responsible for that volume being, on one level, a definition of Larkin's own aesthetic. What Larkin saw as Coltrane's bloatedness led to his honing his poetry into a kind of compressed, intense minimalism both lean and multi-layered. What struck him as Coltrane's deliberate rejection of the audience's pleasure (or even involvement) inspired him to even greater demoticism, with no hint of condescension or compromise. But from Coltrane he also learned, or had invigoratingly confirmed, the power that can attend shock and 'ugly on purpose' aggression.

It is a truism that Coltrane was a driven man. That manifested itself during his career as Miles Davis's front-line partner in the 1950s, but it was especially evident during his last few years. Did he sense that his death (at the age of 40) was imminent? Analogously, did Larkin sense that his time as a poet was running out, that his Muse would soon depart? No one can answer either question, but just asking them throws light on the contradictions that both artists exemplify.

The American poet Walt Whitman declaimed:

Do I contradict myself?
Very well then I contradict myself.
(I am large, I contain multitudes.) [21]

Remarks like that can be dismissed as shallow conceited attitudinizing, the default excuse of those whose art has lost coherence and purpose. However, they can equally be heard as elaborating on Blake's 'Without contraries there is no progression.' In Larkin's case, those contradictions are partly a matter of mask-wearing, which grew in sophistication the longer he wrote: as Nietzsche observed, 'Upon every profound spirit a mask is continuously growing.' But they also point to a dialectic that increasingly informed his writing and its underlying ideology.

The persona of Larkin the Little Englander – in literature and in politics – is well known. I've already looked at some of the key exhibits for the prosecution, but to those must be added his alleged aversion to non-English poetry, neatly conflated with his dislike of 'abroad'. Consider this exchange from the *Paris Review* interview:

Q: *In one early interview you stated that you were not interested in any period but the present, or in any poetry but that written in English. Did you mean that quite literally? Has your view changed?*

A: It has not. I don't see how one can ever know a foreign language well enough to make reading poems in it worthwhile. Foreigners' ideas of good English poems are dreadfully crude: Byron and Poe and so on. The Russians liking Burns. But deep down I think foreign languages irrelevant. If that glass thing over there is a window, then it isn't a *Fenster* or a *fenêtre* or whatever. *Hautes Fenêtres*, my God! A writer can only have one language, if language is going to mean anything to him.

As on several other occasions in this interview and the *Observer* one, for all his apparent forthrightness Larkin is evasive here. Only his second sentence actually answers the question asked – and then it is highly suspect, given his acquaintance with the French *symbolistes* (the witty use of Gautier for 'Sympathy in White Major', for example). The rest of his reply has nothing to do with being 'interested' in other poems as a *reader*: its primary focus is on his own writing, with some incidental aperçus about the problems of translating poetry thrown in.

An analogous caution needs to be exercised when Larkin talks about what he reads. His response to Miriam Gross's request, 'Tell me what you like reading,' is representative:

> I read everything except philosophy, theology, economics, sociology, science, or anything to do with the wonders of nature, anything to do with technology – have I said politics? I'm trying to think of all the Dewey decimal classes. In point of fact I virtually read only novels, or something pretty undemanding in the non-fiction line, which might be a biography. I read almost no poetry. I always thought the reading habits of Dylan Thomas matched mine – he never read anything hard.
>
> I tend to go back to novelists, like Dick Francis, for instance: I've just been through his early novels again which I think are outstandingly good for what they are. And Barbara Pym, of course, whom I've written about. Dickens, Trollope – sometimes you go back to them for about three novels running. And detective stories: Michael Innes – I don't know why there's never been a serious study of him: he's a beautifully sophisticated writer, very funny and, now and then, very moving. Anthony Powell, Rex Stout, Kingsley Amis, Peter de Vries.

This is differently evasive but no less so. This time he does answer the question. For Larkin, as for all of us, there is reading for pleasure and reading in the way of business, and with one exception his is a literal response to Gross's verb: these are the writers he 'like[s]'. But what he lists is not *all* he read: the sardonic self-deprecation of those first two sentences is contradicted by a great deal of his prose work (and not a little of his poetry), where knowledge of and response to those subjects is invariably evident.

The exception cited is the assertion 'I read almost no poetry,' rendered absurd by his very next answer. After citing Betjeman, Amis, Gavin Ewart, Hardy, Christina Rossetti and 'Shakespeare, of course' – a fairly hefty list for an abstainer – he relates a story both funny and moving about nearly crashing on the M1 because a reading of Wordsworth's 'Immortality Ode' suddenly blinded him with tears. 'Poetry can creep up on you unawares,' he reflected; it is clear that it did so, often.

It is answers such as those above which persuade even some sympathetic to Larkin that 'Books are a load of crap' really does represent his stance on 90 per cent of literature and academic commentary on it. What better place to start the necessary corrective than the poem whose last line that is, 'A Study of Reading Habits'?

Like many Larkin poems, the ostensibly casual–chat diction conceals a subtly formidable narrative. It is important that the first two stanzas are in the past tense, the last one in the present. We are witnessing the progression of a life – that of a speaker who had a hard time then and in a different way still does.

In stanza one, the 'I' is, I'd say, about eight or nine. And he has a rotten life: 'Cured most things short of school' is eloquent of hatred and fear – exactly what any kid who's being bullied would feel. We know this because of the stuff he reads to compensate and *fantasize* with: pulp fiction (in this case Westerns, which were as common then as soap operas are now) enables him to act out flooring 'dirty dogs twice my size' – the big boys giving him playground hell in real life.

In stanza two, the protagonist is anything from 11 to 15, but probably somewhere in the middle. The governing condition here is puberty, plus the no-less-important fact that he's deeply unattractive to the opposite sex, chiefly because of his NHS milk-bottle-bottomed 'inch-thick specs'. So once again he fantasizes, via another form of pulp fiction, vampire comics: this time he is Superstud rather than crypto-Clint Eastwood. The delicious rhyming of 'fangs' with 'broke them up like meringues' is full of vengeance as well as excitement and adolescent horniness; its buried violence confirms how forlorn and unfulfilled the speaker's actual life has been like.

In stanza three, the 'I' is adult/early middle-aged. And the crucial question to be asked is: *why* doesn't he 'read much now'? The types then mentioned return us to pulp Westerns – but now it's the 'yellow' store-keeper rather than John Wayne, the two-timing 'dude' rather than the romantically heroic Gary Cooper. And these seedy types are 'far too familiar' – they remind the protagonist of his own life, status and moral worth: that's why he '[doesn't] read much now'![22] Which brings us to that pivotal, and to many baffling, phrase: 'get stewed'.

A lot of people, of all ages, assume this to be the equivalent of 'get stuffed', 'get out of it' or 'don't waste my time'. As a result, they take the last line literally and, in doing so, completely misinterpret the poem and its true 'thesis'. 'Get stewed' means nothing of the sort: 'stewed' was mainstream 1960s slang for 'drunk'. What he is saying is

> I don't read much now because reading no longer offers me any escape from my own dismal life/self. If escape's what you want, hit the bottle, not the book.[23]

And so that last line emerges as virtually the opposite of what it appears to argue. It's saying that 'books are a load of crap' if you're looking to fantasize and get away from yourself: they are all too good at reminding you what real life is like. He is paying books a major compliment, defining their often pitiless authenticity. It is not quite a celebration of books: the poem is too bleak for that. But it is emphatically not a dismissal of literature either – more a recognition of a power that the protagonist finds too painful to enjoy any more.

It is remarkable how many professional commentators *did* take that last line literally, apparently not pausing to reflect that it was an odd thing for the Librarian of Hull University to have said. This was a job he did for over 30 years, which he loved[24] and was still doing when he died. The poem is yet another example of mask. But such disguising does not excuse those

misinterpretations: after all, decoding and properly 'reading' a poem is supposed to be commentators' work. Clive James puts it with imperious precision:

> To believe Larkin really meant that 'Books are a load of crap' you yourself have to
> believe that books are a load of crap. The arts pages are nowadays stiff with people
> who do believe that, even if they think they believe otherwise: all they really care
> about is the movies. There are people reviewing books, even reviewing poetry, who
> can read only with difficulty, and begrudge the effort. No writer, alive or dead, is any
> longer safe from the fumbling attentions of the semi-literate literatus.[25]

Now to a poem which I would say has some claim to be called the most
deceptive of all Larkin's pieces.

'Homage to a Government' was completed in January 1969. The date is
important for several reasons – not least because, uniquely in Larkin's *oeuvre*, it
forms part of the poem's text. That month marked the beginning of the last
full year of Harold Wilson's Labour Government, of which Larkin was not an
admirer. In common with several Larkin critics, I happen to think he was not
so much pro-Right as anti-Left; nevertheless, the poem seems to dramatize a
virulent strain of Blimpish frustration, even rage. That impression can be
strengthened by considering the vinegary clerihew he composed at the same
time:[26]

> When the Russian tanks roll westward, what defence for you and me?
> Colonel Sloman's Essex Rifles? The Light Horse of L.S.E.?

The same angry irony is readily detectable in 'Homage to a Government'. Its
rhetorical technique is strongly reminiscent of Mark Antony in *Julius Caesar*:
the more he repeats the refrain, 'For Brutus says he was ambitious / And
Brutus is an honourable man', the less the crowd believes him, which is exactly
what he wants and intends. Analogously, Larkin's 'it is all right', 'And this is all
right' and 'Which is all right' makes it cumulatively clear that it certainly *isn't*
all right, so far as Larkin is concerned. The final dismantling of our once-
glorious military empire and its attendant responsibilities is just another
symptom of the disease characterized three years later in 'Going Going': 'And
that will be England gone.'

That is, I trust, a properly observant reading, and one in line with the
supposed attitudes of Larkin the man at this time. And yet it does not begin to
satisfy. A minor biographical objection might be that such Disgusted-of-
Tunbridge-Wells bellicosity is right out of character, but I don't need to go
down that precarious path, since it is also right out of character with Larkin's
previous work. Such hawkish views do not sit easily, if at all, alongside two
poems written less than ten years before: 'MCMXIV' and 'Naturally the
Foundation Will Bear Your Expenses'.

The former's gently elegiac tone and heartfelt sympathy for all those
'archaic faces' who died cannot conceal the quiet rage that drives the poem.

The repeated 'Never such innocence again' is both an historically acute statement and a form of prayer. From a vantage point nearly 50 years on, the poet knows that the Great War was not only a story of hideous and useless carnage but the end of an era, including the beginnings of the end of the British Empire. But there is also the fervent implicit hope we will never again be that 'innocent', in the sense of deluded, duped or just plain stupid.

The latter poem contains three lines which have not been sufficiently dwelt on. In another reference to World War I (and also World War II), the speaker reflects sourly on the 'solemn-sinister / Wreath-rubbish in Whitehall' that is Remembrance Day, and then comments:

> It used to make me throw up,
>   Those mawkish nursery games:
> O when will England grow up?

Offensive to some, doubtless, those 17 words evince a hard-hitting sensibility that is neither left-wing nor right, just properly 'grown up'.

So the alternative reading I'm about to advance has some considerable provenance. Even if I'm mistaken, and Larkin really *did* alter his views on Britain's global role and military pride so quickly, I would point out anew what so many have done before me: that the wonderful thing about art is that it has a life of its own. That life can run radically counter to the artist's apparent purposes and motivations; it can even emerge as totally opposite to those surface meanings.

First, consider the rhyme scheme. By Larkin's standards it is crude; lazy; almost approaching the cretinous. The rhymes are not even (to borrow a term from French linguistics) 'feminine', i.e. weak/partial: they are mere repetitions – 'home'/'home', 'right'/'right', 'orderly'/ 'orderly', and so on throughout the poem. It conjures up mindless marching – a resonance enriched by that very repetition of 'right', which on one level is a sergeant-major's drill command. There is a similar pun on 'orderly' (a low-ranking soldier), and the pun on 'right' is tripled if one thinks of the political dimension mentioned earlier. And although the observation 'We want the money for ourselves at home / Instead of working' may seem to be – indeed *is* – a scarcely veiled reference to unemployment benefit (the number of strikes during the late 1960s was prodigious), its virulence is superbly undercut by the poem's final line.

Furthermore, the second stanza is notable for its deliberate vernacular vagueness. It is forthright but bereft of knowledge, lacking any exactitude, approximating nothing so much as cheap journalism.[27] Are we *really* to assume that this is Larkin talking – the Oxford First, the immensely clever and learned scholar, the dedicated librarian and the unimpeachable craftsman? I do not think so – or if it is on one level, it certainly isn't on another. The speaker's voice is constantly being satirized, as are the tough-mouthed bromides it comes out with. The pattern continues in the final stanza's lazily sentimental reference to 'The statues ... in the same / Tree-muffled squares' and the maudlin repetition of the speaker's shame at 'living in a country / That brought its soldiers home for lack of money.' It's the kind of thing you expect from a not very bright correspondent to the *Daily Telegraph*.

And so to that last line. On the surface, 'All we can hope to leave them now ... ' is a forlorn structure, whether the grammatical object is 'money' or anything else. Yet the word 'hope' is the only affirmative note struck in the entire poem, and that is decisive. It *celebrates* leaving the money to advance the prosperity of future generations rather than wasting it on anachronistic and futile sabre-rattling. In the previous line he has cited 'Our children': if the cessation of that aftermath-of-Empire military posturing did indeed lead to greater domestic prosperity for subsequent generations, with taxes spent on our own people rather than those we patronizingly assumed we must 'guard' and keep 'orderly', all I want to say is: *good*.[28]

In sum: the full import of this poem is remarkably at odds with its blaring 'up front' message. It is not simply about Wilson's Government and the 1968 defence cuts; indeed, it is not necessarily about Wilson's Government *at all*. The indefinite article 'Homage to *a* Government' is crucial: that shortest and most basic of grammatical devices removes the poem from its ostensible historical immediacy, making its assertions not only more general but potentially universal.

One of the better literary jokes is to be found in Virginia Woolf's *Mrs Dalloway*, whose final sentence is followed by 'THE END'. It is quite a shock to find a writer of genius indulging in the kind of thing one associates with primary-school compositions – until one realizes that she is using that sign-off as a controlling, forward-looking paradox. It is only 'the end' of a single day[29] in the lives (or in Septimus Warren Smith's case, the death) of the various characters we encounter. We are left, thanks to that gnomic valediction, not only to reflect that their lives will go on but to ponder on how they *might* so do.

Equally though differently ludic is Larkin's decision to end 'Homage to a Government' with '1969'. On one level it suggests, 'There! I've made up my mind about *that*. This really was a national watershed.' Much more penetratingly, though, it is, like Woolf's flick, deliciously self-satirizing. There is nothing special about '1969': what the poem addresses could be true of any nation at any time when it finally decides to 'grow up'.

At root the poem is about what might constitute a genuinely fruitful legacy from government to people. Notice that while the speaker is talking about troop withdrawal, the word 'leave' is never cited: it instead takes such paraphrastic forms as 'bringing the soldiers home' and 'brought its soldiers home'. Those too can strike us as affirmative rather than otherwise: what better thing for a soldier than to return home – that is, alive rather than dead? Such affirmation is endorsed by the fact that when 'leave' is used, it follows 'hope' and is completed by 'money'.

Finally: while 'leave' does appear, its participle 'left' does not – in contrast to that triple repetition of 'right'. One way, indeed, of hearing 'And that is all right' is to recode it slightly as 'And that is all *right-wing* – i.e. sentimental attitudinizing. Such a response may be understandable, but in a world where the UK's power is now negligible anyway and not necessarily a good thing even where it remains ('The soldiers there only made trouble happen'), it simply won't do. Larkin the brain and above all Larkin the poet knew that.

Work

Part Three will look in some detail at Larkin's performance as a professional librarian, but it is worth recording straight away the words of Brynmor Jones, the sometime Vice-Chancellor of Hull University, after whom its library is now named. He and Larkin got on very well, both on a day-to-day basis and in more far-reaching ways, and two years after Larkin's death Jones commented:

> I think people who have written about him have made too much of his poems and not enough of him as a librarian.[30]

It might be said that Jones would say that, wouldn't he? – the poems almost certainly mattered less to him. It is nonetheless a handsome imprimatur, albeit one that might seem considerably at odds with Larkin's professed attitudes to 'the day job' as expressed in certain poems and elsewhere.

In the 'Footnote to Second Edition' of *AWJ* he declared that

> Listening to new jazz records for an hour with a pint of gin and tonic is the best remedy for a day's work I know.[31]

– which amplifies and makes explicit the inner thrust of 'Sympathy in White Major'. Larkin is also recorded as saying, 'Anything rather than work,'[32] and when in the course of Larkin's *Desert Island Discs* appearance Roy Plomley asked him, 'What would you be happiest to have got away from?', he replied:

> The instant answer is work ...

All that formidably suggests a deep aversion to 'the toad *work*'.

Yet in his reply to Plomley Larkin at once added

> but over the years I've come to think that I rather like work.

One more 'deliberate disguise'. Those four words, 'I rather like work', are not only charmingly modest, given what he achieved at Hull, but need to be borne centrally in mind when reading 'Toads' and 'Toads Revisited'.

The former is a much richer and subtler poem than some have recognized. Completed on 16 March 1954 towards the end of Larkin's tenure in Belfast, 'Toads' is still too often read as a wittily sour tirade at the drudgery of being in harness, at the incarcerating 'poison' of the cash nexus, and at the underlying, humiliating awareness that the speaker will never really do anything about it. Such an interpretation therefore takes the exasperated rage of the first two stanzas at face value, regards the next six stanzas as the speaker's inexorable progress towards the realization that an alternative lifestyle is precluded him – 'that's the stuff / That dreams are made on' – and finds in the final stanza what Blake Morrison has called 'a rather strained element of self-consoling': the rueful recognition of the need to make the best of a bad job, both literally and metaphorically.

I find the speaker's point of view and his voice much more complex, and that complexity starts with the title. It is *plural*, yet the reference throughout the poem is to a single toad, which is both visualized literally ('sickening poison', 'hunkers') and as a metaphor for the 'sickening' need to work. It is often argued – quite correctly – that the title's plural telegraphs the toad that squats 'on' him and another that is 'in' him; however, a recent account by Graham Landon points to another, arresting possibility.[33]

In 1936, aged 14, Larkin went to Germany with his father, where in Werningerode they met a Herr Niemand. During a discussion with Sydney Larkin about the work ethic, Niemand turned to Philip and said:

> We have an amusing slang word for money in Germany – *Kröten* – toads. If we work hard we can earn *eine menge Kröten* – a packet of money. And if a lazy worker has only a few coppers in his pocket we would say *er hatte nur noch paar Kröten in der Tasche*.

Landon reports that while Sydney 'brayed with laughter', Philip 'listened politely, considered the unlikely image of a lazy German with two toads in his pocket' and 'smiled nervously'. His story ends with Philip back home amusing his friend Jim with an impression of Hitler; he does not connect the incident to either 'Toads' or 'Toads Revisited'.

It may seem curmudgeonly to say so, given the valuable source Landon has provided, but he surely might have done just that. The slang term *Kröten* gives both poems a vibrant new dimension. For a start it increases the force of 'Just for paying a few bills!', which in turn puts one in mind of the 1973 'Money'. Further, the image of a layabout with two toads in his pocket that the young Philip 'considered unlikely' informs stanzas three to five of 'Toads' and four and five of 'Toads Revisited', setting up a wonderful paradox fundamental to the ethos of both: one of the consequences of 'dodging the toad work' is to end up with at best a couple of *Kröten* – and that is not a fate that the speaker views with any pleasure.

Notice, too, how the apparently liberating prospect signalled by 'Lots of folk live on their wits' is instantly torpedoed by the sheer nastiness of the figures cited. The alliteration is decisive: the profusion of 'l' sounds is cumulatively unpleasant, and by the time we reach such phrases as 'windfalls and tinned sardines', 'bare feet' and 'skinny as whippets', the picture is one of horror – not so much 'dreams' as a nightmare. 'No one actually starves' seems to be softened by the preceding 'And yet', but no attentive reader can possibly imagine that the speaker is contemplating such a life. The fantasy of shouting '*Stuff your pension!*' two lines later is inspired by the equally forlorn fantasy of getting 'The fame and the girl and the money / All at one sitting': it has nothing to do with a wish to 'live up lanes'.

Most important of all, there is a residual affection for 'the toad *work*' detectable in 'Toads', and not just because the speaker acknowledges the partially 'toad-like' quality of his own nature. In that list of 'L-words' in stanza three, as Jean Hartley has pointed out with cogent mischievousness, 'Lecturers' is there but 'Librarians' isn't.[34] One appealing inference is that the speaker has a respect for what he does despite its intermittent irksomeness – an idea which the last stanza decisively confirms.

As noted many times already, much of Larkin's *oeuvre* is very demanding, requiring constant attention to detail – including matters of syntax and grammar, which are crucial to the final stanza of 'Toads'. Larkin's formal mastery is at its most audacious here: the antecedents for the pronouns 'one', 'either' and 'both' are located eight stanzas away in the poem's opening two lines – '*work*' and 'life'. And, the speaker admits and we realize, the two are symbiotic. The deft pun in 'bodies' ('giving strength to' and '*em*bodying') contributes to an ending not only positive but serene – a denouement for which one could not possibly have been prepared even by stanza eight.

A similar if more obvious serenity attends the ending of 'Toads Revisited'. Once again, there are traces of wistfulness and the importance of elsewhere; this time, however, the line 'Yet it doesn't suit me' complements, albeit in contrast, an affirmation Larkin made in the *Observer* interview: 'Librarianship suits me.'[35] I return to that important admission shortly; for now it should be emphasized that the resignation signalled by 'Yet it doesn't suit me' not only occurs much earlier than in 'Toads' but is also more direct, as is the horror of witnessing the 'Palsied old step-takers', the 'Hare-eyed clerks with the jitters' and the 'Waxed fleshed-out patients'. There is, too, a profound sense of relief: 'Think of being them!'. The modulation into 'No, give me my in-tray' and the rest of the penultimate stanza is much more predictable than the finale to 'Toads', and despite the grim resonances of 'Cemetery Road', the poem ends, almost predictably, as a quiet celebration of work and purposefulness.

Ultimately, 'Toads' is the more interesting poem of the two, but it is illuminating to consider them together as well as separately. The fact that Larkin should wish to resuscitate the topic of 'work' as a poetic theme after eight years might be thought eloquent enough in itself, especially as he was now in a completely different environment (Hull, not Belfast). To echo some of my observations about Larkin's jazz journalism, why return to a subject if it is hateful? While I would not suggest that the irritation (sometimes worse) he expressed about his professional duties was bogus, it is worth placing it in a more ordinary, even homely context.

In 'Poetry of Departures', completed less than two months before 'Toads', the speaker notoriously declares, 'We all hate home and having to be there.' If one substitutes 'work' for 'home', an additional and less provocative insight is fashioned – one which every single employee has felt at one time or another, no matter how satisfying his or her job may generally be. To resent being in harness is part of being human; nevertheless, as 'Poetry of Departures' and 'Toads' dramatize so deftly, the alternatives are often worse, or simply impossible. All of us have at some time dreamed of *'chuck(ing) up everything'* or of *'walk(ing) out on the whole crowd'* or some such thing, but the suspicion remains that a 'move' ostensibly 'audacious, purifying' and '[e]mental' will not only in all probability prove futile but be morally questionable to boot. The speaker in 'Poetry of Departures' goes even further: it's not so much futile or immoral as simply 'artificial', a 'step backwards' – possibly even a recipe for a life leading to 'them sending a van'.

Jean Hartley has argued that Larkin may have fantasized about a life dedicated to art but that he never took the idea seriously.[36] That is confirmed by Larkin's 1979 reflections on his burgeoning career –

> In any case, I could never have made a living from writing. If I'd tried in the Forties and Fifties I'd have been a heap of whitened bones long ago.

– and even more by his abhorrent vision of what *was* now possible:

> Nowadays you can live by being a poet. A lot of people do it: it means a blend of giving readings and lecturing and spending a year at a university as poet in residence or something. But I couldn't bear that: it would embarrass me very much. I don't want to go around pretending to be me.[37]

That last sentence could serve as a definitive warning about the danger of equating Larkin with any given speaker in any given poem; here its import is more straightforward. He forbears to mention that by this time, thanks to his editorship of the *Oxford Book of Twentieth Century Verse*, he would not have needed the money such campus antics would have provided, that indeed he could have lived solely off such royalties if he had wanted to. The point is that he *didn't* want to: 'Librarianship suits me.' Just how congenial he found it may be gauged from the remarks that surround that assertion:

> Looking back [becoming a librarian] was an inspired choice ... I love the feel of libraries – and [librarianship] has just the right blend of academic interest and administration that seems to match my particular talents, such as they are.

That could not be further removed from the whingeing time-server popularly assumed to be the Larkin of 'Toads', nor could the deceptive playfulness with which he concludes:

> And I've always thought that a regular job was no bad thing for a poet. Indeed, Dylan Thomas – not that he was noted for regular jobs – said this; you can't write more than two hours a day and after that what do you do? Probably get into trouble.[38]

Beneath the throwaway humour lurks a hint of the Protestant work ethic that was an important part of Larkin's make-up. He had as little time for the work-shy as he did for the second-rate, and why Andrew Motion feels compelled, several times, to judge him 'lazy' is one of the more bizarre mysteries of *A Writer's Life*.

Moreover, for all his profound sense of vocation, Larkin was never entirely comfortable with the idea of being A Poet. He disliked subsidized art, he loathed pretension and cant, and he found his later fame 'an inhibiting burden'[39] despite enjoying certain aspects of it. And while he was never other than proud of the poems he deemed wholly successful, he was 'in many ways his own best, certainly his most severe critic'.[40] He would not, I think, have been displeased by a recent declamation from an Oxford Professor of English Literature, 'Art is a regressive, infantile and ferociously self-centred affair'.[41] Certainly that caveat is very much in line with the second section of Larkin's 'The Literary World', written in 1950 (*CP*, p. 38), where Larkin provides an extensive inventory of all that 'Mrs. Alfred Tennyson' attended to as secretary, wife, chatelaine, mother, hostess and protective friend before commenting that she did all this while 'Mister Alfred Tennyson sat like a baby / Doing his poetic business.'

The scatological connotations of that last line are crucial, and – quite unlike 'Books are a load of crap' – must be taken at face value (as must the poem's residual feminism: its thrust could not be less misogynistic). 'The Literary World' is only a squib and it is not hard to see why it was never anthologized; even so, Larkin's waspish impatience is instructive in rejecting the cosily self-regarding, indulgent world sometimes supposed to be the Poet's territorial right. Despite James Booth's and others' cogent observations to the contrary, I don't think Larkin had any time for the 'ivory tower' approach to poetry.[42] He was as realistic as dedicated, and as good a businessman as he was a craftsman. It is wholly significant that when Larkin was first accorded an entry in *Who's Who*, he gave as his Occupation not Poet but Librarian, 'because one should say what one is paid for'. Vestigial suspicion of self-indulgence and a quiet pride in the taking full care of business form an apt blend – one which not only testifies further to the *sprezzatura* side of his personality but characterizes his work as a librarian, to which I now turn.

Part 3

Larkin the Librarian

Chapter 8

Larkin the Librarian

Listening to new jazz records for an hour with a pint of gin and tonic is the best remedy for a day's work I know.

Philip Larkin, 'Footnote to Second Edition', *All What Jazz*[1]

Anything rather than work.

Philip Larkin, as quoted by David M. Baker[2]

This final chapter was partly inspired – and certainly energized – by *The Modern Academic Library: Essays in Memory of Philip Larkin*, edited by Brian Dyson and published in 1988 by the Library Association. A stimulatingly heterogeneous collection, it is regrettable that it seems to be less well known than it should be: references to it in the corpus of critical work on Larkin are few, and if there has been a detailed discussion of any of its ten essays, I have missed it.

I am not going to compete with Dyson's contributors, all of whom are expert in their fields. Instead, I want to make use of that memorial's insights, and those of others, into Larkin's working life as a librarian and his signal achievements in that profession. I have already, in Chapter 7, drawn attention to the enduring liking for work that underpins (in my view entirely subverts) the antipathy and sense of poisonous entrapment which apparently characterize 'Toads' and 'Toads Revisited'. I also quoted there four words Larkin uttered early on in his *Desert Island Discs* appearance – 'I rather like work': they should be borne in mind throughout this chapter, which aims to show that Larkin's professional life emerges as no less deceptive than his work as jazz critic and poet.

Thanks chiefly to *Required Writing* and *Further Requirements*, the facts of Larkin's career are well known. His poor eyesight precluded him from military service, so midway through World War II he twice tried to join the Civil Service, though without success. A polite enquiry from the Ministry of Labour about what he was doing 'scared' him into seeking other employment, and he ended up as the (sole) librarian in Wellington, Shropshire. Thereafter he moved on to Leicester (1946), Belfast (1950) and Hull (1955–85).

At almost every point in interview reminiscences about his work, Larkin's humorous modesty borders on self-deprecation, be it this picture of his Wellington days –

It was an ordinary public library where one lent books to old age pensioners and children and performed the various simple tasks like putting newspapers in the newsroom ... I stoked the boiler and opened the doors in the morning and closed them at night. I can really claim to have started at the bottom. The previous Librarian used to scrub the floors as well but I said I didn't want to do that. ('Desert Island Discs', *FR*, p. 105)

– or this answer to Roy Plomley's enquiry about how much Hull's Library had grown under his stewardship:

there must have been about 120,000 books when I went and there must be just over half a million now. But this is only really due to the natural expansion of the University. This has been a tremendous boom period ... (Ibid.)

The composite impression created is that of an unremarkable jobbing professional whose achievements boil down to being in the right place at the right time; about the only remark that could be taken to express professional satisfaction is 'Librarianship suits me', and even that strikes a note of gratitude rather than pride.

The Dyson collection and other sources reveal the real picture to be quietly startling in its difference. Larkin was a top-class professional who had as little time for the work-shy as he did for the second-rate, who was imaginative in all he did as well as meticulously efficient, and who, *pace* his implication that the 1960s 'boom' would have seen the library's transformation from 'nice little Shetland pony' into 'Grand National winner'[3] whoever had been at the helm, was an innovator whose administrative vision and bibliophilic dedication were decisive.

As I move to a detailed consideration of Larkin *qua* chief executive, I return briefly to 'Toads' and 'Toads Revisited'. In the former, the speaker's advertised attitude seems so alientated as to prompt the further thought that to work with or for him would be bad news. And even the more genial persona who voices the latter poem hardly seems an ideal boss: the sarcasm within 'loaf-haired secretary' and 'shall-I-keep-the-call-in-Sir' may be affectionate, but could still be heard as mildly wounding. In that respect more than any other in Larkin's case, life did not imitate art: the two were, indeed, wholly other.

* * *

At Hull Larkin ended up with over 100 people in his charge – five times the number he inherited – and the overwhelming consensus is that he was a very fine chief. While he worked his staff hard and was irritated by sloppy or second-rate work, he was also solicitous and supportive, eager to see them fulfilled and prospering; furthermore, all accounts of his time at Hull emphasize the warmth of his working environment and an almost tangible mutual affection.

However, there were occasional flies in this particular ointment, and the largest appears to have been his deputy, Arthur Wood. The publication of *A Writer's Life* and the *Selected Letters* must have caused Wood's relatives some distress[4] on encountering such descriptions of him as 'the same grinning subnormal gnome that has plagued me for fourteen years' and 'the sawn-off little rocking horse of stupidity', and for that reason reading those remarks oneself induces something other than just mirth. On the other hand, they *are* funny – and in contentiously wondering if I am alone in finding them extravagantly so, I return to a variant of a previous point.

In Chapter 7, I manufactured the Larkinesque 'We all hate work and having to be there', suggesting that to be a universal experience, however fleetingly it is felt. Similarly, nearly all of us know or have known colleagues who drive us crazy. It may be their voice, their pomposity, their punctiliousness, their oleaginous leeriness; it may just be that their clothes grate on us or that their faces resemble an incompleted join-up-the-dots drawing. It can be *anything*, and saintly indeed is the soul who has not experienced such stress in the workplace. And I use that much over-used abstract noun because for once it is *true*: the stress is caused not so much by the irritation itself as the awareness that you will never confront said person – it would be cruel and in every way destructive.

His 1990s reputation notwithstanding, Larkin was a man of rare courtesy to whom good manners mattered very much. Since he operated at a very high voltage, it cannot have been easy for him to work with plodders, however much he recognized their value in the overall scheme of things, and in public he kept himself in check. In private, however, there was a paramount need to let off steam – and to regard his remarks about Wood in that light is both the kindest and the most accurate interpretation. When Larkin penned them, it was in the context of that 'willing suspension of accountability'[5] that characterizes any correspondence. And in answer to any huffy retort that by that time Larkin knew there was a very good chance his correspondence would be published one day, I share Larkin-advocate Joseph Epstein's right-minded suspicion of 'people who, along with being impressed with their own virtue, cannot stand too much complication in human character'.[6]

So much, for the time being, for Larkin's attitudes and conduct. What was he like as a Librarian and what did he achieve? The quick answers appear to be, respectively, 'outstanding' and 'a prodigious amount'. He may have complained that the 'nice little Shetland pony' that was Hull's university library when he took it over had under his guidance grown into 'a frightful Grand National winner',[7] but while the care-worn anxiety was possibly genuine, it is impossible not to hear in those words professional satisfaction as well.

Maeve Brennan confirms that when Larkin arrived at Hull in March 1955 the Library's stock was 120,000 volumes; she also reveals that its book grant was £4,500 and its staff numbered 11.[8] By 1974 there were 91 staff, the stock was just short of half a million volumes and the grant had risen to £180,500. Admittedly, 20 years is a long time and one would expect a significant rise anyway from those 1955 figures, especially in view of the Robbins Report, whose implementation transformed British university provision. Nevertheless, the growth over which Larkin presided and much of which he directly effected was remarkable: if he'd done nothing else his tenure would still have been considered successful. But he did a great deal more.

His first major contribution was substantially to revise the plans for the first phase of a new library building, which opened in September 1959. Thereafter he supervised stage II (completed in 1969); he pioneered the use of audio-visual equipment and self-paced workbooks; he greatly increased the University's store of rare books, fought hard to stem the purchase of manuscripts by foreign libraries[9] (with considerable success: at least all his own papers are at Hull) and expanded the University's provision for specialist fields of study. Despite his affectation of cynicism about what nowadays is called INSET – 'Anything but work' – he encouraged his staff to update and widen their training; David M. Baker considers Larkin's commitment to educational pro-grammes for library staff to be one of his most laudable achievements. Last but not least was his role in enacting the Library's comprehensive automation. Privately a Luddite when it came to computers, Larkin nevertheless recognized that they had become a *sine qua non*, and although Hull's programme did not begin till 1979–80 it was completed by 1982 – an outcome that borders on the amazing. Larkin was responsible for little of the actual work, delegating it to three Deputies, but the enterprise says much for his vision and determination.

Baker's essay makes extended and telling use of the confrontations in *A Girl in Winter* between Katherine Lind and Anstey. The latter's vainglorious unpleasantness is duly nailed, but the extract that most caught my eye was Baker's reference to Anstey's 'frustration at his inability to complete "original and it may be even valuable work on classification" for the simple reason that he has been too busy "worrying about fiddling little details that won't matter in six weeks ... while the really important things go hang"'. One suspects – with good reason – that Anstey is no good at either the little things or the big ones. In contrast, Larkin was equally good at taking care of 'fiddling little details' and 'the really important things': the two must go together. I have already outlined his successes in the latter area; for an instance of his expertise in matters less glamorous, I offer a personal anecdote.

In 1998 I spent a large part of my (sabbatical) summer piecing together the volume that is now *Philip Larkin: Jazz Writings*. The work was both exciting and largely trouble-free, but one reference did cause undoubted angst. It occurs at the end of 'A Racial Art', Larkin's review of Paul Oliver's *Blues Fell This Morning*:

> [Oliver's] kind of exegesis teaches his readers the difference between a buffet flat and a barrelhouse flat, but not Bogardus's race-relations cycle.

I had never heard of Bogardus; neither had my co-editor John White, who as the historian in the partnership undertook to find out. It took him two weeks of phone calls to other distinguished academics, various false trails and dis-appointments before a professor of American history solved the problem – and even he could not supply the answer as such, just where to look for it. Only then were we able to insert this footnote:

Sociologist Emory S. Bogardus applied the concept of 'social distance' to race relations. White Americans, he suggested, have been willing to associate – in varying
degrees – with members of some forty ethnic groups, based on perceptions of skin
colour. African-Americans, Hindus, Japanese, and Koreans were at the bottom of the
list; the English, Canadians and Scots were at the top. See Emory S. Bogardus,
'Comparing Racial Distance in Ethiopia, South Africa, and the United States',
Sociology and Social Research, 52 (1968), 149–56.

Why spend so much time on one 'fiddly detail'? Two reasons. I think it
impressive anyway that Larkin knew exactly who Bogardus was and what he
promulgated – arcane information then and now. How he came across it is
neither pertinent nor possible to ascertain; the significant thing is that it went
in, stayed in and was instantly available when an appropriate occasion arose.

Second, the quasi-casual expertise that rounds off a 750-word jazz review
written in 1960 is definitive. Part One of my study indicated how wide-ranging
and detailed was Larkin's scholarly knowledge of jazz, and the same goes for a
great many other subjects. In the course of our research John White and I were
constantly struck by Larkin's familiarity with American social and political
history (not just Bogardus), English social and political history, all the arts, and
English and foreign literature. And that was just one, jazz-focused book: as I
trust by now I have demonstrated, there is abundant evidence elsewhere to
indicate that Larkin was unusually erudite.

Naturally, in his own inimitably Castliglione-esque fashion, he denied that,
or at any rate went to considerable pains to mask it. Yet another deliberate
disguise – in this case, the near-paradoxical one that characterizes the
nineteenth-century tradition of 'the amateur', the apparent *flâneur* who is in
fact dedicated, expert and razor-sharp. It is with two further tributes to that
'Toad' mastery that I conclude.

The first has already been logged in Chapter 7: Brynmor Jones's reflection
that 'people have made too much of [Larkin's] poems and not enough of him
as a librarian'. Here I will simply add that all conscientious professionals
appreciate above all the laudatory respect of their colleagues and peers, and
that Larkin would have treasured that tribute, however embarrassedly he
might publicly have downplayed it.

The second appears in Kingsley Amis's *Memoirs*, in which the author relates
overhearing a conversation on the train between two men, one of whom (a
Welshman, as it happens) had recently visited Hull University:

> The chap was full of praise for everything he had seen, 'especially the library. This
> fellow Larkin there … has transformed the place. Designed a new building to hold a
> million volumes. Oh, a real live wire, myn.' When I told Philip about this, *he showed,
> not the gratification I had unthinkingly expected, but the look of a man whose guilty secret has
> been revealed.*[10]

[My emphasis]

The three areas of Larkin's life and work that I have examined indicate that he
was nothing if not tenacious. His jazz journalism spanned nearly 30 years,

including an intensive decade of record-reviewing necessitating monthly copy. He published poetry for close on 40 years, and we now know there was a host of poems he did not publish or did not finish. Almost 40 years, too, was his career as a librarian, and he was still in office when he died.

However, tenacity could never be the only or even main reason for thus remaining in harness. To echo the end of Part One: nobody does anything for those amounts of time who doesn't enjoy it, no matter what other motivations there may be, and it would be ridiculous to suggest that Larkin did not derive as much satisfaction from his salaried work as he did in different ways from listening to or reviewing jazz and writing poems. And it would be just as absurd to imagine that he did not know how good a librarian he was. Amis's observation italicized above could not be more eloquent – the perfect exemplar of *sprezzatura* blended with Puritan shyness that was Larkin the dedicated professional. On several occasions I have celebrated Larkin the minimalist; closely allied to that is his predilection for litotes. 'I rather like work': you can say that again. He was superb at it, and even if he arrived at 'Cemetery Road' rather earlier than anyone would have wanted, the 'toad *work*' did indeed 'help' make his life as successful as it was fulfilled and fulfilling.

Appendix

A Skeleton Discography

In the hope that the foregoing pages may have stimulated readers to investigate not only Larkin's writing on jazz but the music itself, there follows a list of records cited during my text. The majority are albums reviewed in 'A Record Diary', but I have also included other records to which I refer from time to time.

The provision has no pretensions to discographical thoroughness: I identify merely artist, album title and original issuing label. A specialist shop like Ray's Jazz at Foyle's should be able to identify all current incarnations, and also trace any individual track that might be desired.

Artist	Album Title	Label
Adderley, Cannonball	*Cannonball Takes Charge*	Riverside
	In San Francisco	Riverside
	Jazz Workshop Revisited	Riverside
	Bohemia	Columbia
	74 Miles Away	Capitol
Armstrong, Louis	*The Hot Fives & Sevens I–IV*	Columbia
	Meets Oscar Peterson	Verve
Ayler, Albert	*Spirits*	Transatlantic
Basie, Count	*The Best of the Roulette Years*	Roulette
Brown, Ray	*This Is Ray Brown*	Verve
Brubeck, Dave	*Time Out*	Columbia
	Time Further Out	Columbia
	Time In	Columbia
	Greatest Hits	Columbia
Coltrane, John	*John Coltrane Quartet*	Impulse!
	Ballads	Impulse!
	Africa/Brass	Impulse!
	Ascension	Impulse!
	Meditation	Impulse!
	Live At Birdland	Impulse!
	Impressions	Impulse!
	A Love Supreme	Atlantic
	Coltrane Jazz	Impulse!
	Expression	Impulse!
	Cosmic Music	Impulse!

	Live At The Village Vanguard	Impulse!
	Selflessness	Impulse!
	Plays The Blues	Atlantic
Coltrane, John & Jackson, Milt	*Bags And Trane*	Atlantic
Davis, Eddie & Griffin, Johnny	*Tough Tenors*	Riverside
Davis, Miles	*At Carnegie Hall*	Columbia
	ESP	Columbia
	Seven Steps To Heaven	Columbia
	Milestones	Columbia
	Nefertiti	Columbia
	Miles In The Sky	Columbia
	In A Silent Way	Columbia
	Bitches Brew	Columbia
	Birth of the Cool	Capitol
	Modern Jazz Giants	Esquire
	Kind Of Blue	Columbia
Desmond, Paul	*Take Ten*	RCA
Ellington, Duke	*Harlem Air Shaft*	RCA
	The Ellington Era I–III	Columbia
	Things Ain't What They Used To Be	RCA
Evans, Bill	*Sunday at the Village Vanguard*	Riverside
	Conversations With Myself	Verve
Evans, Bill & Hall, Jim	*Undercurrent*	United Artists
Getz, Stan	*At Large*	Verve
Getz, Stan & Byrd, Charlie	*Jazz Samba*	Verve
Getz, Stan & Gilberto, Joao	*Getz/Gilberto*	Verve
Getz, Stan & Johnson, J.J.	*At The Opera House*	Verve
Gillespie, Dizzy	*Something Old, Something New*	Philips
	Gillespiana	Verve
	The New Continent	Verve
	Best of the DG Small Groups	Limelight
	A Portrait of Duke Ellington	Verve
	An Electrifying Evening	Verve
	The Ebullient Mister Gillespie	Verve
	Have Trumpet, Will Excite	Verve
	The Melody Lingers On	Limelight
	Jambo Caribe	Limelight
	The Complete RCA Collection	RCA
Hawkins, Coleman	*The High And Mighty Hawk*	Decca
Jarrett, Keith	*Tribute*	ECM
Jones, Quincy	*Big Band Bossa Nova*	Mercury
Krupa, Gene	*Drummin' Man*	Columbia
Loussier, Jacques	*Play Bach (4 LPs)*	London
Mingus, Charles	*Plays Piano*	Impulse!
Modern Jazz Quartet	*European Concert*	Atlantic

Monk, Thelonious	*Misterioso*	Riverside
	Straight, No Chaser	Columbia
	Work	Transatlantic
Parker, Charlie	*Historical Masterpieces*	MGM
	Pick of Parker	Verve
	Bird Symbols	Verve
	Parker Panorama	Verve
Peterson, Oscar	*At the Blue Note* (4 CDs)	Telarc
	Salutes the Count and the Duke	Verve
	Exclusively for My Friends (6 LPs)	MPS
	The Jazz Soul	
	Swinging Brass	Verve
	Night Train	Verve
Powell, Bud	*The Vintage Years*	Verve
Rollins, Sonny	*The Bridge*	RCA
	Our Man In Jazz	RCA
	On Impulse!	Impulse!
	With Coleman Hawkins	RCA
	Way Out West	Contemporary
	The Cutting Edge	Milestone
	The Sound of Sonny	Riverside
Russell, Luis	*The Louis Russell Story*	Parlophone
Smith, Bessie	*Bessie Smith Story*	Columbia
Tatum, Art	*Alone And With Friends*	Verve
Thigpen, Ed	*Out of the Storm*	Verve
Various	*Swing Trumpet Kings*	Verve
Various	*Treasury of Jazz*	Columbia
Webster, Ben	*Angry Tenors*	Columbia
Young, Lester	*The Legendary*	Verve
Zawinul, Joe	*Zawinul*	Polydor

Notes

Preface

[1] The conversation in question must have taken place during the Christmas–New Year period, because Reeves urged me to get hold of a copy of the 23 December edition of *The Times Literary Supplement*, in which 'Aubade' appeared. He also told me he thought Larkin not only the finest poet alive but one of the century's greatest. I was embarrassed: I knew of Larkin and was vaguely familiar with a few of his poems, but I had never studied him in any proper sense. I therefore owe Reeves a great debt of gratitude.

[2] It prefaces Alvarez's anthology *The New Poetry* (Harmondsworth: Penguin, 1962), pp. 21–32. The passage quoted appears on pp. 24–5.

[3] For my analysis of the poem, see Chapter 6.

[4] I say 'regrettably' because 'This be the Verse' is not only very far from being amongst Larkin's best work: it is in several respects highly untypical. Neither fully coherent nor organically crafted, the poem amounts to a collage of quasi-epigrams that are inner-directed rather than edifying. An exception is the haunting clause, 'It deepens like a coastal shelf', but elsewhere the tone is harsh, even brutal. It is unfortunate that when so many finer and more characteristic Larkin poems are known only to the initiated, 'This be the Verse' should have become, largely on account of its first stanza and especially its opening line, part of the national consciousness on a folk-myth level.

[5] James Booth, 'Living Rooms and Dying Rooms in Larkin's Poetry'; a lecture delivered at the Larkin Study Day held at King Henry VIII School, Coventry, 25 March 2000.

[6] Ernst Cassirer, *Language and Myth* (Toronto: Harper & Brothers, 1953, Dover edition), p. 99.

I sense an almost irresistible concordance between Cassier's words and these comments Larkin made during his 1955 'Statement' (RW, p. 79): 'As a guiding principle I believe that every poem must be its own sole freshly created universe, and therefore have no belief in "tradition" or a common myth-kitty ... '.

[7] The term 'The Movement' derives from a 1954 article in the Spectator by Blake Morrison; the poets thereby bracketed together included Robert Conquest, Kingsley Amis, D.J. Enright and John Wain.

Larkin's own take on 'The Movement' was agnostic, if not impatient. So, as it happens, is mine: I very much endorse James Booth's observation that '[Larkin] resisted the implication that what was most essential to his poetry was anything shared with a group.' I would add that whether the judgements are approving – 'They aimed to communicate clearly and honestly their perceptions of the world as it was' (David Lodge) – or hostile – the aforementioned Alvarez essay (see note 2 above) and Charles Tomlinson's summary of the Movement's aesthetic as 'a stepped-down version of human possibilities' – what is being argued and the criteria on which those arguments are based do not reflect the true nature of Larkin's style or preoccupations.

All that said, those more sanguine about the importance of 'The Movement' are directed to Booth's excellent discussion of it in *Philip Larkin: The Poet's Plight* (Basingstoke: Palgrave Macmillan, 2005), pp. 122–9, from which all the quotations cited in this note are taken.

[8] 'Statement', Cahiers d'Art (Paris), April/May 1939. Quoted in Margit Rowell (ed.), *Joan Miró Selected Writings and Interviews* (London: Thames & Hudson, 1987), p. 166.

[9] Those wishing to investigate further my linking of Larkin and Thomas might wish to consult the latter's *Collected Poems 1945–1990* (London: Dent, 1993).

[10] Jane Austen, *Emma,* ch. 12.

[11] Nikolaus Pevsner, *The Englishness of English Art* (Harmondsworth: Penguin, 1978), p. 79.

[12] That last is spectacular evidence of how much England has changed, even since Larkin's death. When he wrote 'The Explosion', coal-mining was one of the UK's largest industries; now it hardly exists.

[13] In the event, the Department objected to the fifth stanza and it was removed when the poem was first published; Larkin restored it in *High Windows.*

[14] Neither, it would appear, was being commissioned. 'Going, Going' and 'Bridge for the Living' were the only two poems he wrote 'to order', and they are amongst the least satisfying of his mature *oeuvre.*

[15] 'Friday Night in the Station Hotel' evinces a similarly evocative gift.

[16] There have been at least three full studies since Motion's, and any number of reminiscences, dramatizations and articles which address his life in one way or another.

[17] *All What Jazz,* p. 156.

[18] 'Duke Ellington' in Justin Wintle (ed.), *Makers of Modern Culture* (London: Routledge & Kegan Paul, 1981). This forms Piece 56 in *Philip Larkin: Jazz Writings,* co-edited by Dr John White and me.

Chapter 1: Prologue: 'Useful to Get That Learnt'

[1] Remarks made to me in 2002. Dr John White was a friend of Larkin; he is also a distinguished Larkin scholar, and it was my great fortune to be his co-editor. See note 3 below.

[2] Ed. Richard Palmer and John White, its first incarnation was as *Reference Back* (Hull University Press, 1999). It was reprinted as *Larkin's Jazz* by Continuum in 2001, and in 2004 that house republished it under the current title as part of its 'Impacts' series.

[3] Richard Bradford, *First Boredom, Then Fear: The Life of Philip Larkin* (London: Peter Owen, 2005); James Booth, *Philip Larkin: The Poet's Plight* (Oxford: Palgrave Macmillan, 2005).

[4] Three recent instances are Richard Gottlieb, the editor of *Reading Jazz* (London: Bloomsbury, 1997), whose use of a phantom question mark in citing *All What Jazz* is of a piece with the rest of his remarks: 'Larkin, Britain's most famous postwar poet and misogynist, was for several years jazz critic for the *Daily Telegraph*. In 1970 he reprinted his reviews in a book called *All What Jazz?* [*sic*], the introduction of which appears below. No one who knows Larkin's work will be surprised at his biting contempt for jazz's latest directions' (p. 798). Then there's Alyn Shipton: in the course of his *Out of the Long Dark:*

The Life of Ian Carr (London: Equinox, 2006) he refers (as if to a matter of fact) to Larkin as 'that most curmudgeonly jazz critic'. And even Miles Kington's article for *The Independent*, 'Why I Never Got to Talk Jazz with Philip Larkin' (19 September 2003), has, amidst its wit and warmly sympathetic tone, a good deal of the 'nice prose, shame about the ears' line to it.

[5] See Larkin's essay on Ellington for *Makers of Modern Culture*, 1981. Collected in *PLJW*, pp. 147–9.

[6] A detailed analysis of 'For Sidney Bechet' forms the core of John Osborne's 'Larkin, Modernism and Jazz', *Hungarian Journal of English and American Studies*, 9/2 (Fall 2003), 7–28. The poem is also examined extensively in B. J. Leggett, *Larkin's Blues: Jazz, Popular Music and Poetry* (Baton Rouge, LA: Louisiana State University Press, 1999), pp. 69–79.

[7] Notwithstanding the parenthesis, I consider this an extremely important remark in terms of Larkin's poetic themes, preoccupations and performance; I return to it in full in Part Two.

[8] I am certain that I am not the only jazz enthusiast who would identify totally with that remark. Rhythm is indeed the defining essence of jazz: one will search the entire classical repertoire in vain for anything which even approximates its unique pulse, its floating power and virtually unnotatable patterns. These definitive properties are fully explored in Chapter 4.

[9] Larkin's *Desert Island Discs* was broadcast on BBC Radio Four on 17 July 1976. A full transcript can be found in *FR*, pp. 103–11.

[10] *FR*, p. 110. The one he finally nominated was Bessie Smith's 1933 'I'm Down In The Dumps'. Having commented that 'a more misleading title couldn't be imagined', Larkin revealed the quality of his ears and his jazz scholarship by voicing his suspicion that this recording was the first time the great blues singer had recorded with a string bass.

[11] Richard Palmer, 'Guest Editorial', *Jazz Journal International*, 36/8 (August 1983), 2.

[12] The comparisons with Beatlemania that frequently characterize accounts of the reception accorded to Benny Goodman's work in the late 1930s are the definitive case in point, but similarly bloated claims are sometimes advanced concerning the rise of bebop in the mid-1940s. The latter solecism briefly tarnishes Alyn Shipton's splendid *Groovin' High: The Life of Dizzy Gillespie* when he unwisely declares, 'at its height the bebop craze rivaled Beatlemania ... ' (New York: Oxford University Press, 1999, p. 5).

[13] *PLJW*, p. 142. Enchanting though those words are, the definition of jazz they advance needs to be precisely understood. His words stand up very well provided their exact meaning – and nothing further or larger – is grasped. Yes, jazz had reached virtually all parts of the globe by the time World War II broke out, but that does not mean it had became a mass taste in all those countries, or indeed any of them. In short, to read Larkin's 'equally' as a synonym for 'universally' would be a mistake.

[14] The *locus classicus* is his 1982 'Interview with *Paris Review*'; *RW*, p. 72.

[15] Letter to Charles Monteith, 3 August 1971 (*SL*, p. 443).

[16] To be fully glossed shortly.

[17] [18] *PLJW*, p. 113.

[18] Edited by journalist George Scott, *Truth* was a weekly magazine which enjoyed a limited vogue in the 1950s, and has been typified by Anthony Thwaite as 'left wing Tory in sympathy' (personal communication with the author). In addition to Larkin, Bernard Levin and Katharine Whitehorn were among its regular book reviewers.

Writing to a friend in 1957, Larkin confided, 'I am contemplating refusing all further reviewing jobs, bar jazz ones for *Truth*: my poor brain finds them too much trouble.' To Robert Conquest, 26 June 1957: *SL*, p. 277.

[19] *PLJW*, p. 141.

[20] Ibid., pp. 108–10.

[21] Intriguingly, the thrust of these aesthetic reflections, and indeed the focus on jazz itself, links Larkin to T. S. Eliot and *The Waste Land*, a congruence I investigate further in Part Two.

[22] 9 August 1939.

[23] Much like Larkin's own poetry.

[24] Larkin was not the first leading literary figure to be inspired by jazz. One thinks of Jean Cocteau, Hermann Hesse, Jean-Paul Sartre and (as just telegraphed above) T. S. Eliot. For an overview of this theme, see Michael Tucker, 'Music Man's Dream', in *Alan Davie* (London: Lund Humphries Ltd., 1992), pp. 71–92. See also Elizabeth Goldson (ed.), *Seeing Jazz: Artists and Writers on Jazz* (Washington, DC: Chronicle Books/The Smithsonian Institution, 1997).

[25] Oddly enough (to extend a point made briefly early on) none of that 'potentiality' is even hinted at in his early work. I explore that fully in Part Two, but here it's worth repeating that his first poem to deal even obliquely with jazz was the 1946 'Two Guitar Pieces' – by which time bebop (his alleged abomination) was in full cry.

[26] I shall be arguing that one of the (several) reasons why 'The Dance' was never finished had to do with its sheer burgeoning size: despite the success of 'The Whitsun Weddings', Larkin was rarely comfortable with large-scale projects.

[27] For a thorough and illuminating study of this topic, see Alfred Appel, Jr, *Jazz Modernism: From Ellington and Armstrong to Matisse and Joyce* (New York: Alfred A. Knopf, 2002).

[28] *PLJW*, piece 53, pp. 147–8.

[29] Leonard Feather, 'The New Life of Ray Brown', *Downbeat*, 9 March 1967, 25.

[30] 1953–8. Peterson, Brown and Ellis were reunited on a number of subsequent occasions, most notably for a World Tour in 1990–1 and a triumphant engagement at New York City's Blue Note Club (which yielded four Telarc CDs).

[31] Gene Lees, *Oscar Peterson: The Will to Swing* (Toronto: Lester & Orpen Dennys, 1989; revised edn, 2000, Cooper Square Press), pp. 251–2.

[32] The (admittedly splendid) phrase is Andrew Motion's; *AWL*, p. 280.

[33] That principle does not, of course, apply to drama or opera: it is perhaps significant that Larkin cared very little for either genre. He cared even less for 'Poetry & Jazz' (P & J), which enjoyed a brief vogue in the 1960s and has been continued today by such figures as Michael Horovitz, Amira Baraka (formerly Leroi Jones) and Ted Joans. My own view approximates to (perhaps even exceeds) Larkin's. Such fare is invariably inadequate on any literary basis one might care to nominate; moreover it cruelly exposes the silliness of what can be seen as the *fons et origo* of P & J, the American poet Hart Crane's 1920s declaration, 'Let us invent an idiom for the proper transposition of jazz into words!' That is a forlorn fantasy, vainly seeking to capture publicly what can only be a private, perhaps unrecordable experience, and Larkin may have had some such thoughts partly in mind when he remarked, 'I find it impossible to imagine what a "spontaneous" poem would be like.'

Chapter 2: *All What Jazz*: Larkin's Most Expensive Mistake

[1] 'An Interview with the *Observer*', *RW*, p. 19.

[2] 'Dockery and Son', 1963.

[3] A pleasingly Larkinesque observation delivered by the eponymous hero of David Nobbs's *The Return of Reginald Perrin* (London: Gollancz/ Penguin, 1977: Penguin edn, p. 246).

[4] In a letter to the author written in the week after Larkin's death.

[5] 'You're Driving Me Crazy'. Their follow-up hit 'Pasedena' reached number two.

[6] 'Blue Moon', a still exhilarating recasting of one of Rodgers and Hart's finest songs.

[7] Darin had already had a number one with the jazz-tinged 'Mack the Knife' in 1959 and could, I believe, have become a jazz singer of comparable distinction to Sinatra and Tony Bennett if he had reached middle age.

[8] Sleeve essay to *Swing Trumpet Kings*, Verve 2-CD 533 263-2.

[9] See the letter to Mitchell of 20 November, 1968, discussed in detail later in the main text.

[10] *The Times Literary Supplement*, 16 June 2000, p. 21. That 'infernal trilogy' is glossed in full below, pp. 29–31.

[11] This especially characterizes his unflagging attention to the work of Coltrane. During his *Telegraph* stint he reviewed 21 of the tenorist's records – more than by his beloved Armstrong and only three fewer than the most 'populous' figure, Duke Ellington (24 entries).

[12] Significantly, it comes from the column of July 1964, 'All What Jazz?': the question mark (absent in *AWJ* itself, of course) signals Larkin's baleful view of jazz-meets-the-classics experimentalism in general and Johnny Dankworth's *Shakespeare and All That Jazz*, Dave Brubeck's *Time Changes* and Loussier's *Play Bach* series in particular. His governing charge of 'frivolity' is damning, and one he never levelled at Coltrane or any of his acolytes.

[13] The phrase is Alan Plater's in his Foreword to *PLJW*, p. ix.

[14] Max Harrison, 'The Pleasures of Ignorance', *Wire* 34/35 (December 1986/January 1987), 61.

[15] *Further Requirements*, p. 113; my emphasis.

[16] 'Credo'; *AWJ*, pp. 175–6.

[17] Larkin was one of 19 critics consulted, and the poll results were published on 20 February 1965. A number of his nominations will astonish those who know only *ITAWJ*. Charles Mingus is his Big Band runner-up and sole Bass citation; Bud Powell, that quintessential bopper, is his number one Piano; Tadd Dameron, no less quintessentially a modernist, his only choice as Arranger; and his two chosen drummers are another doyen of bop, Roy Haynes, and Elvin Jones, the man who by now had been for years the engine room of the quartet led by the musician Larkin apparently hated most, John Coltrane. Finally, and perhaps most striking of all, his Musician of the Year is Thelonious Monk.

[18] The reference is to Parker, Gillespie and Monk.

[19] Larkin's 'Annus Mirabilis' was completed in June 1967.

[20] The Who hits were 'I Can't Explain', 'Anyway Anyhow Anywhere' and 'My Generation'. Williams comments: 'If [they'd] packed it all in at Christmas, they'd have been regarded as the greatest rock group ever, no contest.' However, he is no less mindful

that 1965 featured 'a parallel boom in complete rubbish'; as he mordantly observes, Ken Dodd's 'Tears' spent five weeks at number one.

²¹ The phrase is Baudelaire's, quoted in *AWJ*, p. 45.

²² Letter to the author, 8 May 2000.

²³ See my *Sonny Rollins: The Cutting Edge*, p. 141, n. 24.

²⁴ Original meaning 'a place where records are sold' (cf bibliothèque) and soon to be known universally by the shortened form 'disco'.

²⁵ Trevor Tolley, *Larkin at Work: A Study of Larkin's Mode of Composition as Seen in his Workbooks* (Hull: Hull University Press, 1997), pp. 110–11.

²⁶ // signifies the start of a new stanza.

²⁷ See Chapter 1, note 17.

²⁸ Larkin had – yet another 'deliberate disguise' – an assured grasp of social history. Indeed, that quality underscored what has emerged as one of his most unexpected strengths as a poet: he has become an at-times-definitive historian of the social mores, habits and preoccupations of the post-war generation and its successor.

²⁹ An idea which drives an essay by John Osborne to which I will shortly return.

³⁰ This was Larkin's response to John Haffenden's suggestion that 'you see [that] as true, but others might dispute it' (*Further Requirements*, p. 53). They were in fact discussing the last four lines of 'Dockery and Son', but the rejoinder applies to the governing diagnosis of *RFJ* no less decisively.

³¹ In my view a bizarre, even devious decision; see note 53.

³² In January 1965, responding to Charles Monteith's proposal that Faber reprint the anthology, Larkin wrote '[The poems] are such complete rubbish, for the most part, that I am just twice as unwilling to have two editions in print as one' (Motion, p. 358). By the time the edition came out in September 1966, he had grown even more derisive – 'When I came to read the poems they seemed so abysmally *bad* to me that I felt the Introduction should have a much more apologetic tone.' (ibid., p. 359) – and as late as 1981 he declared, 'There are some pieces in the book I hate very much indeed' (*Further Requirements*, p. 50). It is abundantly evident, therefore, that he acceded to Faber's initiative for solely business reasons. First, it allowed him to acquire the copyright; second, royalties would accrue – and no doubt he thought that he was 'owed' some money, given that the shabby R. A. Caton had seen to it that the original brought him none.

Further observations about the *The North Ship* can be found in Part Two.

³³ 'The Sicilian might almost be better classed as a fighting counter-attack than as a defence. Few players adopt it with the intention of achieving mere equality or being satisfied with a draw.' Harry Golombek, *The Game of Chess* (London: Penguin, 1954), p. 159.

³⁴ An initiative which, *pace* Motion, I infer Larkin was at least half hoping for.

³⁵ Hitherto a studiedly donnish figure who had been a highly successful Minister of Health at the start of the 1960s, Powell's sudden and sensational démarche catapulted him from Opposition obscurity into national fame (which many argued was the chief and wholly cynical reason for his infamous 'Rivers of Blood' speech of March 1968). Edward Heath quickly expelled him from the Shadow Cabinet, but that served only to increase Powell's appeal: as a putative alternative to Heath, he found himself attracting widespread support from many traditional Labour voters as well as the Tory Right.

³⁶ Anthony Thwaite, 'Introduction' to *SL*, p. xiii.

³⁷ *LJ*, pp. 34–5; the piece originally appeared in the *Guardian*, 30 September 1958. Larkin put the sentence quoted into italics: the most dignified of stylists, he kept

typographical emphases to a minimum, and any such instance therefore signals something of unusual importance to him.

[38] Kingsley Amis, *The James Bond Dossier* (London: Panther, 1966), p. 141. The italics are Amis's.

[39] *Required Writing*, p. 60.

[40] The piece was written for August 1967's column; the *Daily Telegraph* chose not to print it. To be found in *AWJ*, pp. 186–8, it is largely devoted to the work of John Coltrane, who had died the previous month; the inference is that Larkin's words were deemed insufficiently respectful or out of tune with the prevailing threnodic hagiography. Even then Larkin was falling foul of Political Correctness.

[41] John Osborne, 'Larkin, Modernism and Jazz', *Hungarian Journal of English and American Studies*, 9/2 (Fall 2003), 7–28.

[42] Specifically, the concept of 'swing'. This property is investigated fully in Chapter 4.

[43] Osborne, *op. cit.*, 9.

[44] See note 16 to Chapter 1 above.

[45] See note 12 to Chapter 1 above.

[46] How many of Larkin's readers then, let alone now – and not excluding English Honours undergraduates in both eras – were likely to have read Pound's work or know anything much about him beyond (possibly) his role as Eliot's 'editor' for *The Waste Land?*

[47] I am indebted to Trevor Tolley for this point, made during his 'On First Looking into Larkin's *Less Deceived*' at the Second International Conference on the work of Philip Larkin, 'Larkin In Context', held at Hull in June 2002. Tolley's paper was delivered on Sunday 30 June.

[48] Wilfrid Mellers, *Musical Times*, May 1970.

[49] Charles Fox, *New Statesman*, 13 February 1970.

[50] Derek Jewell (Philip Larkin Papers, Brynmor Jones Library, University of Hull).

[51] Ten of these reappear in the final section of *Required Writing*: it is very hard to see why. With the exception of 'What Armstrong Did' and 'Wells or Gibbon?' (which amounts to a final manifesto) their selection seems to have been random. He later told the volume's dedicatee, Anthony Thwaite, that 'The jazz scraps at the end are a mistake.' It is not clear whether he means just the columns or *ITAWJ* as well. My own opinion (as opposed to interpretation) would endorse the latter. To reprint *ITAWJ* was unnecessary: unlike everything else in *Required Writing*, it was very well known, and many putative readers of this 1983 collection were likely to possess its original incarnation already. I repeat my belief that the inclusion of *RFJ* instead would have been far more illuminating; however, that might well have given Larkin's game away, and it would seem he did not want that.

[52] Osborne, *op cit.*, 10, 24.

[53] See Chapter 1 above, p. 6: 'Everyone should know this.'

[54] *Required Writing*, p. 73.

[55] See epigraph and note 1 to Chapter 1.

Chapter 3:'Essential Beauty': Larkin's Righteous Jazz

[1] Given my controlling theme of deceptiveness and Larkin's masterly use of personae, such 'what you see is what you get' straightforwardness is striking enough. But it is

remarkable in another way too. Published diaries are invariably and almost by definition ambivalent, even suspect enterprises. Ostensibly they are presented as a private log; yet they are often planned for publication from the outset, which presupposes a (sought) public response. It could be suggested that Larkin was playing a similar game: almost every item in his 'Record Diary' had been published before. However, he changed nothing in its text apart from restoring a few of his original titles in place of those favoured by the *Telegraph*'s subeditors, and in spectacular contrast to the Introduction there is no attempt to memorialize the writer-as-subject. It is a diary about jazz records, and jazz is the 'hero', not Larkin.

² *AWJ*, pp. 40–2; see p. 16 above.

³ That decision may partly have been motivated by the 'trad boom' then at its height. Modern jazz was restored to 'Jazz Club' some time later.

⁴ All collected on the Verve album *Pick of Parker*; the compiler was Alun Morgan.

⁵ '[It] sounds more like a rather screwy Ellington record than Duke interpreted in an entirely different tradition' (*AWJ*, p. 39).

⁶ 1961, with pianist Lalo Schifrin and Leo Wright on alto and flute.

⁷ Larkin's appraisal of the young Davis is shared by many, including a veteran Parker-worshipping acquaintance who has never been able to forgive Davis for tarnishing so many of Bird's records. That was the gist rather than the letter of his words to me, most of which remain unprintable even today. However, what *is* printable – memorably so – is this 1960 observation by Max Harrison: 'Davis was temperamentally a member of the "cool" school of jazz ... and his presence on so many of Parker's recordings is regrettable' (*Kings of Jazz: Charlie Parker*, London: Cassell, 1961, p. 36). Such congruity is all the more diverting in view of Harrison's fatuous dismissal of Larkin's jazz credentials cited on p. 17 above.

⁸ *Daily Telegraph*, 22 December 1969. See *PLJW*, pp. 166, 167: for some reason Larkin also voted for *Miles In The Sky* in 1970.

⁹ The remaining two are what I'd call 'neutral'. The albums in question are *In a Silent Way* and *Bitches' Brew*. His remarks on the latter encompass its electronic predecessor as well and are worth relishing simply for the prose: 'I would many times sooner listen to this than the cut-yourself-a-slice-of-throat-Whitey stuff some artists produce, but its Muzak-like chicka-chicka-boom-chick soon palls' (October 1970; *AWJ*, p. 265). Larkin did not consider such stuff 'jazz' even if he admits to a modicum of enjoyment from it, and indeed says so in the column of March 1970 (*AWJ*, p. 250) which briefly reviews *In a Silent Way*.

If he were still alive, it is hard to say how surprised Larkin would be to witness the quite extraordinary hype and mythologization which still characterizes the discussion of Davis's work and shows no sign of stopping, but a remark in that earlier column – 'can Miles be turning into one of those fortunate artists who can do no wrong?' – suggests that he would stop short of amazement. As will doubtless be evident, I share Larkin's agnosticism about the two records in question; I also think – and despite the current hype just mentioned, I am far from alone – that Davis's subsequent work has been absurdly lionized by those mythologists and a number of others too. No one seriously questions his achievements during the 1950s and 60s, but overall the jury is still out on post-1970 Davis. Larkin would have been a compelling member of the 'twelve good men and true'.

¹⁰ He did so in a letter of 27 October 1984 to his Hull friend, the late Mike Bowen. The full text reads:

'Dear Mike,

My sarcasms about L. Feather ranking C. Shavers among the 'nine best trumpeters' leads me (in small hours) to pick my own. Armstrong, Bix, W Bill, Allen, Miley all pick themselves, then (more subjectively) Spanier, Bunk, Joe Smith, and Coleman.

Who wd yours be? Oliver, I don't doubt. G. Mitchell? I'd love to know. Tell me some time, unless you take the line that one can't do this sort of thing – well, I suppose one can't, really.

Ever,

Philip

P.S. By Jove, I forgot Miles.'

Is the PS a mordant joke or a genuine afterthought? This writer would favour the latter, but not all that assuredly: that's why the main text calls the endorsement 'gnomic'.

[11] It is instructive to compare Larkin's summaries of Davis and Coltrane with those offered by Kingsley Amis in 'The Metaphysical Hangover' chapter of his book *On Drink*:

If badly hungover, try any slow Miles Davis track. It will suggest to you that, however gloomy life may be, it cannot possibly be as gloomy as Davis makes it out to be.

Warning: Make quite sure that Davis's sometime partner, John Coltrane, is not 'playing' his saxophone on any track you choose. *He* will suggest to you, in the strongest terms, that life is exactly what you are at present taking it to be: cheap, futile and meaningless.

Motion and Thwaite have drawn attention to the streak of competitiveness that informed the two men's friendship, and while there can be no question of Larkin trying to outdo Amis here – *On Drink* was not published until 1974 – there is also no question of who is the more authoritative.

[12] See note 12 to Chapter 2.

[13] 'On His Wit', *Larkin at Sixty* (ed. Thwaite), p. 99.

[14] B. J. Leggett, *op. cit.*, p. 94.

[15] Ibid., p. 37.

[16] The concept of the jazz pulse and that ever-problematic, elusive term 'swing' are explored in Chapter 4.

[17] Rightly so, too. It continues to amaze me that anyone, even if they are a fervent admirer of Coltrane, can read it without breaking into embarrassed laughter or just blowing a raspberry.

[18] *LJ*, p. 164. The citation is devoid of any of the irony or implicit rancour of the original review: 'a four-part attempt by the sheets-of-sound father of the New Thing to say "Thank You, God" in his own angular fashion, moving from frenzy to faith in doing so'.

[19] At least one reader/fellow-listener couldn't agree more: I find it a horrible record, the perfect anti-advertisement for the half-baked Easternish philosophy it seeks to dramatize.

[20] In addition, he is spot on in his (understated) judgement that 'Mrs Coltrane and Rashied Ali are inferior on piano and drums to McCoy Tyner and Elvin Jones', both of whom he warmly admired and about whose work he was always illuminating.

[21] Stuart Nicholson, 'Jazz Collector: John Coltrane', *The Times*, 4 August 2000, II, 13.

[22] See *inter alia* the discussion of 'Going, Going' in my Preface, p. xvi.

[23] 'On His Wit', *op. cit.*, p. 98.

[24] Stanley Crouch, *Considering Genius: Writings on Jazz* (New York: Basic *Civitas* Books, 2006), p. 214.

[25] Ibid., p. 37.

[26] Ibid., p. 212.

[27] See note 14 of Chapter 1 above.

[28] Crouch, *op. cit.*, p. 207.

[29] After his 1960s *succès fou*, Shepp reverted to being a perfectly competent but unremarkable player of hard bop.

[30] Michael Tucker, jazz critic and author of *Dreaming with Open Eyes: The Shamanic Spirit in Twentieth-Century Art and Culture* (HarperCollins, 1992), points out that shamans often wear hats: they hold the view that doing so concentrates the visionary power in the head. I am not sure this intriguing idea (which Tucker develops) can be applied in full to Gillespie, Monk and Shepp; however, there is no question that the first two were jazz gurus and, beneath the 'Uncle Tommery' Larkin cites, serious and innovative musical thinkers. Shepp certainly – and insistently – thought of himself as both: it is not easy to concur. See Tucker also for a shamanically inflected interpretation of the Lascaux–Picasso development of modern art.

[31] Even Ornette Coleman, who is granted warm praise at times, has a degree of 'silliness' that 'prevents one taking him quite seriously' (*AWJ*, p. 66).

[32] Kingsley Amis reports that Larkin was a great deal ruder about Art Hodes, another pianist with a line in studied primitivism who is mentioned in passing in *AWJ*. '[He] remarked of him that he sounded as if he had three hands and didn't know what to do with any of them.' Kingsley Amis, *Memoirs* (London: Hutchinson, 1991). Penguin edn (1992), p. 70.

[33] *PLJW*, p. 134.

[34] Hobsbawm was writing here under his 'jazz pseudonym', Francis Newton, in *The Jazz Scene* (London: MacGibbon & Kee, 1959). Revised edn, Penguin, 1961, p. 41.

[35] *PLJW*, p. 132.

[36] Tony Tanner, note 4 in his edition of Jane Austen, *Mansfield Park* (London: Penguin, 1966), p. 458.

[37] In truth, some young whites were equally enthusiastic. The most extraordinary jazz concert I have ever attended was the climax to the Jazz Expo 67 package at the Hammersmith Odeon, whose first attraction was The Miles Davis Quintet. The second half featured the Archie Shepp group: a quarter of the audience walked out within 20 minutes, and that fraction had grown to half before the hour was up. Those that remained gave the music a tumultuous reception; I saw out the affair for reasons of journalistic duty rather than pleasure, and seemed to be the only non-disciple left at the end. More than any other single thing, that experience brought home to me just how splintered, even polarized, the (already small) world of jazz had become. In that respect, it seems to me that Larkin's governing diagnosis is unanswerable.

[38] An irony not lost on Larkin was that the 'recent and extravagant ... vogue for "beat" music' (*RB*, p. 142) suddenly made blues artists such as Howlin' Wolf, Muddy Waters and Roosevelt Sykes newly marketable, for they were lauded by groups like the

Rolling Stones, the Animals and Manfred Mann, all of whom also used the bluesmen's material.

[39] E.g. the 'scandalous efficiency' of pianist Lennie Tristano (p. 230) and this defence of Coleman Hawkins: 'Before we criticize the milestone for walking we should compare it with milestones that stand still' (p. 210).

Chapter 4: Conclusion: 'The Natural Noise Of Good'

[1] Coined during a tribute to that magnificent drummer Billy Higgins (ob. 2001). Crouch, *op. cit.*, p. 32.

[2] Larkin, 'Reasons for Attendance'.

[3] To be found on *Stan Getz & J.J.Johnson at the Opera House*, Verve CD 831 272-2.

[4] On the sleeve note to *This Is Ray Brown*, Japanese Verve (LP) UMV 2117.

[5] Ian Carr, Digby Fairweather and Brian Priestley, *Jazz: The Rough Guide* (London: The Rough Guides, 1995), p. 750.

[6] See Chapter 1 above, p. 9.

[7] The full provenance of all the performances just cited, along with all other records referred to in my text, may be found in the Appendix.

[8] Martin Williams, *The Jazz Tradition* (New York: Oxford University Press, 1970), pp. 6–7. Intriguingly, OUP engaged Larkin as a referee for the manuscript in January 1970. See *PLJW*, pp. 141–2.

[9] I repeat my opinion that the essay is not all that well written, but would like to add that it is astonishingly mature in its insight, ambit and bravery. In view of this, and notwithstanding his perceptive gloss on the essay itself, it bewilders me that Andrew Motion thought Larkin 'lucky' to get his Oxford First. I find it equally strange that anyone could fail to recognize that Larkin had a prodigious and major intellect. To revisit an idea voiced in Chapter 1, he was always '*heavy*'.

[10] He offered this valuable perception during questions and discussion following my paper at the 'Larkin in Context' International Conference, Hull, 29 June 2002.

[11] Milton, *Paradise Lost*, XII. 646.

[12] By Frederic Ramsey, Jr and Charles Edward Smith; see *LJ* No. 2, pp. 26–7.

[13] See above, p. 49.

[14] 'Lives of the Poets', *PLJW*, pp. 35–6. The book in question was the celebrated French discographer Charles Delaunay's *Django Reinhardt* (London: Cassell, 1961).

[15] That is the view of Martin Williams in *The Jazz Tradition*, and his case is persuasive.

[16] Antonin Dvorak, 'Real Value of Negro Melodies', *New York Herald*, 21 May 1893.

[17] Over a million sheet-music copies of *Maple Leaf Rag* had been sold by the time of Joplin's death in 1917.

[18] I do not have uppermost in mind here the bigots who simply cannot face the idea of the hated inferior producing anything worthwhile or indeed other than evil rubbish. All societies have such people, but while they are by no means negligible in their mindless corrosiveness, they very rarely take whole nations with them.

[19] Duke Ellington speaking to Nat Hentoff in 1965. Quoted in John Edward Hasse, *Beyond Category* (New York: Omnibus, 1995), p. 397.

[20] 'Cultural Politics: The Betrayal of Jazz', *A Jazz Odyssey: The Life of Oscar Peterson* (London: Continuum, 2001), p. 329.

[21] Ira Gitler, *Swing to Bop: An Oral History of the Transition in Jazz in the 1940s* (New York: Oxford University Press, 1987), p. 303.

[22] 'A New James Bond', *Whatever Became of Jane Austen?* (London: Cape, 1970). 1972 Panther edition, p. 68.

Chapter 5: Departures and Arrivals

[1] Having closely perused Zachary Leader's monumental 2006 *The Life of Kingsley Amis*, I am still none the wiser. That is not to berate Leader's admirable work, but to observe that Amis seems to have taken quite a while not so much to get going as to discover what he really wanted to do/write. Just like Larkin, in fact.

[2] He quotes from Larkin's 18 July 1943 letter to Jim Sutton – 'Oh how clever I am! How infinite and wise in all my faculties! A star descends onto my forehead! It is all the more remarkable because I made numerous blunders and know sweet bugger all about my subject' – and proceeds to take it at face value, commenting, 'Larkin's tutors, more soberly, agreed that he was lucky to have done so well' (*AWL*, p. 103). No provenance is given for that intelligence, though of course it could be true; however, Motion's later use of 'snatched his First' (p. 167) is gratuitous, not least because he compares it unfavourably to Monica Jones's equivalent accomplishment – a woman who subsequently published nothing and who, despite Motion's almost pathological determination to prove otherwise, emerges from his account notably less gifted than her lover.

[3] 'I always favoured the view that people's laundry lists should be published: if they're any good at all, they've got interesting laundry lists.' Clive James in conversation with Mark Lawson, *Front Row*, BBC Radio Four, 4 January 2001, prompted by the publication of *FR*. I like James's observation as a guiding principle, but (as will be evident) can acquiesce only wanly in the case of *Trouble at Willow Gables*.

[4] 'Evelyn Waugh: The Paris Review Interview', conducted by Julian Jebb. *Writers at Work: 3rd Series* (London: Secker & Warburg, 1967) 1977 Penguin edn, p. 110.

[5] Curiously, I find myself linking the limp, unsatisfactorily realized figure of Kemp with one of the outstanding triumphs of post-war comic writing – Kingsley Amis's Jim Dixon (*Lucky Jim*). Perhaps I am historically ignorant or naive, but just as I have never been able to understand how Dixon (or come to that his equally philistine pal Beesley) could land a job as a university lecturer, it baffles me that Kemp ever got to Oxford. He displays no real academic prowess or intellectual vigour: the (admittedly haunting) early scene on the train which charts his excruciating sandwich-embarrassment nails him as a hapless overgrown Boy Scout more or less devoid of focus.

[6] Letter to Norman Iles, 17 April 1941.

[7] Forty years later Northrop Frye observed in remarkably congruent fashion: 'The teacher, as has been recognized at least since Plato's *Meno*, is not primarily someone who knows instructing someone who does not know. He is rather someone who attempts to re-create the subject in the student's mind, and his strategy in doing this is first of all to get the student to recognize what he already potentially knows, which includes breaking up the powers of repression in his mind that keep him from knowing what he knows. That is why it is the teacher, rather than the student, who asks most of the questions.' *The Great Code: The Bible and Literature* (London: Routledge & Kegan Paul, 1982), p. xv.

[8] 'An Interview with the *Observer*'; *RW*, p. 49.

[9] Made while comparing Johnny Hodges with John Coltrane (p. 257).

[10] *Observer* interview; *RW*, p. 49, within the same answer as the 'I wanted to write novels' admission quoted just above.

[11] The thought occurs that much the same could be said of Larkin's early poetry.

[12] 'The Poetry of Hardy' (1968), *Required Writing*, p. 175.

[13] *A Writer's Life*, p. 141.

[14] This aspect of Larkin is explored in Chapter 7.

[15] 1950; never anthologized until the 1988 *Collected Poems*.

[16] The rather pleasing thought occurs that Larkin would have been at his sardonic best on the (in part) idiotic reverence now afforded the internet, which has replaced the cloth-bound word as the new inviolable *auctoritas*. As Alan Plater said in 1998, Larkin could 'sniff the crap at a hundred paces, especially when it was on the page'.

[17] A possible exception is 'Brushing her hair … ', which was – in my view incongruously – added to the 1960s reprint of *The North Ship*.

[18] See also my 'Religious Resonances in Philip Larkin's Poetry', *About Larkin*, 22/23 (2007).

[19] Jonathan Smith, 'That Poem', in *The Learning Game* (London: Cape, 2001), p. 237.

[20] See my 'Teaching and Learning Larkin: "Helping the Old Too, As They Ought"', *About Larkin*, 21 (Summer 2006), 18–21.

[21] Ronald de Leeuw, the editor of *The Letters of Vincent Van Gogh* (Harmondsworth: Penguin, 1997), cites a 'well-nigh endless series of studies' (p. 284).

[22] Ibid., p. 291.

[23] Michael Tucker, *Dreaming with Open Eyes: The Shamanic Spirit in Twentieth Century Art and Culture* (London: HarperCollins, 1992), p. 114.

[24] Ibid., p. 1.

[25] Van Gogh, quoted in David Sweetman, *The Love of Many Things: A Life of Vincent Van Gogh* (London: Hodder & Stoughton, 1990), p. 92.

[26] Booth, *op. cit.*, pp. 67–71.

[27] *Required Writing*, p. 74.

[28] The phrase calls to mind another great Romantic artist, J. M. W. Turner.

[29] John Bayley, 'Larkin, Pym and Romantic Sympathy', *About Larkin*, 14 (October 2002), 13.

[30] *Desert Island Discs*, BBC Radio Four, December 1996.

[31] Ten years or so ago, a student of mine (who went on to become an art teacher) drew my attention to an exhibit in Tate Britain by conceptual artist Michael Craig Martin. It took the form of a flask of water, arranged prismatically to catch the light. The student immediately thought of 'Water', which we had recently been reading. I suspect this is a matter of coincidence rather than inspiration, but it is telling nonetheless.

[32] Occasionally that desire has less than felicitous, strained results. 'Show Saturday' is uncomfortably twee at times, and there's a faintly preacherly quality to it (especially the last line) which jars: like Van Gogh, Larkin is at his least effective when he mounts a soapbox (cf. 'The Potato Eaters' once more). Like him, too, Larkin did not perform well when commissioned: see the observations on 'Going, Going' in my Preface.

[33] Booth, *op. cit*, p. 14.

[34] Written in the course of a review for the *Independent* (13 December 1986) of Terry Whalen's *Philip Larkin and English Poetry*.

[35] *Required Writing*, pp. 53–4.

[36] Ibid., p. 67.

[37] Teacher and colleague Linda Caldicott in a letter to the author, February 2006.

[38] To my mind the same anger, though much more quietly expressed, underpins the last stanza of 'Money'.

[39] A similar contrast in tone and attack attends another poem whose title Larkin borrowed, 'I Remember, I Remember'. Thomas Hood's original was an affecting elegy for a brother who died young; Larkin's is an extremely funny demolition of the clichés of childhood and adolescence which simultaneously reflects with sour envy on a childhood 'unspent' (not necessarily Larkin's own).

[40] The three ellipsis-separated extracts are drawn from *AWL*, p. 358; *AWL* p. 359; *Further Requirements*, p. 50; they span 1965, 1966 and 1981.

[41] *Required Writing*, p. 62.

[42] *The Letters of Vincent Van Gogh*, p. 53.

Chapter 6: Larkin and Religion

[1] The phrase is taken from Larkin's 1950 poem 'Strangers' (not published until *CP*).

[2] 'The Other Larkin', *Critical Quarterly*, 17/4 (Winter 1975), 360.

[3] *A Writer's Life*, p. 486.

[4] Letter to the author, 15 August 2006.

[5] *Critical Survey*, 5 (Winter 1971), 224–33. James Booth quotes briefly from both this and Watson's article in his 2005 *The Poet's Plight* – which is indeed how both came to my attention.

[6] So frequent is such diction, in fact, that the temptation is to 'recode' the anthology's title into an abstract noun, *Northship*.

[7] It is adumbratively reminiscent of the lines which close 'Days', explored later.

[8] It is fitting that Larkin's last words were 'I am going to the inevitable' (*AWL*, p. 485).

[9] The words quoted are J. R. Watson's, *op. cit.*, p. 348. They occur during a passage arguing that the poet Larkin most closely resembles is Browning.

[10] That lifelong reluctance is entirely in keeping with my book's title: Larkin had a fondness for hiding his light under bushels (an appropriately biblical phrase).

[11] The fact that Larkin was clearly conversant with Hopkins's verse strengthens my governing contention here; it also points up his *sprezzatura* persona, particularly in wearing his learning lightly, His many (and gloriously mischievous) 'I-am-dumb' interview-sallies notwithstanding.

[12] See Chapter 7.

[13] It is still used in church ceremony today, and is also a symbol of the last rites, in which oil is administered in the same places.

[14] His name is Toby Forward. He remains one of the best students I've ever taught anywhere; unsurprisingly he obtained a Distinction. Toby has since gone on to become a successful author of fiction.

[15] I am indebted for that paraphrase to Michael Tucker in his *Jan Garbarek: Deep Song* (Hull: Eastnote, 1998), pp. 31–2.

[16] Alan Bennett, *Untold Stories* (London: Faber, 2005), p. 302. The remarks quoted were written in his diary for 27 December 2001.

[17] 'An Interview with John Haffenden', in *Further Requirements*, ed. Anthony Thwaite, p. 55.

[18] i.e. each 'ship' which forms that 'Sparkling armada of promises'.

[19] It is not insignificant that the word 'ignorance' appears in 'Arrival', in effect coupled with 'innocence'.

[20] Philip Marlowe in Raymond Chandler's *The Long Goodbye*, 1953.

[21] James Bond in Ian Fleming's *Diamonds Are Forever*, 1959.

[22] Though apparently not renowned enough for all critics to get their facts right. In a piece that has the dubious distinction of being the first full-scale posthumous attack on Larkin, the music critic Max Harrison prefigured the drastically revisionist responses occasioned by the publication of *A Writer's Life* and the *Selected Letters*, although it should be admitted that he did not exhibit the salacious glee that characterized a number of his successors. Instead he did something more immediately injurious – shooting himself in both feet with a double-barrelled shotgun that he imagined was aimed at Larkin's ghost. Unsurprisingly, his main concern was Larkin the jazz critic, but he unwisely strayed into literary territory also, thereby inviting ridicule with the clause ' ... poor Larkin began a poem, "Life is first boredom, then fear"'. Poor Harrison, actually: the remark quoted is the *antepenultimate* line of 'Dockery and Son', which is not a short poem. (Max Harrison, 'The Pleasures of Ignorance', *Wire*, 34/35 (December 1986/January 1987), 61.)

[23] It is improbable that Larkin suffered no 'regret' in his late middle age; however, he never underwent retirement, and the only real ill-health he suffered was the short-ish illness which killed him.

[24] The reference is to the final paragraphs of 'Armageddon?', ch. 8 of *Armageddon?* by Gore Vidal (London: André Deutsch, 1987).

[25] Cf. 'A Study of Reading Habits'.

[26] That sardonic appraisal of the Church's interest in Mammon also informs the wonderful final stanza of 'Money'.

[27] See Chapter 5, note 34.

[28] 'Sad Steps' is in that respect reminiscent of 'Vers de Société'; see Chapter 7.

[29] Just like steam, water, ice (spirit, essence, substance), light, heat, fire is a tryptych symbolic of the Holy Trinity – the Light of God, the Heat of the Holy Spirit and the fire/substance that was and is the Incarnation.

[30] In exploring this Christian reading of 'Solar', I have been much indebted to friend and teaching colleague Linda Caldicott, whose insights were as crucial as they were further enabling. The enabling strength of this reading is borne out by examples to be found in the work of figures as diverse as Boethius (480–c.524) and the twentieth-century poet Charles Causley. See Helen Waddell, *Songs of The Wandering Scholars* (London: The Folio Society, 1982), pp. 73–9 and Causley's 'I Am The Great Sun' in *Collected Poems 1951–1997* (London: Macmillan, 1957), p. 57.

[31] For a muscular and illuminating survey, see J. E. Cirlot, *A Dictionary of Symbols* (London: Routledge, 1988), pp. 317–20.

[32] Michael Tucker looks at this matter in some detail in his *Jan Garbarek: Deep Song* (Hull: Eastnote, 1998), p. 259 and *passim*.

[33] As a double postscript to 'Solar': first, it is fascinating to read the poem in tandem with Thom Gunn's 'Sunlight', whose last two stanzas, and especially its final line – 'Petals of light lost in your innocence' – are extraordinarily akin to Larkin's poem in ethos and thrust. 'Sunlight' closes Gunn's 1971 collection *Molly* (London: Faber, 1971) and appears to have been written during the 1960s. I am not suggesting for a moment that Gunn was 'influenced' by 'Solar' or anything similar; that said, the congruence is as notable as the two poems are pleasing.

Second, Louise Tucker has brought to my attention that in a side-chapel directly opposite 'The Arundel Tomb' sculpture in Chichester Cathedral is a 1973 piece by Cecil Collins, 'The Icon of Divine Light'. All Larkin devotees know that the former inspired the 1956 poem which closes *The Whitsun Weddings*. While I am of course not suggesting that Collins's piece exerted any effect, its synchronistic pertinence to 'Solar' is remarkable. The artist uses as epigraph Revelation 21.5, 'Behold, I make all things new,' and the image depicts the sun. Both poems in question hinge on love and Larkin's enduring belief in it (a property evident in many other poems too). That serendipitous Chichester coincidence illuminates the broader concerns and spiritually engaged ethos of Larkin's work which have so far eluded the majority of his critics.

[34] To underline that surreptitious masterliness, it amuses me that the alliterative 'Parchment, plate and pyx' foreshadows Larkin's (in)famous 3-P trilogy 14 years later in the Introduction to *All What Jazz*: 'Picasso, Parker and Pound'.

[35] Cf. 'Money' (written nearly 20 years later: 1973), which includes a searing reference to 'churches ornate and mad'.

[36] In the light of which it is pertinent to quote Francis Wheen in his *How Mumbo-Jumbo Conquered The World*: 'When people cease to believe in God, they don't believe in *nothing*: they believe in *anything*.' Splendid – but it should be pointed out that the aperçu was originally G. K. Chesterton's, not Wheen's. As T. S. Eliot wryly observed, 'Immature poets imitate; mature poets steal.' – a *bon mot* he himself stole from Ralph Waldo Emerson!

Chapter 7: Fears, Antipathies and Aversions

[1] I would especially cite the 1984 'Pleasing The People' (*Larkin: Jazz Writings*, pp. 108–10), which cuts to ribbons James Lincoln Collier's biography of Larkin's greatest hero, Louis Armstrong.

[2] The book in question was Roger Woddis's *The Woddis Collection*. All the material quoted forms part of 'Correspondence Bundle #1' [DLP (2) 1/54/2], housed in the Larkin Suite of the Brynmor Jones Library, Hull University.

[3] Peter Ackroyd, *T. S. Eliot* (London: Faber, 1984), p. 93.

[4] 'Reminiscences of Larkin', delivered at the Larkin Study Day held at King Henry VIII School, Coventry, 25 March 2000.

[5] Milton, *Paradise Lost*, X.770–1, 773–9.

[6] Tennyson, *Tithonus*, 1–6, 27–31, 66–72. Tithonus was loved by Aurora, the goddess of dawn, who gave him immortality but not eternal youth. Although he grew old and shrunken, he could not die; nor could she rescind the gift.

[7] Cf. the speaker in both 'Annus Mirabilis' and 'High Windows'.

[8] That conjugation of emptiness, plenitude and underlying/resultant compassion attends 'I Remember, I Remember', 'Love Songs in Age' and perhaps most notably 'Mr. Bleaney'.

[9] Another jazz connection can be noted here. Those lines from Psalm 103 are quoted by Keith Knox in his sleeve essay to Swedish saxophonist Lars Gullin's *Like Grass*, recorded on 27 August 1973 and issued on Odeon Records E 062 34574; they also govern the album's concept.

[10] Philip Marlowe in Raymond Chandler's *The Long Goodbye*, 1953.

[11] James Bond in Ian Fleming's *Diamonds Are Forever*, 1959.

[12] In addition, I doubt I'm the only reader who winces at the lines, 'And that letter to her mother / Saying *Won't you come for the summer*'!

[13] That view underpins the team's spoof of Christ, *The Life of Brian*, but the name featured in a good number of their TV sketches before that film was conceived.

[14] *AWL*, p. 311.

[15] 'Larkin's Money', in James Booth (ed.), *New Larkins for Old: Critical Essays* (London: Macmillan, 2000) pp. 11–28.

[16] A gloriously audacious, Cole Porterish rhyme that is almost the equal of 'fangs' and 'meringues' in 'A Study of Reading Habits'.

[17] Unless he was stuck for a rhyme with 'save' – and as I hope I've already intimated, the mature Larkin was rarely stuck for a rhyme. Or if he ever was, he abandoned the poem forthwith: like any even halfway decent poet, he knew that once you let the rhyme scheme govern the poem, you're finished.

[18] As an afterthought, it is possible that such meaninglessness made Larkin simply *mean*. Given that 'Money' hinges on *saving* money – reluctantly, but the speaker can think of nothing better or indeed as good to do with it – then this is one area where art and life were closely congruent. In his 1993 essay 'Don Juan In Hull', Martin Amis declared:

> He was, by the way, a genuine miser. In his last weeks, he lived off 'cheap red wine and Complan'. He left a quarter of a million pounds.

In that one respect at least, Eric Homberger was perhaps not far off the mark in calling him 'the saddest heart in the post-war supermarket'.

Such an impression of Larkin tends to be confirmed when one notes that in Georgina Battiscombe's anthology of poems on old age, *Winter Song* (London: Constable, 1992), Larkin is one of the most represented poets. Only Yeats (16), Wordsworth (10), Hardy and Herrick (7 apiece) outnumber Larkin's six. Incidentally, the poems Battiscombe chose are 'The Old Fools', 'Age', 'Heads in the Women's Ward', 'The Winter Palace', 'Long Sight in Age' and 'Continuing to Live'. Intriguingly, only the first two did Larkin anthologize himself: we are returned to the governing thesis of my Preface, i.e. the need to challenge and indeed correct popular misconceptions of Larkin's image, worth and indeed what he was like and what he valued.

[19] *RW*, p. 51.

[20] Analogous (albeit entirely unobscene) is the use of 'MCMXIV' as that poem's title instead of the Arabic '1914'. There are several other, adumbratively trenchant reasons why Larkin uses Roman numerals, but the most immediate one is to engage his readers by requiring them to decode the very title.

[21] 'Song of Myself' (1855), Canto 51 *Poet to Poet: Walt Whitman*; selected by Robert Creeley (Harmondsworth: Penguin Books, 1973), p. 113. Also, see the 'Introduction' to Frances Nesbitt Oppel's *Mask and Tragedy: Yeats and Nietzsche* (Charlottesville: University Press of Virginia, 1987), pp. 1–5.

[22] Actually, 'don't read much now' is not only a compressed form of '*I* don't read much now': it can also be read/heard as an imperative verb, an order or advice to the audience.

[23] I am tempted to apologize for such a laborious prose paraphrase of what Larkin brings off with superb poetically compressed economy.

[24] I look to justify that claim in Part Three.

[25] *Postscript (2001)* to 'Four Essays on Philip Larkin', *Reliable Essays*, pp. 70–1.

[26] It follows 'Homage to a Government' on the very next page of the *Collected Poems*.

[27] *Cf.* the similarly misunderstood 'Annus Mirabilis'. See Chapter 5, pp. 84–6.

[28] In passing, it is not entirely irrelevant to my reading of this poem that a key factor in President Clinton's (admittedly praiseworthy) success in turning round the US budget deficit in such spectacular fashion was that after 1989 or so America had no Cold War to fight – a phantom engagement that from the sixties onwards had accounted for 70 cents of every tax-dollar.

[29] 23 June 1923.

[30] Quoted in *AWL*, p. 302.

[31] *AWJ*, p. 29.

[32] By David M. Baker. See Chapter 9, p. 140, including note 2.

[33] Graham Landon, 'Toad Tale', *About Larkin*, 9 (April 2000), 21.

[34] She made the observation during her 'Reminiscences of Larkin' talk at the Larkin Study Day held at King Henry VIII School, Coventry on 25 March 2000.

[35] *RW*, p. 51.

[36] 'Reminiscences of Larkin', Coventry, 25 March 2000.

[37] *RW*, p. 51.

[38] Ibid.

[39] Anthony Thwaite, Introduction to *CP*, p. xviii.

[40] Ibid., p. xxiii.

[41] The fact that the words are those of perhaps his most ardent disparager is a satisfying irony. They were spoken by Terry Eagleton in his 'Philip Larkin: Poetry and Politics', the Distinguished Lecture given to the Annual General Meeting of the Philip Larkin Society, Hull, 25 November 2000.

[42] Booth's discussion is valuable nonetheless. See *The Poet's Plight*, pp. 21ff.

Chapter 8: Larkin the Librarian

[1] *AWJ*, p. 29.

[2] Baker recalls this as Larkin's 'standard response' to any 'suggestion that a training programme be introduced or a member of [Hull University Library] staff sent away on a conference'; the phrase is the title of his contribution to Dyson's 1988 collection. However, as Baker then goes on to chart in some detail, Larkin was in fact both assiduous and quietly passionate about staff training. Yet another instance of a throw-away, jocular remark that it would be most unwise to take literally.

[3] I revisit that description (Larkin's own) shortly.

[4] Wood died in 1970; Larkin attended his funeral.

[5] The remark is Martin Amis's: *Independent on Sunday* (magazine section), 29 November 1992.

[6] Joseph Epstein, 'Mr Larkin Gets a Life', *Life Sentences* (New York: Norton, 1997).

[7] Thwaite, Introduction to *CP*, p. xviii.

[8] Maeve Brennan, 'Philip Larkin: a biographical sketch' in Dyson (ed.), *op. cit.*, pp. 1–19.

[9] See, e.g., 'A Neglected Responsibility: Contemporary Literary Manuscripts'. A talk to the Manuscripts Group of the Standing Conference of National and University Libraries (SCONUL) at King's College, London, 1979. Reprinted in *RW*, pp. 98–108.

[10] Kingsley Amis, *Memoirs*, p. 59. Amis's final clause is interestingly analogous to my suggestion, concerning Larkin's failure to republish or even mention 'Requiem for Jazz', that to have done either 'might have given [his] game away' (see note 45 to Chapter 2).

Bibliography

Those requiring a comprehensive Larkin bibliography are referred to the late B. C. Bloomfield's monumental survey detailed below. What follows is a list of sources from which I have quoted, to which I refer or which were instrumental in the shaping of my text.

Ackroyd, Peter, *T.S. Eliot* (London: Faber, 1984).

Alvarez, A., 'The New Poetry, or Beyond the Gentility Principle', *The New Poetry* (Harmondsworth: Penguin, 1962), pp. 17–28.

—*The Writer's Voice* (London: Bloomsbury, 2005).

Amis, Kingsley, *Lucky Jim* (London: Gollancz, 1955).

—*I Like It Here* (London: Gollancz, 1958).

—*The James Bond Dossier* (London: Panther, 1966).

—*Whatever Became of Jane Austen?* (London: Cape, 1970).

—*On Drink* (London: Cape, 1972).

—*Memoirs* (London: Hutchinson, 1991). Penguin edition (1992).

—*The Letters of Kingsley Amis*, ed. Zachary Leader (London: HarperCollins 2000).

Appel, Alfred Jr, *Jazz Modernism: From Ellington and Armstrong to Matisse and Joyce* (New York: Alfred A. Knopf, 2002).

Austen, Jane, *Emma*.

— *Mansfield Park*, ed. Tony Tanner (London: Penguin, 1966).

Banville, John, 'Homage to Philip Larkin', *The New York Review of Books*, 53/3, 23 February 2006.

Battiscome, Georgina (ed.), *Winter Song* (London: Constable, 1992).

Bayley, John, 'Larkin, Pym and Romantic Sympathy', *About Larkin*, 14 (October 2002).

Bennett, Alan, *Writing Home* (London: Faber, 1994).

—*Untold Stories* (London: Faber, 2005).

Betjeman, John, *Collected Poems* (London: John Murray, 1973).

—*Trains and Buttered Toast,* ed. Stephen Games (London: John Murray, 2006).

Bloom, Harold, *The Anxiety of Influence* (New York: Oxford University Press, 1973).

Bloomfield, B.C., *Philip Larkin: A Bibliography 1933–1994* (revised & enlarged edn; London: The British Library, 2002).

Booth, James, *Philip Larkin: Writer* (Hemel Hempstead: Harvester Wheatsheaf, 1992).

—*Philip Larkin: The Poet's Plight* (Basingstoke: Palgrave Macmillan, 2005).

—(ed.) *New Larkins for Old* (Basingstoke: Palgrave Macmillan, 2000).

Bradford, Richard, *First Boredom, Then Fear: The Life of Philip Larkin* (London: Peter Owen, 2005).

Brennan, Maeve, 'The Larkin–Sutton Correspondence', *Paragon Review*, November 1992.

—*The Philip Larkin I Knew* (Manchester: Manchester University Press, 2002).

Browning, Robert, *Men and Women*.

Campbell, Joseph, *The Masks of God*, 4 vols (Harmondsworth: Penguin, 1976–82).

Carr, Ian, Digby Fairweather and Brian Priestley, *Jazz: The Rough Guide* (London: The Rough Guides, 1995).

Cassirer, Ernst, *Language and Myth* (Toronto: Harper & Brothers, 1953, Dover edition).

Castligione, Baldassare, *The Book of the Courtier*.

Causley, Charles, *Collected Poems 1951–1997* (London: Macmillan, 1957).

Chandler, Raymond, *The Long Goodbye* (London: Hamilton, 1953).

Cirlot, J. E., *A Dictionary of Symbols* (London: Routledge, 1988).

Collier, James Lincoln, *The Making of Jazz: A Comprehensive History* (London: Macmillan, 1978).

—*Louis Armstrong* (London: Michael Joseph, 1984).

Conrad, Joseph, *Heart of Darkness*.

Cookson, Linda and Brian Loughrey, *Philip Larkin: The Poems* (Harlow: Longman, 1989).

Cooper, Stephen, *Philip Larkin: Subversive Writer* (Brighton: Sussex Academic Press, 2004).

Crouch, Stanley, *Considering Genius: Writings on Jazz* (New York: Basic Civitas Books, 2006).

Cunningham, Andrew, 'Rebel with an Age-old Cause', *Times Educational Supplement* ('English Curriculum' Supplement), 25 May 2001.

De Leeuw, Ronald (ed.), *The Letters of Vincent Van Gogh* (Harmondsworth: Penguin, 1997),

Dyson, Brian (ed.), *The Modern Academic Library: Essays in Memory of Philip Larkin* (London: The Library Association, 1989).

Eliot, T. S., *The Complete Poems and Plays* (London: Faber, 1969).

Epstein, Joseph, 'Mr Larkin Gets a Life', *Life Sentences* (New York: W.W. Norton, 1997).

Everett, Barbara, 'Larkin's Money', in James Booth (ed.), *New Larkins for Old: Critical Essays* (London: Macmillan, 2000), pp. 11–28.

—'Larkin and the Doomsters', *The Times Literary Supplement*, 3 June 2005.

Feather, Leonard, 'The New Life of Ray Brown', *Downbeat*, 9 March 1967, 25.

Feinstein, Sascha, and Komunyakaa Yusef (eds), *The Second Set: The Jazz Poetry Anthology, Vol. 2* (Bloomington: Indiana University Press, 1996).

Frye, Northrop, *The Great Code: The Bible and Literature* (London: Routledge & Kegan Paul, 1982).

Gardner, Philip, '"One Does One's Best": Larkin Posthumous', *Critical Survey*, I/2 (1989), 194–9.

Gelly, Dave, 'Swing Trumpet Kings', Verve 2-CD 533 263-2 (liner essay).

Gitler, Ira, *Swing to Bop: An Oral History of the Transition in Jazz in the 1940s* (New York: Oxford University Press, 1987).

Goldson, Elizabeth (ed.), *Seeing Jazz: Artists and Writers on Jazz* (Washington, DC: Chronicle Books/The Smithsonian Institution, 1997).

Goodby, John, '"The Importance of Being Elsewhere", or '"No Man Is an Ireland": Self, Selves and Social Consensus in the Poetry of Philip Larkin', *Critical Survey*, I/2 (1989), 131–8.

Gottlieb, Richard (ed.), *Reading Jazz* (London: Bloomsbury, 1997).

Gunn, Thom, *Molly* (London: Faber, 1971).

Hamburger, Eric, *PL: A Retrospect* (London: Enitharmon Press, 2002).

Hardy, Thomas, *The Complete Poems*, ed. James Gibson (London: Macmillan, 1979).

Harrison, Max, *Kings of Jazz: Charlie Parker* (Cassell, 1961).

—'The Pleasures of Ignorance', *Wire* 34/35 (December 1986/January 1987).

Hartley, Jean, *Philip Larkin: The Marvell Press and Me* (London: Sumach Press, 1989).

Hasse, John Edward, *Duke Ellington: Beyond Category* (New York: Omnibus, 1995).

Heaney, Seamus, *New Selected Poems 1966–87* (London: Faber, 1990).

—*The Redress of Poetry: Oxford Lectures* (London: Faber, 1995).

Hentoff, Nat, *American Music Is* (Cambridge, MA: Da Capo, 2004).

Hollindale, Peter, 'Philip Larkin's "The Explosion"', *Critical Survey*, I/2 (1989), 139–46.

Hopkins, Gerard Manley, *Poems*, ed. W.H. Gardner (London: Oxford University Press, 3rd edn, 1948).

Hughes, Ted, *Collected Poems* (London: Faber, 2003).

James, Clive, 'On His Wit', in Anthony Thwaite (ed.), *Larkin at Sixty* (London: Faber, 1982).

—*The Meaning of Recognition: New Essays 2001–2005* (London: Picador, 2005).

Jones, LeRoi (now known as Amiri Bakara), *Blues People* (Edinburgh: Canongate, 1995).

Joyce, James, *Portrait of the Artist as a Young Man*.

Kington, Miles, 'Why I Never Got to Talk Jazz with Philip Larkin', *The Independent*, 19 September 2003.

Kirsch, Adam, 'Green Selfconscious Spurts', *The Times Literary Supplement*, 13 May 2005.

Knapp, Bettina L., *Music, Archetype and the Writer* (Pennsylvania: Pennsylvania State Press, 1988).

Kuby, Lolette, *Uncommon Poet for the Common Man: A Study of Philip Larkin's Poetry* (The Hague: Mouton Press, 1974).

Landon, Graham, 'Toad Tale', *About Larkin*, 9 (April 2000), 21.

Langridge, Derek, *Your Jazz Collection* (London: Bingley, 1970).

—*Early Poems and Juvenilia*, ed. A. T. Tolley (London: Faber, 2005).

Larkin, Philip, *Jill* (Fortune Press 1945; London: Faber, 1975).

—*The Less Deceived* (Calstock: Marvell Press, 1955).

—*The Whitsun Weddings* (London: Faber, 1964).

—*A Girl in Winter* (London: Faber, 1965).

— *The North Ship* (London: Faber, 1966).

—*All What Jazz* (London: Faber, 1970; revised edn, 1985).

—*High Windows* (London: Faber, 1974).

—*Required Writing* (London: Faber, 1983).

—*Collected Poems*, ed. Anthony Thwaite (London: Faber, 1988).

—*Selected Letters*, ed. Anthony Thwaite (London: Faber, 1992).

—*Further Requirements*, ed. Anthony Thwaite (London: Faber, 2001).

—*Trouble at Willow Gables*, ed. James Booth (London: Faber, 2002).

—*Jazz Writings* (formerly *Reference Back: Philip Larkin's Uncollected Jazz Writings 1940–84*) (London: Continuum, 2004/Hull: Hull University Press, 1998).

—(ed.), *The Oxford Book of Twentieth Century Verse* (Oxford: Oxford University Press, 1973; revised edn, with a Foreword by Andrew Motion, 1997).

Leader, Zachary, *The Life of Kingsley Amis* (London: Cape, 2006).

Lees, Gene, *Oscar Peterson: The Will to Swing* (Toronto: Lester & Orpen Dennys, 1989; revised edn, 2000, Cooper Square Press).

Leggett, B. J., *Larkin's Blues: Jazz, Popular Music and Poetry* (Baton Rouge, LA: Louisiana State University Press, 1999).

Lerner, Laurence, *Philip Larkin* (Tavistock: Northcote, 1997; 2nd edn, 2005).

Lyttelton, Humphrey, *Second Chorus* (London: MacGibbon & Kee, 1958).

Milton, John, *Paradise Lost.*

Miro, Joan, *Selected Writings and Interviews,* ed. Margit Rowell (London: Thames & Hudson, 1987).

Morrison, Blake, *The Movement: English Poetry and Fiction of the 1950s* (Oxford: Oxford University Press, 1980).

Motion, Andrew, *Philip Larkin* (London: Methuen, 1982).

—*Philip Larkin: A Writer's Life* (London: Faber, 1993).

Newman, Henry (Cardinal), *The Dream of Gerontius.*

Newton, Francis (Eric Hobsbawm), *The Jazz Scene* (London, MacGibbon & Kee, 1959; revised edn, Penguin, 1961).

Nicholson, Stuart, 'Jazz Collector: John Coltrane', *The Times,* 4 August 2000, II, 13.

Nietzsche, Friedrich, *Beyond Good and Evil.*

Oakes, Philip, 'The Unsung Gold Medallist', *Sunday Times* (colour magazine), 27 March 1966.

Oppel, Frances Nesbitt, *Mask and Tragedy: Yeats and Nietzsche* (Charlottesville: University Press of Virginia, 1987).

Osborne, John, 'Larkin, Modernism and Jazz', *Hungarian Journal of English and American Studies,* 9/2 (Fall 2003), 7–28.

Palmer, Richard, 'Guest Editorial', *Jazz Journal International,* 36/8 (August 1983).

— 'All What Jazz: Larkin's Most Expensive Mistake', *Hungarian Journal of English and American Studies* (Fall 2003), 9/2, 27–50.

—*Sonny Rollins* (London: Continuum, 2004).

—Teaching and Learning Larkin: "Helping the Old Too, As They Ought"', *About Larkin,* 21 (Summer 2006).

—'Religious Resonances in Philip Larkin's Poetry'; *About Larkin,* 22/23 (2007).

— and John White (eds), *Reference Back: Philip Larkin's Uncollected Jazz Writings 1940–84* (Hull: Hull University Press, 1998). Now reprinted as *Philip Larkin: Jazz Writings* (London: Continuum, 2004).

Parkinson, R. N., 'To Keep Our Metaphysics Warm: A Study of "Church Going"', *Critical Survey,* 5 (Winter 1971), 224–33.

Peterson, Oscar, *A Jazz Odyssey: My Life In Jazz* (London: Continuum, 2001).

Pevsner, Nikolaus, *The Englishness of English Art* (Harmondsworth: Penguin, 1978).

Plath, Sylvia, *Collected Poems,* ed. Ted Hughes (London: Faber, 1981).

Potts, Robert, 'In Curious Company', *The Times Literary Supplement,* 5 October 2001.

Regan, Stephen, *Philip Larkin* (Basingstoke: Macmillan, 1992).

Rowell, Margit (ed.), *Joan Miró Selected Writings and Interviews* (London: Thames & Hudson, 1987).

Salwak, Dale (ed.), *Philip Larkin: The Man and his Work* (Basingstoke: Macmillan, 1989).

Shakespeare, William, *A Midsummer Night's Dream; King Lear; Measure For Measure.*

Shelly, Percy Bysshe, *A Defence of Poetry.*

Shipton, Alyn, *Groovin' High: The Life of Dizzy Gillespie* (New York: Oxford University Press, 1999).

—*Out of the Long Dark: The Life of Ian Carr* (London: Equinox, 2006).

Smith, Jonathan, *The Learning Game* (London: Cape, 2001).

Stoppard, Tom, *Jumpers* (London: Faber, 1972).

Swarbrick, Andrew, *Out of Reach: The Poetry of Philip Larkin* (Basingstoke: Macmillan, 1995).

Sweetman, David, *The Love of Many Things: A Life of Vincent Van Gogh* (London: Hodder & Stoughton, 1990).

Tennyson, Alfred, *The Poems,* ed. Christopher Ricks (London: Longman, 1969).

Thomas, R. S., *Collected Poems 1945–1990* (London: Dent, 1993).

Tolley, A. T., *My Proper Ground: A Study of the Work of Philip Larkin and its Development,* (Edinburgh: Edinburgh University Press, 1991).

—*Larkin at Work: A Study of Larkin's Mode of Composition as Seen in his Workbooks* (Hull: Hull University Press, 1997).

Treneman, Ann, 'An Ugly Little House', *Times 2*, 13 February 2002.

Tucker, Michael, *Dreaming with Open Eyes:The Shamanic Spirit in Twentieth-Century Art and Culture* (London: HarperCollins, 1992).

—'Music Man's Dream', in *Alan Davie* (London: Lund Humphries Ltd, 1992).

—, *Jan Garbarek: Deep Song* (Hull: Eastnote, 1998).

Vidal, Gore, *Armageddon?* (London: André Deutsch, 1987).

Waddell, Helen, *Songs of The Wandering Scholars* (London: The Folio Society, 1982).

Watson, J. R., 'The Other Larkin', *Critical Quarterly*, 17/4 (Winter 1975), 347–60.

—'Cliches and Common Speech in Philip Larkin's Poetry', *Critical Survey*, 1 (1989), 149–56.

Watt, R. J. C., *A Concordance to the Poetry of Philip Larkin* (Hildesheim, Zurich and New York: Olms-Weidmann).

Waugh, Evelyn, *Decline and Fall.*

—'The Paris Review Interview', conducted by Julian Jebb. *Writers at Work: 3rd Series* (London: Secker & Warburg, 1967) 1977 Penguin edition.

Wheatley, David, Review of *Reference Back, The Times Literary Supplement*, 16 June 2000.

Whitman, Walt, *Poet to Poet: Walt Whitman*; selected by Robert Creeley. (Harmondsworth: Penguin Books, 1973).

Williams, Martin, *The Jazz Tradition* (New York: Oxford University Press, 1970).

Williams, Richard, *Long Distance Call: Writings on Music* (London: Aurum, 2000).

Wintle, Justin (ed.), *Makers of Modern Culture* (London: Routledge & Kegan Paul, 1981).

Woolf, Virginia, *Mrs. Dalloway.*

Wordsworth, William, *Poetical Works*, ed. Thomas Hutchinson; new edition ed. Ernest de Selincourt (Oxford: Oxford University Press, 1969).

Yeats, W. B. *The Poems* (London: Dent, 1990).

Index